I'D LIKE YOU MORE IF YOU WERE MORE LIKE ME

I'D LIKE YOU
MORE
IF YOU WERE
MORE LIKE ME

GETTING REAL ABOUT GETTING CLOSE

JOHN ORTBERG

TYNDALE
MOMENTUM™

*The nonfiction imprint of
Tyndale House Publishers, Inc.*

Library of Congress Cataloging-in-Publication Data
Names: Ortberg, John, author.
Title: I'd like you more if you were more like me : getting real about
   getting close / John Ortberg.
Description: Carol Stream, Illinois : Tyndale House Publishers, Inc., 2017. |
   Includes bibliographical references.
Identifiers: LCCN 2017016982| ISBN 9781414379029 (hc) | ISBN 9781496429568 (sc)
Subjects: LCSH: Interpersonal relations—Religious aspects—Christianity. |
   Individual differences—Religious aspects—Christianity.
Classification: LCC BV4597.52 .O78 2017 | DDC 248.4—dc23 LC record available at
   https://lccn.loc.gov/2017016982

ISBN 978-1-4964-2956-8 ITPE edition

Printed in the United States of America

23 22 21 20 19 18 17
7   6   5   4   3   2   1

To Santiago (Jimmy) Mellado, Nancy Beach,
Doug Veenstra, Fred Vojtsek, Dick Anderson, and the
inimitable Dr. Gilbert Bilezikian, this book is most
affectionately dedicated with gratitude and love.

Contents

Introduction: Table for One?

WHEN I THINK ABOUT LOVE, I think about a table.

I grew up in a Swedish family in Rockford, Illinois, surrounded by other Swedes. We're not the most expressive, demonstrative, or verbal people. Sometimes when I come home at night and my wife, Nancy, asks me, "How was your day?" I tell her, "Sorry, I've used up all my words. I don't have any words left." Nancy cannot understand that because she *never* uses up her words. She is an inexhaustible source of words. She's like the Niagara Falls of words.

One thing Swedes always have, however, is a table. For the people I grew up with, gathering around a table was the primary love language. If someone got hurt, got sick, got married, bought a car, bought a house, had a crisis, had a baby, or died, that's what we'd do. There would always be the rich smell of coffee in the house (not Orange Mocha Frappuccino—just coffee), and we'd gather around the table to talk, laugh, and cry—*together*.

If you think about it, many of the moments that shape our lives are spent around a table. In fact, some of my most vivid childhood memories took place around a glass-topped rectangular table in a small dining room at 227 Brendenwood Terrace in Rockford, Illinois.

If I close my eyes, I can still see it. That's my dad sitting way down at the end. To his right is my little brother, Barton. I'm the guy in the glasses and braces, and my mom is sitting kitty-corner from me on my right.

I remember one time when we were eating breakfast and my mom was holding a piece of peanut butter toast. It was that critical peanut buttering time when the toast is still warm enough to melt the peanut butter a little, and just as Mom was lifting the toast to her mouth, I reached over and smashed it right in her face. Before you knew it, we were all creaming each other in the face with peanut butter and laughing until we cried.

Good times.

And sometimes not so good times.

A couple of years ago, a friend of mine (who also happens to be Swedish) lost his mom. As soon as I heard—just a few hours after his mom had died—I called him on his cell phone. Turned out his whole family was at a local pancake house sitting around a table drinking coffee. I immediately felt a resonance in my spirit.

I know that family.

Throughout the years, there have been other tables, as well.

I remember the first time I sat around a table with Nancy's family. She happened to mention that she had bought a tire from a car dealer, and immediately someone at the table responded, "I would *never* buy tires from a dealership. They charge an arm and a leg. I get 'em at Shell."

"Shell?" someone else said. "You would get a tire at a Shell station? I would never do that. They have terrible tires. You couldn't *give* me one of their tires. I get mine at Goodyear."

"Goodyear?" a third family member chimed in. "Their

service stinks! If you get tires at Discount Tire, you get a free rotation every six thousand miles. Just saying."

And it went on like that.

Later, I said to Nancy, "What was up with that fight?"

"What fight?"

"That tire fight at the table."

"That wasn't a fight," she said. "That was us helping each other."

Really? At *my* family's table, in the unlikely event that I ever bought a tire, my mom would say something like, "Oh, Son, you bought a tire. We're so proud. You know, you raise kids; you try to teach them right from wrong. You never know how things will turn out. And now a moment like this makes it all worthwhile. Let's take a selfie."

Different tables have different styles, different rules. For Nancy, "table talk" involves a gritty commitment to reality—being deeply honest about the difficulties of life. No pedestals, no idealizing. Flowery language sets her on edge.

Once we were in a restaurant in Menlo Park, where we live. As we were laughing about something, a woman came up to our table and said, "I go to your church, and it's so great to see you two enjoying each other. I've been watching the way you interact—the way you look at each other when you talk. You must have a wonderful marriage."

"Sometimes," Nancy immediately shot back. She wants truth to have a place at the table. And I've come to enjoy that. For the most part.

When we were dating, we used to have Sunday dinner at the home of Nancy's grandmother, Gladys. The whole family would sit around an old mahogany table they had brought out to California from Texas. Sitting around that table made me feel like I was part of the family. Nancy loved that table.

When Nancy and I got engaged, I gave Gladys a dollar so we could get the mahogany table after she died. I even wrote a little deed, claiming the table, and taped it on the underside, so Nancy's greedy cousin wouldn't get it after Gladys was gone. When Gladys died, her table found a new home in our dining room.

When it's only two adults at the table, everything may look quite elegant and stylish; but when you have a baby, the table is a mess. Of course, the easiest way to keep your table tidy is not to let anyone sit there. But sometimes a messy table creates a memory that a tidy table never could. Once, when one of our kids had spilled one too many times and punishment was about to ensue, this particular child pulled out a dollar, set it on the table, and said, "Maybe Mr. Washington can change your mind." Turns out he could.

We had all three of our children in pretty short succession, and I remember what a triumph it was when we had our first meal together where nobody spilled, nobody cried, and nobody spit up. Our youngest was twenty-one by then, but that was still a great day in our family.

One thing about tables, at least in my family, is that we always sit in the same places. My spot is across from Nancy and kitty-corner from our daughter Laura. Even after the kids moved out, whenever they came home they reclaimed their old chairs: Laura on one side, Johnny and Mallory on the other; and now Laura's husband, Zack, next to her. We never voted on this. There's no seating chart. Nobody made assignments. There's just something deep in the human soul that says, "I need to have my place at the table." I know it's true for me: I want to have my chair, and I want everybody in my family to have their chairs. And I kind of like it when their chairs are filled.

To have our own place at the table means we belong. We have an identity. We're somebody's sibling, somebody's parent, somebody's spouse. We're *in*.

For me, a table is a reminder that what *really* matters in life is relationships. We are hardwired for emotional connection to other people. We want to be known. We crave being loved. We want to be accepted by someone who is completely aware of our gifts *and* our flaws and yet wants to be with us anyway. In short, we crave intimacy.

On a little study table in my office, there's a card with a quote from Victor Hugo's epic novel *Les Misérables*:

> My coat and I live comfortably together. It has assumed all my wrinkles, does not hurt me anywhere, has molded itself on my deformities, and is complacent to all my movements, and I only feel its presence because it keeps me warm. Old coats are old friends.[1]

On the back of the card, written in pen, are four words: *You are my coat.* It is signed by my wife. That's intimacy.

You may be thinking, *Nancy must be a wonderful person to be married to.*

She is.

Sometimes.

OUR FEAR OF INTIMACY

Although we crave it, intimacy is a scary concept for a lot of people. When I mentioned I was writing a book about intimacy, some people visibly tensed up. Others blushed. Nancy laughed.

I sometimes wonder why people have such strong reactions. Why do we fear intimacy so much?

For one thing, I think we're afraid of being hurt. Intimacy means being *known* by someone—like Nancy knows *me*, for example. She knows my strengths and weaknesses, my hopes and fears. She can use that knowledge to bond with me and grow closer to me, or she can use it to shame, wound, or betray me.

We also fear intimacy because it can set us up for disappointment. If you and I are not particularly close, I won't be crushed if you let me down because odds are, I didn't expect much from you to begin with. But if I desire closeness with you, if I come to depend on your friendship or need your love, it would wound me to the core to be rejected or abandoned by you. I would feel like a fool for trusting you—like Charlie Brown lying flat on his back after believing, yet again, that Lucy really *will* hold the football this time.

Intimacy can also make us feel needy. Or worse, it can *reveal* our neediness. Generally speaking, we don't like to feel needy. We like to think of ourselves as strong. (Ironically, the choice to pursue intimacy—to reveal our weakness and neediness—actually requires great strength.)

Many of us fear intimacy because deep down, we think we don't deserve it. We're afraid that our deficits and flaws are bound to emerge, and it will hurt even more to *lose* intimacy than never to have had it at all. Anytime we let someone in, we run the risk of being hurt or rejected. So we tend to avoid it.

The irony, of course, is that we deeply desire intimacy. We want to be loved, to be liked, to be celebrated, to have someone who accepts us no matter what. We want to have great friendships. We want to have people to turn to when a crisis hits. We want to have someone trustworthy in whom we can safely confide our secrets. We not only *want* intimacy, we were made for it.

Whether you are a man or a woman; whether you're the life of the party or a wallflower; whether you're a thinker or a feeler or a category not yet known to social science, you were made for connection. You were made for relationships. You were made for intimacy.

We see it whenever a freshly minted baby enters the world, looks into its mother's eyes, and—by some miracle—latches on to its mother's breast and begins to feed. My wife had never been a "baby person," but when she held our firstborn, she said with an awestruck voice, "I'd kill for this baby."

"Don't you mean you'd die for her?" I asked, concerned about her maternal instinct.

"No—that'd be stupid," she said. "Then I'd be dead and someone else would get her. I'd *kill* for her."

Intimacy has a fierceness that distance will never know. Inside every one of us is a hunger to be accepted, and it goes deeper than any other hunger.

We see it when two young lovers cannot stop gazing into each other's eyes. We see it when a couple bent with age won't go anywhere without holding each other's arms. We see it when a child comes to us beaming with the knowledge of a secret and wants to whisper it to us. We see it in the Bible when God looks at Adam and declares, "It is not good for the man to be alone," and proceeds to create a partner who is "just right" for him.[2]

When we experience intimacy, we can take on whatever else life throws at us. Without it, even our greatest accomplishments ring hollow. After all, where's the joy in success if we don't have someone we love with whom to share it? That's why I believe the pursuit of intimacy is the greatest, most worthwhile pursuit there is.

Granted, for most of us, pursuing intimacy is not as simple as adding more fiber to our diets. It's not something we can do without thinking about it. We have to work at it. But it's worth it because deep down, we know that being close to another human being matters like nothing else in the world. And being close to God? That takes things to a whole new level.

But maybe when you think about having an "intimate relationship with God," it feels like one more obligation in an already overwhelmed life. After all, intimacy is tricky enough to pull off with a real, live, flesh-and-blood person. How can we hope to have an intimate relationship with someone we can't even see? A spiritual being, no less.

Well, what if I were to tell you that not only did God create you for intimacy, but he also has been pursuing an intimate relationship with you from the very beginning?

Not long after God decided it was "not good for the man to be alone," we find him walking in the Garden *searching* for Adam and Eve. They were his creation; he enjoyed their company, and he wanted to spend time with them. But they were hiding. Finally, he calls out, "Where are you?"[3]

Unfortunately, the serpent had convinced Eve to eat from the tree of life, and she had cut Adam in on some of the fruit. Now their relationship with God had changed—the bonds of intimacy were broken. For the first time, they realized they were naked, and they were embarrassed and ashamed. For the first time, they feared being *seen* and *known* by God. So they hid.

Now, here's the interesting part: God *allows* them to hide—because intimacy can't be coerced. God doesn't want compliance; he wants connection. Intimacy respects distance but isn't content with it. Like God in the Garden, intimacy calls out,

"Where are you?" And God, in his desire for intimacy with us, has been asking that same question ever since.

God wants you and me at his table. Jesus says, "Look! I stand at the door and knock. If you hear my voice and open the door, I will come in, and we will share a meal together as friends."[4]

John, the dear friend of Jesus, was an old, old man when he recorded those words. He must have remembered a thousand meals he had shared with Jesus. And he used this image of sitting at the table with Jesus to describe an experience that is possible for you and me. When I think of love, when I think of intimacy, I think of a table—just like Jesus did.

It's a mystery, no question about it, that we're invited into an intimate relationship with God. But how does that happen? Is it possible that God has been speaking to us all along, and we've been hearing without realizing that the whisper comes from him? Is it possible for us to draw closer to God without realizing that it's happening? I think it is. In fact, I believe God uses our relationships with other people to teach us how to love *him*. The more we pursue intimacy in our other relationships, the more we see and understand God's incredible, audacious love for us.

But that's getting ahead of things a little. For now, let's talk about what I learned about intimacy on my honeymoon.

CHAPTER 1

ARE YOU WITH ME?

WHAT INTIMACY IS

To know and engage with someone intimately is always a crossing of a border, always fraught, even if you've been married fifty years.

AMY BLOOM

ONCE UPON A TIME, in a suburb far, far away, I thought I was going to be the greatest husband anyone had ever seen.

And then I got married.

Back then, I thought I knew everything there was to know about intimacy, but I had no idea how emotionally immature I was. I believed that intimacy was a feeling of closeness into which I would effortlessly fall as soon as the pastor said, "You may now kiss the bride," and that everything would then be a fantastic, blissful Hollywood musical. The idea that intimacy was something I would actually have to *work at* never occurred to me. As you might expect, that led to a few problems.

When Nancy and I were first dating, she would occasionally say or do something I didn't like. Maybe she would disagree with me too vehemently in front of other people or say something that struck me as bossy or too opinionated. Ironically, part of what attracted me to her in the first place was the fact that she was a person who loved to talk and had strong opinions. And she's always been that way. At her very first evaluation in kindergarten, her teacher said, "Nancy is adjusting well, but she does have a tendency to chat during nap time." So even though I was drawn to her outgoing and expressive personality, for some reason it also bothered me.

And I didn't handle it very well.

Whenever we had a disagreement, instead of being able to talk to Nancy about it, something inside me froze up, and I pouted. A lot. It was my spiritual gift. In fact, if I were a superhero, pouting would be my superpower. I would just pout the bad guys into a deep sense of guilt and remorse that would make them want to turn themselves in.

Pouting may be a great (though admittedly unconventional) superpower, but it's also an intimacy killer.

On the night of our rehearsal dinner, I was upset with Nancy about something—I don't remember what. But instead of telling her what was bothering me so we could work through it (you know, like two adults), I became politely withdrawn and distant. Of course she noticed, and as a result, what should have been a time of great joy was actually quite painful.

The next day, without ever resolving our differences from the night before, we arrived at the church, got married, and left for our honeymoon.

You always hear about how your honeymoon is going to be perfect, and I—being the perfect husband—had the perfect plan. Nancy was a California girl born and bred. She has always loved the ocean and the warm coastal climate. So naturally, for our honeymoon, I took her to . . . wait for it . . . Wisconsin.

I thought, *This is going to thrill her!*

Yeah. Not so much. Go figure.

Not surprisingly, our honeymoon was an emotional roller coaster. If Nancy said or did something I didn't approve of, instead of talking about it, I brooded and withdrew. One afternoon we were sitting by the pool (it was a beautiful day for pouting), and I was reading a book as a way of distancing myself from my bride. (That's right, I not only brought a book on my honeymoon, but I was reading it out by the pool.) I had waited my entire life for a honeymoon. Ever since puberty, I had *lived* for my honeymoon. And now here I was, at a beautiful Wisconsin resort, and instead of building intimacy with my wife, I was reading a book. And not just any book, but a biography of Sigmund Freud. (No, I'm not making this up.) As you may know, Freud mostly wrote about sex. So I could have been *having* sex, but instead I was reading about it.

What would Freud have said?

What would Jesus have said?

Here's what Nancy said: "Put down that book!"

Actually, that's the sanitized version. In reality, she used an adjective to describe the book that was the kind of word you would use if you hit your finger with a hammer. It was a very non-Baptist word.

Oh, man, I thought. *We're still on our honeymoon and she's already using bad words.*

See what I did there? Instead of *engaging* with Nancy's frustration, I simply criticized her means of expression. In other words, I totally missed the point.

By telling me to put down my book and pay attention to her, Nancy was *inviting* me to intimacy (in her own non-Baptist way). And I was missing it. I thought of myself as someone who—by virtue of my background and training in clinical psychology and ministry—was an expert in intimacy. But I was, in fact, severely intimacy-challenged.

UNDERSTANDING INTIMACY

Somewhere along the way, in the minds of a lot of people in our culture, the word *intimacy* got all tangled up with sex. But even though there *is* a connection between the two words, they are not interchangeable, and one is not necessarily dependent on the other. We don't need to have sex to be intimate with someone. And we don't need to be intimate with someone in order to have sex. In fact, the vast majority of our intimate relationships have absolutely nothing to do with sex. Intimacy also applies to our relationships with our kids, our parents, our friends, our coworkers—and even with God.

Intimacy is not simply a feeling. It's not a mysterious experience that some people are born for and others are condemned to miss out on. It's not restricted to certain temperaments, or to married couples, or to "feelers" on the Myers-Briggs continuum. And it's not something that mystically occurs the moment we say, "I do."

The best definition of intimacy I know of—and the core of our journey together in this book—comes from my friend Dallas Willard.

Dallas was the head of the philosophy department at the University of Southern California. There's an old saying that if you're the smartest person in the room, you're in the wrong room. Dallas was always in the wrong room. He also knew the Bible better than anyone I'd ever met. People wanted to be around him because he constantly said unforgettable things that could not have come out of any other mouth. Things like these:

- The Kingdom of God is never in trouble. Neither are the people in it.
- Reality is what you bump into when you're wrong.
- Christians are people who are better off dead.

But even greater than his capacity for wisdom was his capacity to experience life as an unhurried gift—and to share this experience with others.

One time, a friend of mine was serving as a teaching assistant for Dallas during a two-week intensive class for ministers. They stayed together in the same home, and in the evening Dallas would change from his more formal teaching clothes into Bermuda shorts and a white T-shirt, but he would leave on his brown wing-tip shoes and brown socks.

One night, they were channel surfing and they landed on a Spanish-language program where people were doing a salsa dance, and Dallas said, "That looks like fun. I should try those moves."

The thought of Dallas Willard—a middle-aged, rural-Missouri-born, Fundamentalist-Baptist-raised expert on Husserlian phenomenology—doing salsa moves wearing Bermuda shorts and brown wing-tips is just priceless, and almost as unforgettable as his teachings.

Anyway, he once told me, "You are an unceasing flow of experiences. To be alive is to have the capacity to experience reality."

This sounds deceptively simple, but it helped me give a name to the craving of my soul. I love to have life-enhancing experiences—the first cry of my newborn child; riding a wave at Cowell's Beach; the beauty of Jean Valjean singing "Bring Him Home"; talking deep into the night in front of a crackling fire with someone I love; watching the Pleiades in sleeping bags on the deck with my children while Don McLean sings, "Starry, starry night . . ."

"Intimacy," Dallas explained, "is shared experience."

Think about it. If our lives consist of our experiences, then to some degree the quality of our lives reflects the quality of our experiences. Our experiences shape our perspectives on life and help to inform our understanding of the world. If you stop to consider how you became the person you are today, it's easy to see the role of your experiences in determining who you are.

Sometimes, we use our cell phones to take pictures of ourselves enjoying these experiences because we want to capture and preserve the good times. Of course, we don't take selfies of moments we want to forget. Nobody captures the moment they flunked a test, got dumped, got fired, or belched on a first date. We take selfies at a ball game, on a hike, at a concert, or even while driving. (Now there's a frightening thought!)

Here's a fun fact I dug up along the way: In 2015, more people died taking selfies than from shark attacks.[1] It's a little surprising that no one takes a selfie during a shark attack.

Not only do we revel in our experiences, but we also have a deep need to *share* them. When we share experiences with other people—the good times, the bad times, and all the mundane in-between times—we're sharing our *lives* with them. And that builds *connection*, which is another essential component of intimacy.

On our honeymoon, Nancy wanted to *connect* with me. She was angry because I wasn't focusing on her. She was angry because I wasn't making myself emotionally available to her. She was angry because I had dragged her to Wisconsin for our honeymoon. But mostly, she was angry because I was not *sharing the experience* of our honeymoon with her. What I had failed to realize—at that critical juncture of our relationship— is that *shared experience* is what intimacy is all about.

Every time we connect with someone in a shared experience, we have the potential to build intimacy. If you're not a planner or overly sentimental, you may think you're doomed to miss out on intimacy. But you're not. Intimacy isn't built on grand, elaborate gestures. It doesn't have to be something deep or dramatic—an elaborate, romantic getaway, a dramatic self-disclosure, or sentimental words. Rather, it's made up of a thousand tiny, everyday moments of *interaction*.

It's asking your kids how their day went when they get home. It's asking—and caring about—what your spouse wore to an event. It's listening to a joke. It's remembering someone's favorite wine, book, or television show. It's a head butt on a football field. It's noticing a downcast face and offering a word of encouragement. It's a private wink to a stressed-out colleague in a fractious meeting that says, "We've got this." It's putting down a Freud book to listen to a disappointed spouse on a Wisconsin honeymoon.

A single note of music is an insignificant thing. But if you put enough of them together in the right way, you get Beethoven's Ninth Symphony. Likewise with sharing our experiences. A single encounter may not amount to much, but if we share enough experiences with someone . . . that's how we build intimacy.

INTIMACY REQUIRES PRESENCE AND TIME

If my honeymoon is proof of anything (aside from the fact that Freud rarely "heightens the mood"), it's that intimacy does not automatically result from being in the same place at the same time with someone. We can share physical space without actually sharing the experience.

There's no such thing as one-way, self-generated intimacy. By its very nature, intimacy must be *mutual.* Consequently, the basic building blocks of intimacy—whether with God or with other people—are shared experiences that build meaningful connections. For the most part, intimacy grows when one person invites another to share the many ordinary—and sometimes extraordinary—moments of everyday life and the invitation is not only accepted but reciprocated.

In order to share an experience, we must be fully present—we must engage with the other person. We have to talk about what we're thinking, feeling, and experiencing, and we must actively listen when the other person does the same. Otherwise, we're just two people who happen to be in the same place at the same time. If my body is here but my mind is distracted—if my thoughts keep drifting back to the stock market or work problems while you're talking about your day—we're not actually sharing the experience.

Two people might sit together at a meal, see a movie, go for a ride to the store, or even face a tragedy such as losing a child, and yet instead of growing more intimate as a result, they may actually lose intimacy.

Not long ago at dinner, my body was at the same table with Nancy, but my attention was on the screen of my cell phone. A few minutes into the meal, I got a text—from Nancy—that read: "I'm sitting right here." Screens are useful, but we can forget their place. Screens are made for man; man is not made for screens.

Is texting together quality time? No. Is checking e-mails together? No. Is watching television together? Well, it depends on what's on. The real-life drama of an NFL play-off game where you're experiencing the ups and downs together—yes, of course it is. If it's *The Bachelor*, that's unbiblical, so use discernment and common sense.

A striking dimension of Jesus' capacity to love was his ability to be totally present with people. In all the Bible, Jesus never says to anyone, "Huh? What did you say? I wasn't paying attention. I was distracted with all my Messiah work." Jesus was constantly aware of how his friends were doing.

Of course, being fully present requires a commitment of time.

Time is precious to us because it is such a limited commodity. We can make more money, but we can't make more time. That's why giving someone the gift of our time is such an intimate act. It's something we can never get back.

Pursuing intimacy means making our top relationships the top priority of our time.

I once had a conversation with Nancy about our relationship and how I was spending my time. I asked her, "Am I working too much?"

Her immediate response was, "It's not terrible."

Granted, that's better than "terrible," but it's kind of a low bar. Jesus didn't say, "By this, everyone will know you are my disciples, if your relationships are *not terrible.*"

Here is the key challenge with time: There's always something else you could be doing. There are always more e-mails to be answered, more stuff to be done, more projects to be finished. But rarely do your kids say, "Hey, Mom. Hey, Dad. Why don't you go and work on your presentation for the office for the rest of the evening."

When it comes to time, you're bound to disappoint someone eventually. Don't let it be the people you love the most.

Because at the end of the day, our relationships—our shared experiences—are what really matter.

I have yet to hear anybody say on his deathbed, "Bring out my résumé so I can read it one last time. Let me review my financial portfolio. Let me tick off that list of impressive achievements I've accomplished."

Time and presence. They are the stuff of shared experience. We can't experience true intimacy without them. And there is no greater gift that we can give to those we love.

Speaking of gifts . . . years ago, my wife and I took our preschool-age children to have a family picture taken at one of those shopping mall photo places. I wanted a happy portrait to send out at Christmastime, so everyone could see what an intimate family looks like.

I don't know who managed this photo shop, but whoever it was should be locked up for a long time, because it was an ugly experience. Basically, a stranger behind a large camera held up a series of odd-looking shapes that frightened the kids until they cried.

Now, I'm no expert, but I'm fairly certain that if you send people a Christmas card featuring three small children crying their eyes out, it's not a good thing. Especially if you're a pastor. So we went through a series of phases as we tried to get the kids to smile for their pictures.

The first was the "happy phase," in which I cheerfully said, "Hey, kids, this is going to be fun! You're going to enjoy this."

That didn't last long before we moved to phase two—the bribery phase.

"Kids, there's a Mrs. Fields just a couple of doors down. If we get a good picture here, with lots of smiling faces, you can go to Mrs. Fields and get a double fudge brownie chocolate chip cookie—if you just smile."

Didn't work.

So we moved into phase three, which is basically a series of threats.

"I told you to smile! You want to cry instead? All right, I'll give you something to cry about."

In case you're wondering, that's a proven and effective way to get small children to smile. I had to go to graduate school for a lot of years to learn that particular technique. And yet—surprisingly—it didn't work. Things just went from bad to worse.

By now, the entire place had filled up with other parents who had brought their kids to have their pictures taken—and all those kids had started crying just watching what was going on with my family.

So I got desperate. I pulled out our middle child—three-year-old Mallory—who was crying the hardest, her little body wracked with sobs, and I said, "Mallory, you're not happy, are you?" (That's called empathy—more help from my grad school years.) "I bet I know what you want right now . . ."

Mallory had always loved little dolls, stuffed animals, and other playthings, and her very favorite at the time was a little doll she called Baby Tweezers. It was the first doll she had ever named, and we don't know why she chose the name she did. Mallory was not a forceps-delivery child, but Baby Tweezers was what she decided to name her doll.

At that moment, I knew that if anything could bring comfort to my daughter, it would be the thought of that little doll she loved so much. So I said, "Mal, I bet if you could have anything in the world right now, you would want to have Baby Tweezers here with you, wouldn't you?"

Fresh tears formed in her eyes, and her bottom lip stuck

out so far that a bird could have perched on it. She didn't even trust herself to speak. She just nodded her head.

Very softly and gently I said, "Well, honey, if you ever want to see Baby Tweezers alive again . . ."

Bottom line, my body was sharing the same space as my children, but I was not sharing in their experience. I was in a hurry. I was worried that other people watching would think I didn't know how to control my family. (As if that were even an option.) I was preoccupied with getting on to whatever the next thing was that I had to do that day. I was concerned about the money we were about to spend on a picture of three crying children that—if we went ahead and sent it out for Christmas—would probably have the social services people coming after us.

The act of "being with" someone requires patience and sacrifice. It means putting the other person's wants and needs above our own and being willing to invest as much time as it takes to make the person feel valued and loved.

THE MASTER OF THE SHARED EXPERIENCE

Jesus was a master of fostering intimacy through time and attention. We see this especially among the circle of people with whom he was closest—the friends who kind of became his family.

The Gospel of Mark highlights Jesus' intention when he chose his disciples: "He appointed twelve that they might be with him."[2]

It was just that simple: *that they might be with him.* When? Well, as it turns out, a lot—when he taught, when he traveled, when he worked, when he ate, when he rested, when the crowds loved him, and when the crowds left him.

He often withdrew from the disciples to pray and be refreshed, but he devoted much of his life to simply being with them. Now, he wasn't always *happy* with them—in fact, they actually made his work a lot harder—nor did he always try to make *them* feel happy. But here's what you never find: You never see one of the disciples come up to Jesus in the Gospels and say, "Hey, Jesus, how come you never have time for us anymore? Now that you're famous, with big crowds coming to see you, everybody calling you Messiah, speaking requests, and healing campaigns, we never see you anymore." From the beginning, when it was just them, through the intensity of when all of the attention and demands of a nation and the weight of the world rested on Jesus' shoulders, his friends always knew one thing: Jesus had time for them.

For three years, Jesus invited his friends to share the experiences of his life. Recently, I took a look at some of the experiences that Jesus shared with his disciples, and I was amazed by how many I found.

They walked together

The most common thing they did together was take walks. In fact, this was the very first experience they shared with Jesus: "One day as Jesus was walking along the shore of the Sea of Galilee, he saw Simon and his brother Andrew. . . . Jesus called out to them, 'Come, follow me.'"[3]

Follow me. That may be the greatest and most life-changing invitation to intimacy ever uttered. Jesus didn't say, "Obey me," though of course obedience is part of following him. He didn't say, "Believe the right stuff about me," though as they grew in intimacy with him, his followers *would* believe. He didn't say, "Serve me," though that would become their greatest purpose. He simply invited them to go for a walk. As it happens, the walk lasted for three years.

Walking together is how it all began, and even after the Resurrection, Jesus went on a seven-mile walk to Emmaus with a couple of disciples.

Taking a walk is so simple. It's very low cost. It's very low skill. And it's very high connection. Jesus utilized walking together so much that "walking with Jesus" became a common way of describing discipleship in the New Testament. To love Jesus meant to walk with him. It still does.

They ate together

Again, so simple. Everybody has to eat. It's low skill. And it can be low cost. When Jesus wasn't out walking with people, he was often at a table eating with people. "While Jesus was having dinner at Matthew's house, many tax collectors and sinners came and ate with him and his disciples."[4]

In fact, the most famous meal in history—the Lord's Supper—is named for Jesus, and the Bible says he "eagerly desired" to share this meal with his disciples, even though he knew he was about to die.[5] Talk about an intimate act!

They learned together

Jesus often spent time teaching his disciples. Time and again, the Bible tells us that "his disciples came to him, and he began to teach them."[6] Something happens in a relationship when we're learning and stretching and growing together. Just think about how much richer the experience of reading a book is when you can engage in a spirited discussion about it with friends.

They did favors for each other

"Now that I, your Lord and Teacher, have washed your feet, you also should wash one another's feet."[7]

Running errands and doing favors isn't a barrier to Kingdom work; it actually *is* Kingdom work, because Kingdom work is about love. If we're too hurried to love, we're too hurried, period.

They rested together

"Then, because so many people were coming and going that they did not even have a chance to eat, he said to them, 'Come with me by yourselves to a quiet place and get some rest.'"[8]

They went for boat rides

"They went away by themselves in a boat to a solitary place."[9]

They went mountain climbing

"Jesus took Peter, James and John with him and led them up a high mountain, where they were all alone."[10]

They prayed

"One day Jesus was praying in a certain place. When he finished, one of his disciples said to him, 'Lord, teach us to pray.'"[11]

They went fishing

"When [Jesus] had finished speaking, he said to Simon, 'Put out into deep water, and let down the nets for a catch.'"[12]

They went for car rides

"On the day of Pentecost, the disciples were together in one Accord."[13]

What we see in Jesus is a presence that doesn't place efficiency above intimacy. He was perfectly willing to accomplish his tasks more slowly if it meant being with his friends more deeply.

THE "10,000-HOUR RULE"

How devoted was Jesus to being with his closest friends? As best we can discern, the Bible indicates that the disciples were with Jesus for about three years. Let's assume they were with him ten hours a day, and for the sake of argument, let's say they had a couple of days off each month. That would give them about 340 discipleship days each year. Now let's do the math:

10 hours/day × 340 days/year × 3 years = 10,200 hours of discipleship with Jesus

Journalist Malcolm Gladwell, in his book *Outliers*, writes about what he calls the 10,000-hour rule. The underlying idea of this "rule" is that it takes time to master a demanding craft, and 10,000 hours seems to be a magic number—whether it's playing a violin or programming a computer or doing surgery or hitting a curveball.[14]

If we were to apply this idea to Jesus' disciples, what "craft" would we say they were mastering during their 10,000-plus hours with Jesus? Well, right about the time they hit the 10,000-hour mark, he told them, "A new command I give you: Love one another. As I have loved you, so you must love one another. By this everyone will know that you are my disciples."[15]

So it might be said that time spent together—shared experience—is the key to mastering the art of living in an intimate relationship with Jesus and with each other, and that *love* is what defines our success.

THE GREATEST GIFT

As they did with the disciples, the same principles apply whether we are seeking intimacy with God or with each other: Share experiences. Carve out time. Be present.

Because God is *always* present, intimacy with him is possible every moment of our lives. He's already here. We just have to show up and spend time with him.

When you need help, tell him. Then pay attention and look for him to give you the strength or wisdom or the right idea you need to keep moving forward. When you are joyful, recognize his goodness behind the joy and take time to praise him. When you see beauty, recognize the hand of the Artist and thank him. And ask him to open your eyes even more, so that you can see the world from *his* perspective. Ask God to share his experiences with you. Say, "Father, what do you feel when you look at this person? What was in your heart when you created this tree? How much joy do you experience when you look at the vast beauty of what you created?"

People who are intentional about being connected with God have a way of finding him in the unlikeliest places. St. Ignatius spoke of finding God in all things.[16] Missionary Frank Laubach called it playing the "game with minutes," in which the goal is to "bring God to mind at least one second out of every sixty."[17] Brother Lawrence, a seventeenth-century Carmelite monk, described it like this:

> During my work, I would always continue to speak to the Lord as though He were right with me,

offering Him my services and thanking Him for His assistance. And at the end of my work, I used to examine it carefully. If I found good in it, I thanked God. If I noticed faults, I asked His forgiveness without being discouraged, and then went on with my work, still dwelling in Him.[18]

Give it a try. You may just find that an ordinary day—such as *today*—can become the most intimate day with God you have ever spent.

But wait—there's more.

If intimacy is shared experience, then perhaps the ultimate example of an invitation to intimacy is the Incarnation—that mystical, miraculous moment when God chose to become more like us—coming to earth, taking on flesh, and living with all the joys, sorrows, temptations, and triumphs that we do, so that we would better understand how to become more like him.

He could have loved us from a distance. But he wanted to do more than just love us. He wanted to be intimate with us. So God became fully human to fully share the experience of humanity. Through Jesus, God shared our experience of loneliness, fatigue, anxiety, and sorrow. He shared in our joy and our pain. He shared in our comfort in being held and our despair at feeling forsaken.

The Incarnation tells us that the story of our world is the story of God's hunger for intimacy; his pain at its loss in the Fall; his determination to recapture it; and his fierce joy at its redemption.

If that's the case, then maybe we're already closer to God than we think we are. Maybe intimacy with God isn't just something we can *do*, but something we can also *receive*.

And maybe, just maybe, we can rest in that for a while.

CHAPTER 2

LET'S GET THIS STRAIGHT

WHAT INTIMACY ISN'T

Inside every child is an "emotional tank" waiting to be filled with love.
DR. ROSS CAMPBELL

IN THE EARLY DAYS of the Model T, Henry Ford decided to cut costs by not supplying a gas gauge. As a result, motorists were constantly getting stuck by the side of the road. Some people actually painted lines on a stick that they could dip into the tank to find out how much fuel they had left. Even today you can find Model T owners forums online with endless discussions about fuel-measuring sticks.[1]

It would be nice if people came with intimacy gauges on their foreheads so we could tell how full their emotional tanks are. But they don't. What's worse, we're often misled by our own internal misconceptions about intimacy. In this chapter, we'll look at some myths about intimacy, and ask some questions that will give you a chance to gauge your own IQ (intimacy quotient).

MYTH #1: INTIMACY SHOULD BE EASY

A few months after Nancy and I got married, we traveled to Aberdeen, Scotland, so I could do some postgraduate work. We were the only two people we knew there. The only other person we saw with any regularity was an old woman named Ruby, who checked IDs at the cafeteria.

For the next year, I studied and Nancy worked as a maid. We were home together every evening. Because we had no money, no TV, nowhere else to go, and no one else to hang out with, we learned how to be together. And without knowing what we were doing, we developed rituals that strengthened our relationship.

Every night, we read Charles Dickens's *Nicholas Nickleby* to each other. Every Saturday, we took the bus to downtown Aberdeen and imagined what we'd buy if we had money. If we had a little extra cash, we might splurge, buy a *Time* magazine, rip it in half, read it together, and talk about world affairs.

Most mornings, I got up early to study while Nancy was still sleeping. One morning, I found a note on my desk that read: "Good morning, sweetheart. I love you with all my heart. I'm probably fast asleep while you're reading this, but I'm dreaming of you. There's no sight in the world to me like looking into your face." (I'll stop quoting here because it starts to get mushy.) It was signed *Ruby*—the old lady who worked in the cafeteria. (Nancy is fond of pointing out to me that she was voted class comedienne in high school.)

What made our Aberdeen experience so great was that it was just the two of us. Apart from my studies—which had their place—we had no deadlines, no schedule, no responsibilities, and no demands. We had all time in the world, and we had each other. We learned to argue, play, fight, make up, and depend on each other. And at the end of our time in Scotland, we felt as if we'd built a solid relationship.

Then we had children. (If you know some couples who have a preschool kid or two, let's observe a moment of silence for them right now—because it's probably the last one they'll have for a long, long time.)

When Adam and Eve sinned and disobeyed God, they were punished with increasingly severe news: They had to leave Paradise; they would have to eat by the sweat of their brow; they would eventually die; and they were given two preschoolers, Cain and Abel.

Early parenthood is the best of times and the worst of times—bottles, diapers, meals, dishes, meltdowns, books, baths, negotiations—"More light, Daddy." "Less light, Daddy"—sleep deprivation, less sex, more trips to the bathroom—and I believe the technical term for the period from 3:00 a.m. to 5:00 a.m. is the Arsenic Hour, because that's usually when you either want to take it yourself or give it to someone small.

Suddenly, all the work of our year in Scotland—while not lost exactly—was swamped by new conflicts over division of labor, parenting styles, money problems, and conversations that always had the phrase "my day was harder than yours" running an inch beneath the surface.

Nora Ephron said, "A child is a grenade. When you have a baby, you set off an explosion in your marriage, and when the dust settles, your marriage is different from what it was. Not better, necessarily; not worse, necessarily; but different."[2] Lest you think the challenge ends there, she also wrote, "When your children are teenagers, it's important to have a dog so that someone in the house is happy to see you."[3]

The point is, intimacy is messy. It's also seasonal. Just

when you think you've reached a happy place, something—or someone—changes, and a whole new set of challenges arises. You go from being friends to being a couple, from being a couple to being a married couple, from being a married couple to being parents. You finally get used to your boss, and you get assigned a new one. You spend years working on your relationship with your mom or dad and then dementia sets in. You love your team at work and then the World's Crankiest Person gets assigned to it. Your child goes prodigal on you, and you suddenly find yourself jealous of your best friend's children and estranged from your own.

Sometimes people will say that they don't want to get married because they're afraid their spouse will change, and they might not like him or her anymore. As a friend of mine says, "If you don't want change, marry a cat." (By the way . . . cats are also messy.)

So where are you in your current season?

- Do you have at least one person nearby you could call in times of personal distress?
- Do you have several people you could visit with little advance warning—and without apology?
- Do you have several people with whom you can share recreational activities?
- Do you have people who will lend you money if you need it, or those who will care for you in practical ways if the need arises?

If your answers to these questions are mostly negative, your intimacy tank may be running a little low.

MYTH #2: INTIMACY TAKES AWAY YOUR SENSE OF IDENTITY

Back when Nancy and I got married, weddings often featured two lit candles, which represented the bride and the groom, and then a large third candle, called the unity candle.

The bride and groom would take their separate candles and together light the unity candle. Our debate was, after we've lit the unity candle, should we blow out the two candles representing our separate lives or should we leave them lit? I voted to blow them out, though what I really wanted—metaphorically—was to blow out hers and leave mine lit. (Future grooms, I don't recommend that.)

Some people mistakenly assume that becoming intimate with someone means you have to think, want, and do every-thing the same way—*their* way. In other words, if I blow out my candle, *I* cease to exist; I've been replaced by *us*. But there's a difference between *intimacy* and *fusion*.

Intimacy involves two persons coming together, but their individual identities remain intact. I'm still fully John, and Nancy is still fully Nancy. Together, we're the Ortbergs—but we complement each other; we don't absorb each other.

Fusion results when two vacuums come together and the boundaries between the two separate selves get lost. In fusion, one person's neediness wants to suck the life out of the other. They take hugs, but they don't give them. They don't say what they really think—they might not even know what they really think. They avoid conflict. They collude with each other so as not to face difficulties. ("Don't you think it's terrible what she said?") They enable each other's denial. They use each other as a crutch. They lose the capacity for independence and strength.

Fusion is not intimacy. Intimacy does not absorb. It does not misappropriate. It does not collude. Intimacy provides balance. It is reciprocal. It doesn't divide or subtract. It adds or multiplies. Intimacy doesn't take away our identity; it enhances it.

Take a look at your current relationships, and ask yourself:

- Does one person most often end up choosing which movie to see and which restaurant to eat at, or is there a balance of decision making?
- Are you comfortable living in disagreement, or do you feel a need to smooth things over or capitulate?
- When you're alone at night, can you enjoy the evening, or do you feel the need to fill it with another person or activity?
- Are you a person who knows what you believe and value?

If you tend to depend on others for your decision making, sense of happiness, and self-worth, you may be at risk of fusion.

MYTH #3: INTIMACY AND LOVE ARE THE SAME THING

I grew up believing that intimacy and love were more or less the same thing. Love is what makes intimacy possible, of course, but love and intimacy are not the same thing; not by a long shot.

Love is not primarily a feeling (though it certainly involves feelings). It is not primarily desire. It is not primarily closeness. It is not being agreeable or doing what someone else wants you to do.

So what is it? Thomas Aquinas said that to love somebody means to will their good.[4] But that doesn't mean simply having good intentions. We might think of it this way: To love someone means both to will and to work for that person to become who God created them to be.

One problem we face when it comes to the word *love* is that we use it for so many different things. We say, *I love you. I love my child. I love my house. I love my job. I love California. I love hot dogs.* What does it mean to *love* a hot dog? It doesn't mean "I will the good" for that hot dog. No. In fact, my love will *consume* that hot dog. It will *destroy* that hot dog. (I really want a hot dog.)

Jesus understood love as a God-powered condition of the heart and mind in which we will the good of everyone we meet. This concept of love was so revolutionary that Jesus' followers had to find a word for it. They took a seldom-used Greek word—*agape*—and used it to explain the nature of love that Jesus taught and modeled.

In the middle of a letter he wrote to the church in Corinth, the apostle Paul rather abruptly shifts to a discussion of love, which includes these amazing words:

> If I speak in the tongues of men or of angels, but do not have love, I am only a resounding gong or a clanging cymbal. If I have the gift of prophecy and can fathom all mysteries and all knowledge, and if I have a faith that can move mountains, but do not have love, I am nothing. If I give all I possess to the poor and give over my body to hardship that I may boast, but do not have love, I gain nothing.[5]

Too archaic? Here's a more contemporary translation:

> Though I tweet like Justin Bieber and have more Facebook friends than the pope; though I get a BA

from Cal and an MBA from Stanford; though I
invented Snapchat and Uber; though I have great
hair and white teeth and low body fat; though I solve
global warming, set philanthropic records, and drive
a Hummer that runs on compost, if I don't have love,
I have nothing.

Prefer math to literature? Here's Paul's claim in equation form:

$$\text{Everything} - \text{Love} = \text{Nothing}$$

Got it? Good. Moving on.

We'll often say things like, "It's easy for me to love this
person, but it's hard for me to love that person." Jesus didn't
qualify love that way. His notion was that we are to become
loving people. It is a condition of being human—like being
healthy—in which we are so firmly rooted in God's love for us
and increasingly free of sin (which always opposes love) that
we are ready to will the good of *any* person, regardless of who
that person is or how he or she feels about us.

In fact, I find that this kind of love—*agape*—will express
itself very differently, depending on the condition of the
people I meet. If I see people who are hungry and I love them
with agape love, I'll try to feed them. If they're lonely and I
love them with agape love, I'll try to connect with them and
listen to them. If they're discouraged and I love them with
agape love, I'll encourage them.

Let's change it up a bit. Let's say I'm with my children and
my children are spoiled brats. (This is completely hypotheti-
cal, of course.) What will I give them if I love them with agape
love? I'll give them discipline.

Here is where love becomes challenging. If I give food to

a hungry guy, he'll think I'm loving. He'll feel grateful. We'll feel close. If I give encouragement to a fearful guy, he'll think I'm loving. We'll feel close. But if I give loving discipline to a spoiled brat, will that child think I'm loving? No, that child will think I'm not.

In order to be a loving person, we must be prepared to be seen as unloving. Our love must come from a source so stable that it enables us to love in kind of a risky way. Only God can supply that kind of love. That's why Paul writes, "I pray that you, being rooted and established in love, may have power, together with all the Lord's holy people, to grasp how wide and long and high and deep is the love of Christ."[6]

That's love. But love is not intimacy. Intimacy must be reciprocated.

The father of the Prodigal Son never stopped *loving* his boy. But they could not experience *intimacy* again until the boy came home.

No one can prevent us from loving them. That's why Paul can make this extraordinary claim: "Love is patient. . . . It always protects, always trusts, always hopes, always perseveres. Love never fails."[7] But anyone can prevent us from being intimate with them. Love can—and sometimes does—go one way. Intimacy must be reciprocated, a two-way street. It must be shared.

When you think of the people in your life with whom you desire intimacy, ask these questions:

- How likely would they be to come to you if they needed help?
- Do they sense that you genuinely like them?
- Are they willing to be their real selves around you, or do they feel the need to hide?

- How well do you understand them? How accurately do you think you are able to gauge their emotional well-being from one day to the next?
- Are you able to discuss differences of opinion without losing your sense of connectedness with one another?

If your answers are mostly in the negative, there's a good chance these people may not be open to an intimate relationship with you—*yet*. That doesn't mean it will never happen. It just means you've got some work to do. Don't stop trying.

MYTH #4: INTIMACY = SEX

People often use the word *intimate* as a euphemism for *sex*. Though I will admit it is slightly less crass to say, "We've been intimate," than to blurt out, "We've had sex," the truth is, the two terms are not interchangeable. Trust me, I've had intimate relationships with plenty of people where there was absolutely no sex involved. And though I can't speak from personal experience, I can also assure you that it is entirely possible to have sex with someone without having an intimate relationship. Sex, in and of itself, is a purely physical act. Intimacy is an emotional investment. When the two go hand in hand, the results can be extraordinary. But when the physical overrides or disregards the emotional, things go downhill quickly.

That's not to say sex is bad. As human beings, we are created by God to be sexual, and our sexuality is integral to who we are. It's part of what adds energy, mystery, and tension to life. In fact, sexual attraction can be a powerful companion, and even a *motivator*, to intimacy. We see proof of this in searing Technicolor in the Song of Solomon, which is essentially a tribute to erotic love. If you haven't read it in a while, here's a quick reminder of why you should:

> How beautiful you are, my darling!
>> Oh, how beautiful!
>> Your eyes behind your veil are doves.
> Your hair is like a flock of goats
>> descending from the hills of Gilead.
> Your teeth are like a flock of sheep just shorn,
>> coming up from the washing.
> Each has its twin;
>> not one of them is alone.
> Your lips are like a scarlet ribbon. . . .
> Your temples behind your veil
>> are like the halves of a pomegranate.
> Your neck is like the tower of David. . . .
> Your breasts are like two fawns . . .[8]

I'll stop, because it gets kind of weird after that. (For what it's worth, I once told Nancy that her hair looked like a flock of goats descending from the hills, and . . . I'll stop, because it got kind of weird after that.) Psychologists call this type of elaborate praise of a loved one "positive sentiment override." This is what happens when one person's positive thoughts and feelings about the other are so numerous and rich that they actually disempower negative feelings and fuel endless curiosity. This is why people in the falling-in-love stage can spend an entire day together talking, only to call each other up the second they part ways, to describe the ride home.

Interestingly, the Bible never tells us to *fall* in love. But it has a lot to say about *growing* in love: "I pray that your love will overflow more and more, and that you will keep on growing in knowledge and understanding."[9]

Beautiful, isn't it? So where did the negative connotation come from? According to Dr. Cliff Penner, who specializes in treating sexual issues, the message many children receive growing up is that sex is something dirty and disgusting—and you should save it for someone you love.[10]

As misguided as that line of thought is, some kids don't get even *that* much input from their parents.

When my father was growing up, for example, he never once saw his parents kiss. They never talked to him about sexual intimacy, how his body worked, what sexual feelings were like, or what to expect as he grew up and got married. The only "sex education" he ever received came from his mom after he graduated from high school.

"Be careful, John," she said. "There are bad girls at college."

Where do I find them? my father wondered.

Of course, kids who grow up not knowing the difference between intimacy and sex eventually become adults who don't know the difference, which often leads to further problems. Gary Chapman, in his book *The Five Love Languages*, tells a great story about a husband and wife who were dealing with sexual issues. The crux of their misunderstanding was that the husband equated love and intimacy with sex, but his wife had something different in mind.

One husband said to me, "I don't like that love tank game. I played it with my wife. I came home and said to her, 'On a scale of zero to ten, how's your love tank tonight?' She said, 'About seven.' I asked, 'What could I do to help fill it?' She said, 'The greatest thing you could do for me tonight is to do the laundry.' I said, 'Love and laundry? I don't get it.'"

I said, "That's the problem. Perhaps you don't understand your wife's love language. What's *your* primary love language?"

Without hesitation he said, "Physical touch, and especially the sexual part of the marriage."

"Listen to me carefully," I said. "The love you feel when your wife expresses love by physical touch is the same love your wife feels when you do the laundry."

"Bring on the laundry!" he shouted. "I'll wash the clothes every night if it makes her feel that good."[11]

The point is, sex is simply one way to express and enjoy intimacy. Words of affirmation, giving gifts, spending quality time together—or even doing the laundry—may be others. How closely do *you* associate intimacy with sex?

- It is virtually impossible for me to imagine an intimate relationship that does not have a sexual component. T/F
- I can become sexually intimate with someone without feeling emotionally connected to him or her. T/F
- I need to feel an emotional connection to someone before I can even think about a physical relationship. T/F

If you answered true to more than one of these questions, you might be confusing intimacy with sex. Let's see if we can clarify the distinction as we go along.

MYTH #5: EVERYBODY RESPONDS TO INTIMACY THE SAME WAY

Early on as a parent, I just assumed that the same words coming from the same parent (me) would have the same effect on all my children. It didn't work out that way. At all.

With one of my daughters, I expressed my love by gushing words of affection as I tucked her into bed. "I love you so much, honey. I love your face. I love your voice. I love your laugh. There's nothing that means more to me than being your dad."

Her eyes locked onto mine and got real big and wide and a little bit moist. Then she said, "I love you too, Daddy."

It was such a tender moment.

Then I went into my other daughter's bedroom with the same approach, the same words of affection. "I love you so much, honey. I love your face. I love your voice. I love the way you laugh. There is nothing that means more to me than being your dad."

She just stared at me, dry-eyed and unmoved. And then she said, "Daddy, I think you have something hanging upside down inside your nose."

Totally different love language, totally different wiring.

Now because my words were not received in the same way by one child as they were by the other, the danger is that I could've taken it personally and felt as if my one daughter didn't care for me as much as the other. But I soon learned that while one daughter might respond well to love talk, the other responded better to something else—like tickling her until she was screaming and laughing and shouting for me to stop (but then hoping I would start again). Two different approaches—same result. It was so interesting.

As people, we also have different temperaments. Introverts like me draw energy from being alone. Emotionally, when I wake up in the morning, I'm like a big balloon filled with air. Then, as I interact with people throughout the day, the air slowly seeps out, and by bedtime, my balloon is empty.

My wife, on the other hand, is a raging extrovert who rarely experiences an unexpressed thought or feeling. When she wakes up in the morning, she's like an empty balloon waiting to be filled. In fact, one of her favorite Bible verses is Proverbs 27:14: "A loud and cheerful greeting early in the morning will be taken as a curse!" (NLT). But as she goes through the day, interacting with people and having lively conversations, her balloon expands and she gets energized.

By the end of the day, I'm a shriveled little balloon and she's the Goodyear blimp. (Remember, we're talking about the fullness of our emotional tanks here.) It took us years to learn that we need to make time for our most important conversations when both our balloons are reasonably full. (And that's often a narrow window.)

Because we all have different personalities and different temperaments, we all give, receive, and interpret gestures of intimacy differently. Learning what types of gestures speak most effectively to those we love is part of what developing an intimate relationship is all about.

Think about the people you are closest to (or want to be closer to).

- Are they introverts or extroverts?
- Do they respond better to physical or verbal displays of affection?
- How about you? Does being around people energize you or exhaust you?

- What is *your* love language? Gary Chapman has identified five: affirmation, quality time, touch, service, and gifts.

If you're not sure how those around you perceive intimacy, spend some time observing, ask questions, and don't be discouraged if you don't connect on the first try. Nurturing an intimate relationship takes time, but it's worth it!

MYTH #6: ONCE YOU'VE ACHIEVED INTIMACY, IT CAN'T BE LOST

Mark Twain once wrote that he could "live on a good compliment two weeks with nothing else to eat."[12] If that were true, his wife, Olivia, would have had to come up with only twenty-six compliments a year (none of which, I'm guessing, would have been about his hair) and she would never have had to cook again.

A word to the wise: The people in your life *might* need to hear from you a little more often than twice a month. After all, intimacy isn't something you check off a list, like letting the dog out or picking up a jar of mayonnaise on your way home from work. It's like a campfire—if you don't continue to add fuel, eventually the flame will flicker out.

That doesn't mean you always have to have a grand gesture at the ready. Intimacy is a *big* feeling, but it's built on small moments. A well-timed hug. Bringing a casserole to a sick friend. Knowing a coworker's favorite coffee concoction and surprising him or her with a cup on Monday morning. Or, if your best friend happens to be Mark Twain, simply paying a compliment can go a long way.

Words of affirmation are some of the most powerful, yet

often neglected, intimacy-building tools in the world. And they can be embarrassingly simple:

"That color looks terrific on you."

"I love the way you encouraged our child."

"I admire the way you connect with people."

In fact, I recently tried an experiment with members of my family.

To my sister, Barbie, I said, "You had a really good idea for a question for all of us to discuss over dinner. We were able to get to know each other a little better and learn how the year went for everybody. Thanks for doing that."

To my brother, Bart: "You let us stay over at your house and fixed up beds and all kinds of fun stuff, and had food for everybody to make it such a joy. Thanks."

To my dad: "You've been through so much (spinal stenosis, a hip replacement, and Bell's palsy), and yet you just keep going. You don't let it stop you. I admire that so much."

To my mom: "I'm amazed at how much you can make me laugh."

It's so simple, yet so effective.

Of course, what we say to those with whom we are intimate doesn't always have to be *affirming*. Authentic intimacy involves painful truths as well as pleasant ones.

For example, I was at a conference with my family once when a woman approached me and told me about reading something I'd written. She said, "You talk a lot about your marriage and your family when you were growing up, and you disclose a lot of their problems, flaws, and shortcomings. When I read this, I thought, *My family would never have been okay with that.* Are the folks in *your* family okay with that?"

I said, "Yeah, they are."

One of my daughters was standing next to me and overheard.

"Dad, what did you say about us in that book?"

"Well, if you ever *read* something of mine," I calmly replied, "you'd *know* what I said. By the way, that color looks terrific on you."

It's important that we let the people we love the most *know* that we love them—and *often*. Sometimes, the smallest gestures have the greatest impact.

Here, let's try it. You're at the grocery store and your spouse says, "Are we out of toothpaste?" What do you say?

A. Nothing. You just shrug apathetically.
B. "How would I know?" (Slight sigh.) "Do you want me to get some?" (The sigh is subtle, but it's critical to indicate ever-so-slight annoyance that someone of your caliber would have to become the toothpaste fetcher.)
C. "I don't know, but let me grab some."
D. "Toothpaste? Who needs toothpaste when they've got you?"

The correct answer is C. Real intimacy isn't built on grand romantic gestures, but on ordinary life moments when we lean into another person instead of turning away. It works the same in friendships, marriages, families, and at work. We listen. We notice. We help out. Again. And again. And again.

MYTH #7: INTIMACY ISN'T FOR EVERYONE

Have you ever met people who seem incompatible with human relationships? You know you should try to get to know them better, but instead, you rationalize: *So-and-so is just too* _____ (fill in the blank: weird, pushy, volatile, self-absorbed, etc.) *to get close to.* And somehow you figure that their "issue" lets you off the hook.

But if every human being bears God's image, then it stands to reason that God *must* have created them with the capacity for intimacy.

Dietrich Bonhoeffer writes: "The exclusion of the weak and insignificant, the seemingly useless people, from a Christian community may actually mean the exclusion of Christ; in the poor brother Christ is knocking at the door."[13]

Simply put, intimacy is not limited to people without flaws and quirks. Love is what gives us the capacity to care for flawed and quirky people. (By the way, we are *all* flawed and quirky people.)

Think for a moment about the twelve men Jesus chose as his closest friends. I sometimes think the reason Jesus chose this particular dozen was to show that God can make a community out of *anybody*. Just look at these guys:

Simon: Though Simon was impulsive and often unreliable, Jesus nicknamed him Cephas (which means "rock" in Aramaic). We get the English name Peter from *petra*, the Greek word for rock. Some have suggested that the name was a play on words—more akin to "Rockhead"—given Peter's hardheaded nature.

James and *John:* Jesus nicknamed them Sons of Thunder, which most likely means they had anger issues.

Andrew and *Philip:* Both men, along with Peter, James, and John, were from Bethsaida—which means the other disciples may have battled a "Bethsaida clique." Even though Andrew met Jesus first and later told Peter about him, he ended up being referred to as "Peter's brother." If the disciples were the Brady Bunch, he was Jan to Peter's Marcia.

Thomas: He was also known as Didymus (the Twin). In the ancient world, twin births were considered bad omens—they complicated both childbirth and inheritance. For Thomas, the nickname was also symbolic of his double nature—a disciple who doubted.

Simon the Zealot: Zealots hated their Roman oppressors, and they hated even more the tax collectors who collaborated with the Romans.

Matthew the tax collector: I'm guessing Jesus had him room with Simon the Zealot.

James: This James was not the brother of Jesus. He was probably known as James the Lesser. Not a great nickname.

Thaddaeus (also known as Judas the son of James): All we know about him is that at the end of Jesus' life, he asked, "But, Lord, why do you intend to show yourself to us and not to the world?"[14] The implication is that he expected Jesus to "show himself to the world" by overthrowing Israel's enemies and establishing military greatness. His question shows a failure to grasp Jesus' repeated teachings that he would be a "suffering messiah." This question does not rocket Thaddaeus to the head of the class. It would be a little like asking on the last day of Science 101: "Tell me again why you teach that the earth is not flat?"

Bartholomew: His name could mean Son of the Furrows. He may have been one of those Jesus referred to as "leaving fields" to follow him.[15] Odds are, Bartholomew was wondering, "Am I crazy to do this?" Jesus probably had some reassuring to do.

Judas Iscariot: Seriously?

These twelve men argued, competed for superiority, and were often jealous or afraid. They misunderstood, blew up, failed, stole, denied, and betrayed. They must have looked at each other and wondered, *What are these other guys doing here?*

What created intimacy in this group wasn't that they were twelve spiritual all-stars. It was having Jesus in their midst. He gave them safety. He settled their conflicts. He showed them grace. He taught them love.

He does the same for us.

How about you?

- How do you respond when a relationship hits a bump in the road?
- What relationships used to be a significant part of your life but are no longer close? What happened? What might you learn from these situations?
- Is there anyone with whom you want to mend fences?
- Who might find *you* to be a difficult person? How can you build intimacy with him or her?

Read that last set of questions again. It's easy to spot qualities in others that might make our connecting with them difficult, but when it comes to evaluating our own readiness for intimacy, we can have some serious blind spots. We'll talk about some of those blind spots later.

In the meantime, remember, if the disciples teach us nothing else, it's that *anyone* is capable of developing a close bond with others.

MYTH #8: INTIMACY GIVES US PERMISSION TO LET OUR NEGATIVE EMOTIONS RUN WILD

Several decades ago, a popular anger-management therapy arose called *ventilationism.* The approach boiled down to this:

When you get angry, let it out. You must discharge your feelings, get it off your chest, blow off steam, let it all hang out, throw something, hit something, scream something—in other words, ventilate your anger.

Proponents argued that keeping your anger all bottled up wasn't healthy. They said it would just build up inside—like steam inside a teakettle—and would eventually explode like a volcano if there wasn't some sort of release.

But why would we think this way about anger and not about other emotions? Nobody says, "I've been holding in joy all these years. People have been telling funny jokes, and I've been repressing my laughter. It's been building up inside of me, and now the joy volcano is about to burst, and I'm going to spew joy all over everybody."

No therapist ever says to a client, "You had better get in touch with your gratitude, because, you know, when you were growing up, people did a lot of nice things for you, and you never verbalized your thankfulness. Now you've got all this gratitude bottled up inside you, and it's not healthy. You're like a walking time bomb of gratitude. Someday, it's going to go off, and you're going to walk up to people you don't even know and just spew gratitude all over them: 'Thank you, thank you, thank you, thank you!'"

As it turns out, ventilating is a bad way to handle anger. Too often, instead of discharging anger, it creates even more anger and becomes self-reinforcing. In other words, when people start shouting or hitting to ventilate their anger, it makes them feel powerful, and they want to shout and hit some more. It becomes a vicious—and violent—circle.

It also turns out that most people do not enjoy getting "ventilated on." The ventilator may experience a cathartic release, but the ventilatee doesn't think very highly of the process at all.

Carol Tavris, in her book *Anger: The Misunderstood Emotion*, writes, "The contemporary ventilationist view, that it is always important to express anger so that it won't clog your arteries or your friendships . . . tends to overlook . . . the consequences of anger. If your expressed rage causes another person to shoot you, it won't matter that you die with very healthy arteries."[16]

The research is very clear on this one. Three major reviews have covered dozens of studies over the last several decades, and not a single one demonstrates that *catharsis* is an effective way to manage anger. It just creates more anger.

Think about it. How often have you seen this scene played out? A driver feels as if he's been cut off in traffic, so he pulls up next to the other driver and screams, "You idiot! Learn how to drive!" To which the other person replies, "You know, that's some good advice. You've touched me deeply, my friend, and I'm going to change. I'm going to become a better driver. And thank you for taking the time to offer me that hand gesture, as well."

Bottom line, just because we're close to someone doesn't give us permission to take out our frustrations on them. In fact, making someone your emotional punching bag is probably the quickest way to *end* a relationship.

But don't take my word for it. Look at Proverbs 29:11: "Fools give full vent to their rage, but the wise bring calm in the end."

We'll look at "bringing calm" rather than "giving full vent" later on, when we talk about rupture and repair. In the meantime, ask yourself:

- How do you express anger? Is it healthy?
- Do you ever take out your frustrations on others?

- How do you feel when others take out their frustrations on you?
- When it comes to expressing anger, what is your end goal? Is it to make you feel better or to make someone else feel worse?

MYTH #9: INTIMACY LOOKS THE SAME REGARDLESS OF GENDER

In her brilliant book *You Just Don't Understand*, linguist Deborah Tannen writes,

> If adults learn their ways of speaking as children growing up in separate social worlds of peers, then conversation between women and men is cross-cultural communication. . . . If you understand gender differences in . . . conversational style, you may not be able to prevent disagreements from arising, but you stand a better chance of preventing them from spiraling out of control.[17]

According to Tannen, male culture tends to be competitive. Men live as individuals in a "hierarchical social order in which [they are] either one-up or one-down."[18] Boys tend to play in large groups—in which communication is about preserving independence and avoiding failure, and status is achieved by winning or by giving orders that stick. They use words to win arguments or demonstrate knowledge. (If you remember, on more than one occasion when the twelve disciples got together on their own, their number one argument was about who was number one.[19]) In male culture, then, words tend to produce stress.

Female culture, on the other hand, is more "a network of

connections."[20] Girls tend to play in small groups or pairs where communication is about preserving intimacy and avoiding isolation. Status is achieved by connecting. Girls tend to use words to affiliate with one another. In female culture, bossiness is to be avoided. Words are used not to prove superiority, but to express bonding. Therefore, words tend to be stress relieving.

If two male friends are in a locker room, they're likely to talk about jobs, sports, or current events, and they express affection by saying things like "That's quite a gut you've got going there. You should give it a name." Men like to play games like racquetball, where you can keep score and know who won. If they're watching a game and decide to have some chips and salsa, they'll negotiate, and the loser will have to fetch the food.

If women are in a locker room (I'm told), they're more likely to say things like "I hate my thighs," or "No, your thighs look great. Plus, you have wonderful hair—I'd kill for your hair." They do things such as aerobics or yoga where it's very difficult to tell who won. If they're watching something on TV, they will come to a consensus about having chips and salsa (after agreeing they shouldn't), and then go to the kitchen together to get them.

If you ask a woman, "How was your day?" she is likely to take that as an opportunity for bonding. She will expect connected listening and empathic responses. If you ask a man the same question, there's a greater chance he'll give you a report on how things went that will demonstrate both his competence and his mastery of details.

So it's no surprise that when the two sexes try to communicate with each other, problems can and do arise. In fact, the idea that men and women are from different planets became the basis of a popular book back in the early nineties.

The truth is, no one is merely a stereotype. There is such a thing as a sensitive male, and I've known many strong, outspoken, competitive women. (I even married one.) Though men and women may have some fundamental differences, what we all want most in a relationship is someone who will hear us, understand us, and value us.

So . . . how do you feel about interacting with the opposite sex?

A. It's my favorite thing!
B. Like I'm still in junior high
C. Utterly confused
D. Once burned, twice shy

If you answered A, that's awesome! If you answered B, C, or D, I get it—and we'll talk about overcoming obstacles to intimacy a little later.

MYTH #10: INTIMACY IS ALL ABOUT FEELINGS

One of the biggest misconceptions about intimacy is that it is all about emotions. Clearly, people who believe that have never forgotten their wedding anniversary or the name of their girlfriend's cat. When it comes to intimacy, details matter.

Deborah Tannen writes about her great-aunt, a longtime widow who was obese, balding, and arthritic, and yet was dearly loved by an elderly man who lived in a nearby nursing home.

One evening she had dinner out, with friends. When she returned home, her male friend called and she told him about the dinner. He listened with interest and asked her, "What did you wear?" When she told me this, she began to cry: "Do you know how many years it's been since anyone asked me what I wore?"

When my great-aunt said this, she was saying that it had been years since anyone had cared deeply—intimately—about her. The exchange of relatively insignificant details about daily life sends a metamessage of rapport and caring.[21]

When we're connected to people, we want to *know* about them. Because I desire connectedness with my children, I make it a point to know their friends. I know what music they listen to, who their favorite authors are, and what foods they like. I know what stresses them out and what brings them joy, and what their recent victories and failures have been.

Unconnected bosses don't know the names of their employees' children. Unconnected coworkers don't know the hobbies or favorite shows of the person at the next desk. Unconnected spouses don't know their significant others' favorite sports teams or perfumes.

In the play *Always a Bridesmaid*, a character named Monette complains to a friend that her husband is more interested in food than he is in her: "Last week I said, 'I bet you don't even know what my favorite flower is, do you?' He said, 'Sure, I do. Pillsbury Self-Rising, right?'"[22]

Intimacy isn't built simply by holding hands at the movies or staring lovingly into someone's eyes (though that's part of it). It's built by taking the time to find out what really matters to the people in your life—and not just the big things.

For example, Nancy and I have a favorite Mexican restaurant, called Lulu's, that's located just a few blocks from our house. We both love the food, but only Nancy likes salsa with hers. (I'm Scandinavian, so the only two spices I really like are butter and sugar.) But Nancy doesn't like just any salsa; she likes one particular kind out of the nine varieties Lulu's offers.

After repeatedly bringing home the wrong kind (or forgetting it altogether), I finally realized I was sending Nancy a message, even though I didn't forget on purpose. If I really care about Nancy (and I do), I should care that she enjoys her takeout as much as I do mine. What she likes matters. I finally took a picture of the *right* salsa, and I keep it on my phone. Now even if my memory fails me, I won't fail Nancy.

By the way, it's just as important that Nancy knows the little things that are important to me. Genuine connectedness runs both ways, and when a relationship lacks attention to detail—no matter how physically connected two people might be—problems are bound to arise.

Think about the people closest to you. People who experience genuine intimacy have what relationship expert John Gottman calls a *love map*—a rich and detailed collection of all the important details they've compiled about the people they love.[23] (You can use the term *database* if you're an engineer.)

For those relationships in your life where intimacy matters, think about some of these questions:

- When's her birthday?
- What does he like to do with his time off?
- What was her first job?
- What kind of music does he like?
- What's her favorite vacation spot?
- What is he most proud of these days?
- What is her biggest fear?
- How does he feel about God?

If you don't already know the answers, get them! And then write them in a journal or on your computer so you'll always remember.

MYTH #11: YOU CAN'T EXPERIENCE GENUINE INTIMACY WITH SOMEONE YOU CAN'T SEE OR TOUCH

Some people think it's impossible to have an intimate relationship with God because we can't see him, hear him, or touch him. But maybe God is to us humans like water is to fish. There's an old Ethiopian proverb that says, "Fish discover water last." The problem for the fish isn't that water is too distant; it's that water is so ubiquitous that they've never known existence apart from it—just like we have never known existence apart from God. So perhaps it's not God's *distance* from us, but our very *dependence* on him that makes us blind to his presence. We have to learn to recognize it.

There's a wonderful scene in *The Grapes of Wrath*, where Tom Joad says a final good-bye to his mother and assures her that his presence transcends physical boundaries—even when she can't see him:

> Wherever they's a fight so hungry people can eat, I'll be there. Wherever they's a cop beatin' up a guy, I'll be there. . . . I'll be in the way guys yell when they're mad an'—I'll be in the way kids laugh when they're hungry an' they know supper's ready. An' when our folks eat the stuff they raise an' live in the houses they build— why, I'll be there.[24]

It is the spiritual nature of God's presence—which at first seems like a barrier to intimacy—that actually makes intimacy with God deeper than with anyone else. He is closer to us than our own skin.

My friend Sean told me about growing up in a home where his mother and father disliked each other so intensely that they would not speak to each other. But for financial reasons, neither was willing to move out of the house. As a boy, Sean literally had to carry messages between them, as if through some science fiction power they were unable to hear what the other one said.

"Sean, tell your mother . . ."

They were occupying the same physical space, but emotionally they were on different planets.

On the other hand, connections in our universe can have a mysterious way of transcending physical distance. Quantum physicists say that two entangled particles can be a universe apart and yet so oddly connected that they *respond* to one another faster than the speed of light.

Like a mother when her son is on a foreign battlefield, or someone whose best friend is critically ill on the other side of the world, there's a spiritual connection, and the "speed of spirit" is even faster than the speed of light.

Another reason we have a hard time picturing ourselves in an intimate relationship with God is the same reason I have a hard time picturing myself chumming around with Mark Zuckerberg, having lunch with a movie star, or trading business ideas with Mark Cuban. Those relationships are above my pay grade. Groucho Marx used to say he wouldn't want to join any club that would accept him as a member. Knowing myself as I do, it's hard to imagine God's standards being low enough for me to join his family. Except they are.

Of course, there's yet another reason why some people have a hard time envisioning an intimate relationship with God: They're not sure he's there.

In *A Secular Age*, philosopher Charles Taylor asks, "Why was it virtually impossible not to believe in God in, say, 1500 in our Western society, while in [the twenty-first century] many of us find this not only easy, but even inescapable?"[25] Everyone knows the story about the emperor having no clothes. But what if there's not even an emperor? We live in an age when belief comes hard because we're much more afraid of being gullible (believing something that's not true) than we are of being skeptical (not believing something that *is* true). We often speak of "honest doubt" and "blind faith," but never of "honest faith" or "blind doubt" (though both exist).

In an intimate relationship, one person often guides the thoughts of the other. Because we're finite creatures, we must use finite means—we make sounds that are words, or write symbols on paper. But because God is infinite, he can guide our thoughts directly without using finite means. God can inhabit our gratitude for a sunrise, our regret over a lie, our burst of creativity, our joy at waking up or contentment after a good night's rest. As Lewis Smedes writes in *Union with Christ*, "The pilgrim journey is not a burdensome trudge up a lonely road; it is a way that cuts through Jesus Christ Himself. Life begins, proceeds, and ends in Christ."[26]

So, how *do* we experience intimacy with God? Easy. The same way we experience intimacy with anyone else.

Everything we've talked about so far—everything that applies to our relationships with each other—applies to our relationship with God. It's messy, sometimes seasonal, requires time and attention to flourish, is reciprocal by nature, fueled by love, and—here's the big one—it is possible for *everyone*.

Likewise, the same obstacles that get in the way of our achieving intimacy with other people tend to get in the way of our relationship with God: not spending enough time with him, not being fully present with him, not getting to know him, taking out our frustrations on him, not paying attention to him, and not seeking his will.

The prophet Jeremiah provides a fantastic litmus test for discerning our intimacy level with God: "Does a young woman forget her jewelry, a bride her wedding ornaments?"[27] (The answer, of course, is no.) "Yet my people have forgotten me, days without number."[28]

I call this *strategic memory loss*—an affliction that strikes us all. We promise to do a chore, take care of a small detail, clean something, buy something, or fix something, and then we forget. But if someone invites us to play golf at a great course, hands us a big check, or gives us a great present, we *don't* forget. We don't just randomly forget things. We remember what really matters to us.

If I forget commitments or acts of service that another dad, husband, pastor, or friend would remember, it says something about my heart. What does it say about our hearts if we forget to spend time with God? Here's what Neal Plantinga, president emeritus of Calvin Theological Seminary, observed:

> To love God intellectually is to become a student of God—a student who really takes an interest in God. Have you ever noticed that a fair number of Christians are not particularly interested in God? Some of them are ministers. These are people who don't ask about God, don't talk about God, and maybe don't even think about God unless they really have to. Their interest in God seems merely professional.
>
> Isn't this strange? Shouldn't we be somewhat *preoccupied* with God? Lovers get preoccupied with their beloved, they notice things about the one they love.[29]

It sounds strange, but I can be guilty of the sin of *not* being preoccupied with God; *not* finding my thoughts turning toward him; *not* asking what his will for me might be from one moment to the next. Eventually, God becomes a stranger to my thoughts. I forget him, I doubt him—not because of honest intellectual questions, but because I fail to love him. I close the door in his face a thousand times a day, and then wonder why he doesn't seem more present.

Ask yourself these questions to help gauge your intimacy with God:

- How much am I experiencing God's presence these days?
- What is my appetite for reading Scripture?
- How naturally do I find myself experiencing gratitude and expressing it to heaven?
- Am I praying more or less than in the past?
- Do I find prayer to be a stress reliever or a stress producer? Why?
- Is my personal and social conscience growing clearer?

Jesus said that the people who called him *Lord* but didn't care for "the least of these" may have thought they were in an intimate relationship with God, but they weren't.[30] People who are intimate with God care for the most vulnerable of those God loves.

- Am I noticing under-resourced people more?
- Am I giving more; wanting to give more?
- Am I more patient?

There is one more aspect of our relationship with God that we should take note of—and it contains a caveat about "gauging" our intimacy: Intimacy with God is a mysterious thing, and no mere human measurement can adequately plumb the depths of God's love. That's why the hollow and empty place inside each of us is our secret, our shame, our sorrow, and our hope.

Sometimes we experience what might be called "the presence of the absence of God."

Sometimes we seek him, we pray, we read the Bible, we give, we want him—but we don't sense his presence.

It doesn't mean he's not there.

It doesn't mean he doesn't care.

In a strange way, we are with Jesus even in these moments. Perhaps especially in these moments. When Jesus was on the cross, when he was doing the highest and most holy act of service, when he had surrendered to the will of his Father like never before, his cry was: "My God, my God, why have you forsaken me?"[31] It was that act of suffering, that experience of human Godforsakenness, that opened up for all humanity the way into God's presence.

It's possible that God is most present with us when we feel him the least.

The only gauge that matters is the one we cannot read—until we get to the other side.

CHAPTER 3

BORN TO BOND

WE WERE MADE FOR INTIMACY

There is the great lesson of "Beauty and the Beast"; that a thing must be loved before it is loveable.

G. K. CHESTERTON, *Orthodoxy*

WHEN OUR ELDEST DAUGHTER was born and we brought her home from the hospital, I was struck by how vulnerable she was. She was way too tiny even for the infant car seat we'd bought. I had to prop her up with blankets and pillows, and I was afraid her head would droop too far down and hurt her neck. On the way home from the hospital, I literally drove twenty-five miles per hour in the slow lane on the expressway with my hazard lights flashing. Meanwhile, Nancy periodically held a mirror under Laura's nose to make sure she was breathing.

When a baby cries, a parent soothes. This is the way of human life. Vulnerability drives us to intimacy.

Parents will instinctively reassure a baby who cries. Nancy always used one of two phrases: "Honey, honey" or "I know, I know." Mothers always say, "I know," even when they don't.

This is how children begin to learn that they have worth. Someone bigger, stronger, and wiser says, "I notice you. I recognize your discomfort, your pain, or your hunger, and I care. I will make things better."

Parents make this connection reflexively. When a baby cries, the mother doesn't immediately smile in response. First she will make a sad face—mirroring the emotion of the child. This is a huge part of intimacy. It says to the baby, "You are known." Not only that, but, "You are *worthy* of being known. Though you are tiny and vulnerable—and even scrawny—you have *value* such that the effort involved to comprehend your experience and serve your well-being is a small price to pay."

When Laura first came home, I often went into her room at night just to look at her and watch her sleeping in her crib. She was born with a little strip of red hair that ran down the middle of her head (it filled out into a lovely profusion of copper-colored hair just in time for college graduation), and if she was lonely or whimpering, I would gently rub her little Mohawk with two fingers and say to her, "I'll stroke your little head." Eventually, my back would start to ache, and I would try to sneak away. But if she was still awake she would object, and I would be right back at it.

"Stroke your little head? Stroke your little head?"

Sometimes, when she woke up in the morning, at around the age of one, if no one went to pick her up immediately, she would become distressed. But instead of crying regular cries, she would sob to herself the words she'd heard us say: "Honey, honey, honey . . . I know, I know . . . stroke your little head."

Hearing this, Nancy and I would lie in bed and laugh.

Looking back thirty years later, I now regret this.

I wish we had gotten up and videoed it.

But this is exactly what attachment looks like. In our

vulnerability, we are driven to someone who cares for us—who, in turn, engages in soothing behavior and promises that things will be okay.

When the little baby takes in these soothing words, the brain rewires itself. Fear diminishes. A sense of safety deepens. The world becomes a safer place.

Honey, honey, honey . . . I know, I know.

In fact, the way a child's brain develops is a staggeringly beautiful reflection of God at work in creation.

In Genesis 1, we're told that in the beginning there was a formless void. Neal Plantinga notes,

> Everything in the universe is all jumbled together. So God begins to do some creative separating: he separates light from darkness, day from night, water from land, the sea creatures from the land cruisers. God orders things into place by sorting and separating them.
>
> At the same time God binds things together: he binds humans to the rest of creation as stewards and caretakers of it, to himself as bearers of his image, and to each other as perfect complements—a matched pair of male and female persons who fit together and whose fitting harmony itself images God.[1]

God uses separating and joining to create what Plantinga calls "the building of shalom, the re-webbing of God, humanity, and all creation in justice, harmony, fulfillment, and delight."[2]

The Bible word for "separate" is *kadosh*. It's often translated as "holy." Over time, "holy" came to be associated with "holier-than-thou," a mind-set of distance and standoffishness. But in the beginning, it was not so. God *separated* so that he could *join together* in ever-more-complex systems of thriving and delight. To be *holy* is to become *useful*.

The human brain consists of about 86 billion neurons.[3] Lined up, they would stretch more than two million miles.[4] It is the most complex structure—natural or artificial—on earth.

Researcher Daniel Siegel writes that the way the mind becomes ordered begins with *differentiation* (through which parts of the brain become specialized and separated from others) and *linkage* (which facilitates the flow of energy and information).[5] Every experience joins certain neural pathways ("cells that fire together wire together"[6]) and separates other ones. This separation and linkage make possible what neurologists call *integration*—the individual brain's version of *shalom*. "In day-to-day terms," Siegel writes, "vitality and harmony emerge from integration. . . . This is the essence of health."[7]

See the connection? It's almost as if God re-creates the universe again with every child. But wait—there's more. Siegel also writes, "The experience of expressing one's emotional state and having others perceive and respond to those signals appears to be of vital importance in the development of the brain."[8] The brain and mind of a little child are literally formed through the power of the word. Such is the awesome influence of attachment.

What's great is that we don't have to be perfect at it. In fact, we can't be. Many moments will invariably get missed. Your baby may want to connect, but then the phone rings, or you're tired, or you're reading a book about connecting, or you misread your child's emotion. One study showed that mothers misread their babies' distressed cues about 70 percent of the time![9] For instance, you might think the baby is hungry, but she's really just tired. Or you may think the baby wants to be bounced on your lap, when he really just needs to be burped. You could do better flipping a coin.

Not surprisingly, the same phenomenon occurs between adults. Like infants, we don't always communicate clearly. And we misread each other's cues. You may think your wife is just tired when she's actually upset and giving you the cold shoulder. Or you may think your husband's not listening to you, but he's actually just trying to think of the right thing to say. Nobody gets it right 100 percent of the time. The key is to stick with it. Over time, two people will learn to read each other's cues better. They just have to keep trying.

When we get it right, though, we *know* they love us. In our vulnerability, we run to them, and while we receive the joy of being comforted, they receive the joy of giving comfort. We "feel felt."[10] Their strength is wired into us. Their voices quite literally get inside our heads.

We are able to say to ourselves, "Honey, honey . . . I know, I know." We can go back into the world to explore, and when we get hurt or hungry or frightened and return for comfort, we know we will hear, "Fear not, for I am with you."[11] And we will be comforted. And so on, and so on—a thousand times over.

Vulnerability. Attachment. Courage. Risk. Fear. Repeat.

We can't survive without intimacy.

HATCHED TO ATTACH

Right after you were born, on that first day you came home from the hospital, you didn't really care who was holding you. Your basic attitude was, "Feed me, clean me, stroke me, burp me, change me, swaddle me, and coddle me." The adults in your life were interchangeable, like spam messages or Ginsu steak knives.

Over time, you began to notice a couple of adults who were with you day after day. (Hopefully this happened before you went off to college.) These folks didn't have to be the smartest or prettiest or strongest people in the universe. They were *your* people. They noticed you. They cared when you were upset. They gave you free stuff. They mourned when you mourned and rejoiced when you rejoiced. You came to prefer them to strangers.

This is called *attachment*. It's a combination of dependence and love. When little children are attached to their mother, they feel calmer when she is around. When Mom's out of their sight, they feel a little anxious.

Attachment is so fundamental to life that entire neuron networks in the brain are devoted to its development. (No wonder the psalmist says we are "fearfully and wonderfully made."[12])

The genius of the attachment system is that it empowers us to cope with life. Your mother's soothing voice telling you "it's okay" literally wires your brain so you are able to say "it's okay" to yourself. Your mother's comforting presence is now inside you (which seems fair since you used to be inside her).

When their parents are near, children are more relaxed, feel safer, and are therefore free to explore. "Be not afraid" is the most common and important command a parent can give. Even young infants, when they are scared, will seek their parents' presence. They naturally believe they are worth caring for, and they are betting everything on their parents' care. As humans, we're made that way. We hatch to attach.

Sometimes we have intimacy problems because of the circumstances of our growing up. These are sometimes called attachment disorders. For example, infants whose parents fail to respond to their cries for help learn to act as if they don't need their parents. They don't cry when their parents leave, and they don't seek them out when the parents come back. (Internally, however, their heart rate and blood pressure reflect the anxiety their faces have learned not to show.) When parents are wildly inconsistent in responding to their children, the children become deeply ambivalent about attachment.

Ironically, when we become adults, the more we try to be attached to others out of immature neediness, the less likely it is to happen. My task as an adult is to become my own person—to deeply own my own values, convictions, and beliefs. To refuse to hide in order to gain acceptance. To take responsibility for myself, but refuse to take responsibility for another.

The more differentiated I am as a separate person, the deeper the attachments I can have with other people because I can love them without using them to fill a hole inside me. This is the shalom of separation and attachment.

People often tell me how much they like my wife. If I travel someplace where she has spoken, that's the first comment I'm likely to hear. If I meet someone who has already met her, she'll be the first topic of conversation.

When I first interviewed to work at the church I now serve, Nancy was offered a job there as well, so we met with the search committee together. Afterward, a member of the committee—whom I have known as a friend for years—was debriefing the interview with me.

"Your part went fine, but the real surprise was Nancy," he said.

"That's great."

"Yep," he went on, "people enjoyed you, but Nancy had a big 'wow' factor."

"I'm glad."

"I mean, there was no problem with your part," he assured me, "but Nancy—holy smokes!—she made the room come alive."

"What's your point, Larry?"

It's not that Nancy is always agreeable. In fact, I'm far more agreeable than she is. But she has a way of completely disagreeing with people that makes them feel even more connected to her than polite agreement would. She has a way of being herself with people and expressing her opinions with great freedom. She's about 90 percent attitude. And people love it.

The apostle Paul puts it like this: "Love must be sincere."[13] When we try to anticipate what will be agreeable to others by hiding our true opinions and modifying what we say, we actually destroy any hope of the very intimacy we desire.

A SEPARATE PEACE

When God created the first woman, he took her from Adam's side. He "separated" her from Adam. His design was to make her into a whole and independent person who could love Adam as an equal. Then God "joined" the man and the woman and created something greater than the sum of its parts: *intimate community*. Two *me's* became a *we*.

If shalom is the webbing together of God, humans, and all creation in justice, fulfillment, and delight, then intimacy is the webbing together of selves that God has separated into *we's* (couples, families, friends, teams).

When we were infants, we needed attachment to survive. But when we become adults, we need *separation* in order for *attachment* to work. In fact, God was so committed to the *separateness* of fully formed people that he *separated* us from himself to allow it to happen. Sometimes that helps me to remember that just because I don't *feel* God's presence, it doesn't mean he's absent.

Rankin Wilbourne writes about an old distinction between *union* with God and *communion* with God. *Union* is an objective connection—for example, I will always be my parents' child; whereas *communion* is a subjective sense of closeness that will wax and wane.[14]

God allows us a kind of separateness from him in order to facilitate the formation of our selves. It's striking that when the serpent tempted the woman in the Garden of Eden, God was nowhere to be seen. Later, we're told that God came to walk in the Garden in the cool of the day. Why hadn't he just stayed the whole time? If he had been present, Eve surely would never have given in to temptation.

Adam and Eve, in their original state, were sinless but not mature. They were not yet guilty of wrongdoing, but they hadn't cultivated a strong attachment to what is right.

God's primary goal for us is *character*, not *innocence*. *Innocence* means I haven't done anything wrong. *Character* means I am habitually devoted to doing what is right. Babies are innocent. Saints have character.

It is only people of sound character who can safely experience intimacy with others. And it's in those moments of temptation, those moments when we feel alone, that we make choices that will uniquely shape our character.

DIVINE ATTACHMENT DISORDER

Whether we acknowledge it or not, this brings us to God, the only one big enough and strong enough to tell us what we all need to hear: "Don't be afraid. It's okay."

Parents will say these words to their children even when

everything is *not* okay (maybe especially then), but we need this foundational truth—that everything's okay—in order to be fully formed as healthy people.

That's the good news, as the Bible assures us: Everything *is* okay—with God, with his Kingdom, and for those who live in his Kingdom. That's why we seek intimacy with God. Our attachment to him is what underscores our foundational beliefs. The only difference is that what psychologists call *attachment*, the Bible calls *faith*.

We are made to live in confident attachment with God the same way a child is made for confident attachment to its mother. Thus, a solid connection with God is the foundation for intimacy with others. In the book of Isaiah, the prophet uses the image of a mother-child relationship to underscore our need for a stronger attachment to God: "Can a mother forget the baby at her breast and have no compassion on the child she has borne? Though she may forget, I will not forget you!"[15]

Dallas Willard writes, "The natural condition of life for human beings is one of reciprocal rootedness in others."[16] We were made to live in what Willard calls "circles of sufficiency," where we can be assured that everything is okay—even though no human circle can *make* everything okay.

Only when rooted in the divine circle of Father, Son, and Spirit can broken individuals recover from the wounds they've received in their circle of origins. Healing must be found there if it is to be found at all. It is no coincidence that the most common command of every mother to her child is also the Bible's most common command of God to his children: "Don't be afraid. I'm here."

I believe we suffer from a kind of Divine Attachment Disorder that renders us unable to receive the words that our heavenly Father most wants us to hear. This disorder can be seen in the Bible as far back as the days of the prophet Hosea:

> When Israel was a child, I loved him. . . .
> It was I who taught Ephraim to walk,
> taking them by the arms;
> but they did not realize
> it was I who healed them. . . .
> My people are determined to turn from me.[17]

Sometimes people assert that our image of God is determined by the relationship we had with our parents. If our earthly father was cold and distant, we imagine our heavenly Father to be the same way. But I suspect that the nature and content of our faith is far more complex than that. Beyond our parents, I believe our faith is shaped by what we learn about God while growing up, by our own genetic predispositions (some people refer to a predisposition toward spirituality as "the God gene"), by our likes and dislikes, by the people we hang around with, and by the goals we set for ourselves.

Maybe you are one who doubts whether God even exists. Maybe you have prayed to him for months or years about a great longing, but haven't seen any answers. Maybe when you read the Bible you find it raises more questions than it answers. Perhaps you're afraid that science or reason have proven that faith is irrational.

Maybe you believe there is a God, but you're not sure he's good. I have a friend who grew up believing that God was just around the corner, waiting to hurt her if she let down her guard. Perhaps you were taught that God must be mean if he's going to run the universe.

Then again, maybe you believe God exists and that he's

good, but you think he's way out there in outer space, worrying about big issues, and your little life is too small to matter. You think of God as uninvolved in the issues of day-to-day life, and without that involvement you find intimacy with him impossible.

Maybe you're afraid that if you were to pursue an intimate attachment with God, you would have to do something you don't want to do or give up something important to you. Maybe the honest truth is that you have a sinful pattern of activity or behavior in your life and you don't want to let go of it.

Or maybe you feel as if you've been burned by faith in the past. You tried it and it didn't work. You asked for help with a problem and the answer didn't come. You joined a community of faith and felt betrayed. You used to feel close to God, but you got tired and are now just drifting. You have felt anxious for years, and all this talk about "peace with God" leaves you feeling guilty and frustrated.

Whatever your image of God, it will shape not only how you interact with others and the world around you, but also how you see yourself. But I can tell you this: The closer you are to God, the greater your attachment, the more secure you will feel—in the world, with yourself, and with others.

WE'RE NEVER ALONE

Our attachments lead us to what some researchers call "a state of mind," a view of the world that is either safe or dangerous; intriguing or boring; generous or stingy. In Psalm 23, we see perhaps the greatest description of the state of mind associated with having a strong attachment to God: "The LORD is my shepherd; I shall not want. . . . Even though I walk through the valley of the shadow of death, I will fear no evil, for you are with me."[18]

Julian of Norwich presents us with a wonderful image of our security with God—that of a hazelnut. She writes, "In this little thing I saw three properties. The first is that God made it, the second is that God loves it, the third is that God preserves it. But what did I see in it? It is that God is the Creator and the protector and the lover. For until I am substantially united to him, I can never have perfect rest or true happiness, until, that is, I am so attached to him that there can be no created thing between my God and me."[19]

A few weeks ago, when I was out surfing, there was no one else in the water. In fact, there was no one around at all, except a guy the size of Goliath doing tae kwon do on the beach.

After I'd been out a little while, a tiny wisp of a kid came paddling up out of nowhere—I couldn't believe he was out there by himself. He pulled his little board right up next to mine. He was so small he hardly needed a board. He could have stood up in the ocean on a Frisbee. Anyway, he started chatting with me like we were old friends. He told me his name was Shane. He asked me how long I'd been surfing. I asked him how long he'd been surfing.

"Seven years," he said.

"How old are you?" I asked.

"Eight."

He asked me about my kids and my family. Then he said, "What I like about surfing is that it's so peaceful. You meet a lot of nice people here."

"You're a nice guy, Shane," I said. "That's why you meet nice people."

We talked a while longer. Then I asked him, "How did you get here, Shane?"

"My dad brought me," he said. Then he turned around and waved at the nearly empty beach. The Goliath doing martial arts waved back.

"Hi, Son," he called out.

Then I knew why Shane was so at home in the ocean. It wasn't his size. It wasn't his skill. It was who was sitting on the beach. His father was always watching. And his father was very big. Shane wasn't really alone at all. Neither are we.

At its core, the gospel is the invitation to an intimate relationship with God. It tells us we are never alone. Although we cannot see him, our Father is always present, always watching. We can turn to him at any moment. We can safely approach and love those around us. We can be okay even if we face storms of rejection or pain. For God is never far away, we are never out of his sight, and his voice is always speaking. In the words of Julian of Norwich, "All shall be well, and all shall be well, and all manner of things shall be well."[20]

Be not afraid.

Honey, honey . . . I know, I know.

Everything is okay.

CHAPTER 4

YOUR BID . . .

INVITATIONS TO CONNECT

They're sharing a drink they call loneliness, but it's better than drinking alone.
BILLY JOEL, *"Piano Man"*

IN 2015, RESEARCHERS at the University of California at Berkeley, announced they would be part of a $100 million dollar project for space travel to see if there's intelligent life in the universe.[1] (Coincidentally, Stanford, which is Berkeley's big rival in the Bay Area, where I live, recently announced a massive project to see if there's intelligent life in Berkeley.) The plan is to send tiny nanocrafts—like spaceship butterflies—traveling at one-fifth the speed of light to Alpha Centauri. Stephen Hawking expressed the purpose poignantly: "It is important to know if we are alone in the dark."[2]

The folks at Berkeley are not the only ones who want to know. It turns out that everyone—including you and me—is constantly sending out tiny little probes, emotional nanocrafts, to find out whether they're alone in the dark. They travel at high speeds, and it's easy to miss them. Those who are skillful at recognizing and responding to these probes have a great gift for cultivating intimate friendships. Those who are blind, or nonresponsive to them, often end up alone in the dark.

These emotional nanocrafts are what John Gottman calls "bids" for emotional connection.[3] We start issuing these bids before we can talk. A baby's cry is a bid to connect. As we grow older, these bids—or invitations—for intimacy take other forms. "A bid can be a question, a gesture, a look, a touch— any single expression that says, 'I want to feel connected to you.'"[4] Intimacy of every kind is either built up or eroded, based on how well we handle the subtle little nanocrafts of relational life.

Gottman's research team at the University of Washington made some interesting discoveries about "bids" made by married couples: "We learned, for example, that husbands headed for divorce disregard their wives' bids for connection 82 percent of the time, while husbands in stable relationships disregard their wives' bids just 19 percent of the time."[5] For wives, the figures are 50 percent and 14 percent, respectively. Not only that, but happily connected couples will engage with each other one-and-a-half times more often in a ten-minute period than a badly connected couple.[6]

We constantly send out these little probes, whether they are acknowledged or not.

They can be small: "Did you see the game last night?"

They can be poignant: "I don't think I'll ever call my dad again."

They can be deep: "I'm not sure my wife loves me anymore."

They can be urgent: "I have no one else to talk to; can I speak to you confidentially?"

They can be funny: "Knock knock." (Well, funny if you're six years old.)

They might appear insignificant: "Will you get me my cell phone while you're up?"

We can either respond in ways that build intimacy: "Yep— want anything else?" or in ways that squelch it: "Why don't you get it yourself."

Sometimes what *isn't* said can communicate just as much as what is. For example, if I pause just long enough before saying "Yep," I can communicate, "What a burden you've put on me. I'll get your phone, but I'll do it with a grudging spirit and take all the joy out of it." (This, by the way, is the standard Scandinavian response.)

An invitation to connect can also be slightly disguised. Toward the end of my freshman year in college, I asked my friend Kevin, "Who are you rooming with next year?" but that's not really what I meant. What I meant was, "I don't have anyone to room with, I feel like a loser, and would you *please* tell me you want to room with me?" When that didn't work, I resorted to inducing guilt by playing the martyr. Fortunately, Kevin finally took pity on me, and he invited me into a friendship and a community that changed my life.

Sometimes we send out fuzzy invitations for intimacy because we're afraid of the pain of rejection. Or because we hope that removing the pressure of a direct request will help the other person respond favorably. Or because we're just poor communicators. The danger in taking the fuzzy route is that sometimes our bids go unrecognized.

On Christmas Eve 1982, I woke Nancy out of a sound sleep at 1:00 a.m., drove her to the parking lot of the church where I grew up (I have a gift for locating romantic settings), and gave her a Christmas present of two small porcelain bears dressed as a bride and groom. To which she responded, "Huh?" Clearly, this was a fuzzy invitation. So I had to spell it out: "Will you marry me?"

People generally respond to an invitation to connect in one of three ways (four, if you include the occasional "huh?"): They either accept it, reject it, or ignore it. For example, if your friend stops by and says, "Hey, I'm going to Starbucks. Wanna come along?" you have three possible responses:

1. *Accept.* Some people have the kind of personality that naturally accepts invitations with flair. *"Not only am I coming—I'm buying!"* Granted, we don't have to respond like a hypercaffeinated version of motivational speaker Tony Robbins. What's most important to remember is that we're constantly sending signals—by facial expression, tone of voice, body language, and pauses—that tell the other person whether we are genuinely interested in connecting with them. Even if we can't accept the invitation outright, we can always find a way to say yes to the bid for connection. *"I'm crunched right now, but how about this afternoon?"*

2. *Reject.* In this case, we actively let the person know their invitation is unwelcome. *"Are you kidding? I've got too much to do."* Sometimes, people who are more attuned to the language of logic than the language of emotion may turn down an offer and unintentionally shut the door to intimacy. For some people, learning to speak "Invitationese" is like learning a foreign language. They may never become as fluent as a true native, but over time they can learn to speak it—albeit with a charming, slightly Spock-like accent.

3. *Ignore.* If we respond with a purely objective caffeine report— *"Nope. Already had some"*—we're sending a message that we didn't notice the *real* invitation—to spend time together. It may be that we genuinely missed it (some of us have a tin ear when it comes to hearing invitations, like we're unable to pick up the frequency of a dog whistle). Or it may be that we heard the invitation just fine, but we don't want to have coffee, so we pretend we didn't notice the underlying invitation to connection. Either way, by ignoring the invitation, we make it less likely that the other person will invite us the next time.

In relationships that move *toward* intimacy, invitations are most often skillfully and playfully issued, and honestly and joyfully received. Each connection is like a deposit into an emotional bank account.

When I call one of my daughters, she literally sings, *"Hello!"* when she answers the phone, as if she were Adele. In response, I sing, *"Hello, how are you?"* like Will Ferrell impersonating Robert Goulet, and we continue singing our call for several lines. It is a tiny, silly, goofy, lovely connection. This is what it looks like to welcome a bid. If I simply started talking as if I hadn't noticed her singing response, I would have ignored her bid. If I said, "Could we just once have a normal conversation?" I would have rejected her invitation.

When invitations are not recognized or embraced, relationships tend to die.

A couple is at a table sharing a meal. They're both looking at their screens, checking Facebook posts and e-mails from work.

"Look at this video of cats playing chess," she says.

He chuckles. Or doesn't. Or grunts. Or shakes his head. Or leans over to take a look.

Depending on how he responds to her bid, he either makes a tiny little intimacy deposit or he doesn't.

Here's the amazing thing: An invitation received usually leads to another invitation.

A friend texts to ask whether I've heard that the Golden State Warriors signed Kevin Durant.

My daughter tells me about the rock star who's writing a post for her website.

My neighbor asks if I know where he could find office space.

My wife tells me about the strategy by which she got the blouse she's wearing for 40 percent off, and how fortunate it was that she already had matching shoes.

Will I notice? Will I smile? Will I ask a question in response? Will I get excited? If I do, the dance continues. In the realm of human intimacy, invitations noticed and accepted are like cells in the human body—the tiny, unnoticed building blocks that add up to make life possible.

THE GRAND INVITATION

Jesus walked through life as a master of intimacy. His invitations to connection were quite fearless in the face of possible rejection:

- He asked a Samaritan woman to give him something to drink. It began an intimate conversation that would change her life.
- He noticed a vertically challenged tax collector named Zacchaeus sitting up in a tree and invited him to come down and join him for dinner.

- He noticed the little children that everyone else shooed away. He invited them to come to him, took them in his arms, and blessed them.

Throughout his life, Jesus pursued intimate fellowship with everyone from fishermen, prostitutes, tax collectors, and soldiers, to Pharisees who came to him by night and lepers who came to him by day.

He gave the greatest invitation ever offered, in two simple words: "Follow me." He extended the invitation to people walking alongside a lake, to a man in a toll booth, to a rich young ruler (who rejected it), and to people who had suffered loss.

Jesus was Peter's intimate friend for three years. Then after Peter had denied Jesus and Jesus had forgiven him, in the very last chapter of the Gospel of John, Jesus issued his invitation to Peter one more time: "Follow me!"[7]

And now Jesus offers the same invitation to you. Just as he offered back then to be with those who would follow him, in the midst of their ordinary lives, so too, he offers to walk with you in the midst of your ordinary life today.

Will you accept, reject, or ignore him?

If you choose door #2 or #3, don't think that's the end of the story. God continually invites us to connect with him. And he doesn't give up.

Each sunrise is no less miraculous just because we've gotten used to seeing the sun rise. Waking up in the morning is a habit, but it's also a mystery and it can be a gift. We might begin to see the start of the day as an invitation to enjoy the gift of life rather than as a burden to be endured with gritted teeth.

Jesus said that seeing a person in need can be an invitation:

"Whatever you did for one of the least of these . . . you did for me."[8] But then we have to be willing to be interrupted and enter into suffering.

Our work might be an invitation: "Whatever you do, work heartily, as for the Lord and not for men."[9] Our computers might become little altars as we're clicking away at the mouse of God.

Even loneliness can become an invitation to intimacy if we're willing to sit quietly and listen rather than distract ourselves with a drink or a screen: "Deep calls to deep."[10]

Light speaks to us of God's goodness; darkness speaks of our need. But both can become offers of God's presence: "By day the LORD directs his love, at night his song is with me."[11]

The heavens declare God's glorious presence, but so do humbler delights on earth—"such created excellences as the velvety coat of a puppy or the honking of geese in a November fly-by or the hitchhiking home of young beetles on the backs of bees."[12]

Stabs of guilt and pangs of regret become invitations to mercy and grace.

Perhaps Elizabeth Barrett Browning was right after all:

Earth's crammed with heaven,
And every common bush afire with God:
But only he who sees, takes off his shoes,
The rest sit round it, and pluck blackberries.[13]

The point is, God sends us invitations to connect every day. We can accept them, ignore them, or reject them. And we can learn to grow more skillful in recognizing these invitations to intimacy with God. Settle back in your chair. Be still. Grab a cup of coffee if it helps. Invite Jesus to experience your day with you. Take a moment to thank God for reaching out to you. Confess and ask God's pardon for those times when you've ignored or rejected his overtures. Ask for God's help in seeing and responding to his invitations. Then hear Jesus issue the Grand Invitation to you once again.

"Follow me."

In spite of your failures and betrayals, he calls you again, just as he did to Peter.

"Follow me."

Tell him *yes*. Invite him to walk with you through every part of your day.

Welcome his presence in your life—if for no other reason than because it's important to know that you're not alone in the dark.

CHAPTER 5

ME, MYSELF, AND LIES

SELF-AWARENESS

He hath ever but slenderly known himself.
WILLIAM SHAKESPEARE, *King Lear*

IN HIS BOOK about developing "emotional intelligence," Daniel Goleman uses an old Japanese parable to introduce the concept of self-awareness, or self-observation.

> A belligerent samurai . . . once challenged a Zen
> master to explain the concept of heaven and hell.
> But the monk replied with scorn, "You're nothing
> but a lout—I can't waste my time with the likes of
> you."
> His very honor attacked, the samurai flew into a
> rage and, pulling his sword from its scabbard, yelled,
> "I could kill you for your impertinence!"

"That," the monk calmly replied, "is hell."

Startled at seeing the truth in what the master pointed out about the fury that had him in its grip, the samurai calmed down, sheathed his sword, and bowed, thanking the monk for the insight.

"And that," said the monk, "is heaven."[1]

There is a world of difference between being caught up in a mood, an emotion, a thought, or a pattern, and being *aware* of its presence in your mind and body.

When I think, *This is a terrible day*, my sadness increases. When I think, *This is sadness I'm feeling*, it actually creates a small but critical distance between me and the feeling of sadness.

Likewise, when I think, *You infuriate me!* my anger increases. When I think, *This is anger I'm feeling*, I actually begin to calm down.

Awareness of what I'm feeling generally brings the awareness that I am *not* my feelings. And then I can begin to see you more clearly and relate to you more intimately. It's a little like shifting my focus from looking *through* a window to looking *at* the window and noticing the streaks and dust and cracks that are distorting my vision.

In the Bible, a lack of awareness is often compared to blindness or a problem with the eyes. And blindness is often portrayed as a central obstacle to intimacy with God and others. Jesus spent a lot of time trying to help people with their blindness—both physical and spiritual.

When Martha complained to Jesus that she was doing all the work while her sister just sat around listening to him, Jesus responded by refocusing her attention: "Martha, Martha, . . . you are worried and upset about many things."[2] Why did he say this? Because Martha wasn't aware that she was anxious and bothered about many things.

Likewise, when a man tried to get Jesus involved in a dispute over a family inheritance, Jesus responded by saying: "Beware! Guard against every kind of greed."[3] Why did he say this? Because the man was unaware of the greed he was feeling.

And after a lifetime of watching judgmental people criticize other peoples' minor flaws while remaining blind to their own major character defects, Jesus asked them, "Why do you look at the speck of sawdust in your brother's eye and pay no attention to the plank in your own eye?"[4] Why did Jesus say that? Because he was surrounded by speck-removers who didn't know they were plank-eyes.

Martha was frustrated with Jesus because to her way of thinking, he wasn't appropriately chastising Mary. (So Martha had to do it.) The greedy man was probably frustrated with Jesus because Jesus wouldn't tell the man's brother to split his inheritance. People walking around with beams in their eyes often try to remove specks from the eyes of others because they think God isn't doing enough speck-removal on his own.

Our capacity for self-deception knows no bounds, and it's a serious problem where intimacy is concerned. Why? Because intimacy is *shared experience*, and we can't share with others if we're not aware of what we're experiencing in our own soul and spirit.

What's more, our lack of self-awareness keeps us from knowing God. Instead of seeing him clearly, we peer at him through the prism of our blind spots.

The ancient oracle at Delphi said to "know thyself" was at the core of human wisdom. In the biblical tradition, self-knowledge is important for an additional reason: It is fundamentally connected to our capacity for intimacy with God.

All great spiritual thinkers understand the deep connection between knowledge of self and knowledge of God.

Augustine, in his *Soliloquies*, prays for what is often referred to as double knowledge: "God, always the same, let me know myself, let me know Thee!"[5]

John Calvin echoes Augustine in book one of his *Institutes of the Christian Religion*: "The knowledge of God and the knowledge of ourselves are bound together by a mutual tie."[6]

Bernard of Clairvaux, a twelfth-century French abbot, said, "Know yourself and you will have a wholesome fear of God; know him and you will also love him."[7]

When we lack self-awareness, we may project onto God and others the fear, anger, greed, and complaints that fester blindly beneath the surface of our lives. In Jesus' story about the talents, the "wicked, lazy servant"[8] blamed his own poor choices on the character of his master: "I knew that you are a hard man, harvesting where you have not sown and gathering where you have not scattered seed."[9]

Healing begins when we become open to the fact that the truth about us is that *we don't know* the truth about us. Healing begins when our desire to face reality is stronger than our desire to avoid pain.

One weekend, as we were debriefing after our services, one of my church staff teammates mentioned in passing that there was a problem with the video of that day's sermon.

"What is it?" I asked.

"You had a big gob of spittle on your lip for most of the message," he explained. "It's always a problem when we videotape the talk and you've got a big gob of spittle on your lips."

I had no idea I had spittle on my lips, and now I'm being told it happens often enough to be a regular problem for the entire video department. I'm the only one who was unaware of my spittle problem. What can I say? Spittle happens.

Now when I speak, one of my colleagues watches me for spittle and flashes a light on a screen to warn me so I can wipe it off. Yes, I actually have a spittle detector.

Here's what King David said about the difficulty of self-awareness: "Who can discern their own errors? Forgive my hidden faults."[10] That's one of the weirdest things about sin—I'm *very* aware of yours, but I'm rarely as aware of my own problems.

Several centuries ago, Joseph Butler preached on our propensity for self-deception. The language is a bit archaic, but the point is too rich to miss:

> There is not any thing, relating to men and
> characters, more surprising and unaccountable,
> than this partiality to themselves. . . . Hence it is
> that many men seem perfect strangers to their own
> characters. They think, and reason, and judge quite
> differently upon any matter relating to themselves,
> from what they do in cases of others. . . . Hence
> it is one hears people exposing follies, which they
> themselves are eminent for; and talking with
> great severity against particular vices, which if all
> the world be not mistaken, they themselves are
> notoriously guilty of.[11]

Often, God uses other people to help us become self-aware. I have a personal spittle detector. In *Peculiar Treasures,*

Frederick Buechner presents a slightly more eloquent story about King David and the prophet Nathan.

> Just about every king seems to have had a prophet
> to help keep him honest. . . . The best example is, of
> course, the most famous.
>   David had successfully gotten rid of Uriah the
> Hittite by assigning him to frontline duty, where he
> was soon picked off by enemy snipers. After a suitable
> period of mourning, David then proceeded to marry
> Uriah's gorgeous young widow, Bathsheba. The
> honeymoon had hardly started rolling before Nathan
> came around to describe a hardship case he thought
> David might want to do something about.
>   There were these two men, Nathan said, one of
> them a big-time rancher with flocks and herds of just
> about everything that has four legs and a tail and the
> other the owner of just one lamb he was too soft-
> hearted even to think about in terms of chops and
> mint jelly. He had it living at home with himself and
> the family, and he got to the point where he even let
> it lap milk out of his own bowl and sleep at the foot
> of his bed. Then one day the rancher had a friend
> drop in unexpectedly for a meal and, instead of taking
> something out of his own overstuffed freezer, he got
> somebody to go over and commandeer the poor
> man's lamb, which he and his friend consumed with
> a garnish of roast potatoes and new peas.
>   When Nathan finished telling him the story, David
> hit the roof. He said anybody who'd pull a stunt like
> that ought to be taken out and shot. At the very least
> he ought to be made to give back four times what the

lamb was worth. And who was the greedy, thieving slob anyway, he wanted to know.

"Take a look in the mirror the next time you're near one," Nathan said. It was only the opening thrust. By the time Nathan was through, it was all David could do just to pick up the receiver and tell room service to get a stiff drink up to the bridal suite.[12]

THE ELICITED SELF

One of the most important "awareness" questions we can ask ourselves in each significant relationship is, "How does my connection with this person impact the person I'm becoming?"

Just as every planet has a gravitational pull on other planets, so too does each person in our lives either pull us *toward* or *away from* our best selves. I call this "the elicited self."

C. S. Lewis writes, "In each of my friends, there is something that only some other friend can fully bring out. By myself I am not large enough to call the whole man into activity."[13]

For example, something about my friend Kent brings out a particular funny streak in my friend Danny like nothing else. When the three of us are together, I get to experience that side of Danny that only Kent can elicit.

This idea of the elicited self applies to all our relationships. When I'm with one particular friend, I find I am more prone to gossip, and we both seem to derive pleasure from pronouncing judgment on others. But a different friend, one who doesn't respond to gossip at all, elicits a non-gossiping me.

Our elicited self is constantly being formed by how we respond to the people around us—people who question or flatter or challenge or laugh or encourage or belittle.

Nathan had a way of eliciting David's true self, even at great risk to his own life.

And of course the master of eliciting our best selves is Jesus.

When a little tax collector named Zacchaeus got close to Jesus, he did a turnaround like Scrooge on Christmas morning.

The Samaritan woman went from a scandalous loner to a spiritual leader in her town.

Simon went from an impulse-control case to Peter, the Rock of Galilee.

A Samaritan leper became a poster boy for the attitude of gratitude.

A thief on a cross exhibited a repentant heart by sticking up for his newfound Savior.

People just generally found they were better when Jesus was around. They called it "being in Christ."[14]

The more intimate we are with Christ, the more we become *like him*—and the more we can become him to others.

THE BIG ME

Fyodor Dostoyevsky once observed, "Every man has reminiscences which he would not tell to everyone, but only to his friends. He has other matters in his mind which he would not reveal even to his friends, but only to himself, and that in secret. But there are other things which a man is afraid to tell even to himself, and every decent man has a number of such things stored away in his mind."[15]

In many ways, contemporary social scientists have merely demonstrated empirically what the biblical writers have always claimed: Our sin blinds us from self-knowledge.

One area of blindness is called the *self-serving bias*—which the Bible refers to as thinking more highly of ourselves than we ought.[16] Most people are average on most traits (by definition), but most of us rate ourselves as "above average." For example, most people rate themselves as above-average drivers (including people in the hospital recovering from car accidents that occurred when they were driving).[17] Only 2 percent of college professors rate themselves as below average; 63 percent say they're above average, and 25 percent say they're truly exceptional.[18] (For the record, self-serving bias is why, in the middle of an argument, we rarely stop and think, *I bet her position is more carefully reasoned than mine.*)

According to another pattern—called *fundamental attribution error*—we tend to attribute our own failures to external causes, but see other people's failures as evidence of character flaws. If my sermon puts you to sleep, you must have been out too late last night. But if *your* sermon puts *me* to sleep, you're obviously a boring preacher.[19]

And these problems are getting worse. David Brooks writes, "We have seen a broad shift from a culture of humility to the culture of what you might call the Big Me, from a culture that encouraged people to think humbly of themselves to a culture that encouraged people to see themselves as the center of the universe."[20]

In 1954, 12 percent of Americans considered themselves to be "a very important person." By 1989, that number had grown to 80 percent.[21]

We live in an age in which self-aware truth tellers like the prophet Nathan would have a hard time getting a job. We'd rather hear about our awesomeness than our faults. As a result, our lives become like a bad *American Idol* audition. We're so convinced of our own greatness that we don't realize how lacking in real talent we actually are—until someone holds up a mirror.

COURAGEOUS GRACE

James writes, "Do not merely listen to the word, and so deceive yourselves. Do what it says. Anyone who listens to the word but does not do what it says is like someone who looks at his face in a mirror and, after looking at himself, goes away and immediately forgets what he looks like."[22]

Self-awareness includes recognizing our strengths and values, but it also includes seeing our weaknesses and sins.

St. Ignatius developed a series of spiritual exercises as a way to make sure that members of his community would allow God to help them become more self-aware. His followers were trained to examine their lives daily the way a doctor examines a patient for symptoms of a disease that might do damage. The late, great management consultant Peter Drucker points out that John Calvin and Ignatius of Loyola incorporated this kind of feedback analysis. "In fact," Drucker writes, "the steadfast focus on performance and results that this habit produces explains why the institutions these two men founded, the Calvinist church and the Jesuit order, came to dominate Europe within thirty years."[23]

Sometimes faith—which should make us *more* self-aware—actually causes us to be more self-deceived. We confuse our aspirations with our achievements. "Christians are usually sincere and well-intentioned people," writes Richard Rohr, "until you get to any real issues of ego, control, power, money, pleasure, and security. Then they tend to be pretty much like everybody else."[24]

Brené Brown talks about what she calls *wholehearted living,* which involves coming out of hiding, letting go of perfection-ism and shame, and being vulnerable enough to live in the reality of the truth about ourselves. People who live whole-hearted lives, she says, share one belief—that they are "*worthy* of love and belonging."[25]

People who call for greater self-awareness often speak of the need for courage to face the truth about themselves—courage that comes from believing we have worth, value, and well-being.

No one has ever called people to more courageous self-awareness than Jesus did. The foundation of his call was grace. And this grace is grounded in a story.

Some years ago, when my family was on a long car ride, one of my daughters (who was maybe six or seven at the time) asked me to tell her a story. I used to make up stories for my kids all the time, but this is the only one I can still remember. It was a story about a prince and his horse.

The prince was brave and handsome, but he was also quite proud, quite arrogant. The horse was fabulous. He was also humble, faithful, and loyal, and he served and loved the prince far more than that prince deserved. The prince never really val-ued the horse, but the horse lived his whole life for the prince.

One time, when they were in battle and the prince was engaged in swordplay on foot, somebody shot an arrow at him. Realizing that the arrow was going to hit the prince and the prince was going to die, the horse leapt in front of the prince, took the arrow in the heart, and fell to the ground. All of a sudden, the prince realized that his horse was the best friend he'd ever had, and that he didn't deserve him. He started weeping, but it was too late. The horse had died.

By now, my daughter was sobbing in the back seat of the

car, and Nancy said to me, "Really? The horse has to die? This will mean years of therapy. Do you understand that?"

Yes, he had to die, because that's the way ultimate love stories work.

"There is no greater love than to lay down one's life for one's friends."[26]

Jesus said that.

Jesus' great love for us is evidence that we are *worthy of love and belonging.* His love gives us the courage to face the truth about ourselves. And that sense of self-awareness makes intimacy with others possible.

THE SELF-AWARENESS PARADOX

Here's the paradox of self-awareness: Although it is a necessary bridge to intimacy, it is also a great obstacle. When we become even partially aware of our brokenness or ugliness, intimacy becomes our fear. Our world is filled with bright, accomplished, beautiful, successful, lonely, and fearful people.

So self-awareness alone isn't enough. Intimacy requires a gift of acceptance that self-awareness cannot provide.

Henri Nouwen writes of being haunted by a great loneliness, even though he was a brilliant writer and teacher. He felt God calling him to leave his teaching post at Harvard to live in and serve a community of severely disabled men and women.

The first thing that struck me when I came to live in a house with mentally handicapped people was that their liking or disliking me had absolutely nothing to do with any of the many useful things I had done until then. Since nobody could read my books, [the books] could not impress anyone, and since most of them never went to school, my twenty years at Notre Dame, Yale, and Harvard did not provide a significant introduction. My considerable ecumenical experience proved even less valuable. When I offered some meat to one of the assistants during dinner, one of the handicapped men said to me, "Don't give him meat. He doesn't eat meat. He's a Presbyterian." . . .

These broken, wounded, and completely unpretentious people forced me to let go of my relevant self—the self that can do things, show things, prove things, build things—and forced me to reclaim that unadorned self in which I am completely vulnerable, open to receive and give love regardless of any accomplishments.[27]

In finding Jesus in "the least of these," Henri Nouwen himself began to be healed.

The message of the Incarnation is that God loves us not because of what we do or accomplish, but because he made us and has chosen to be with us. It is one thing for us to be aware of ourselves. It's another thing to know that God—the holy Creator of the universe—is fully aware of us, and yet still loves us, wholly, without reservation, and without end.

BEGINNING TO BECOME THE REAL YOU

In one of C. S. Lewis's Narnia books, a boy named Eustace is turned into a dragon. Later, he's invited by Aslan the lion—the Christ figure in the story—to bathe in a pool that can cleanse Eustace, remake him, and rebirth him. But first, he's told, he must undress. Eustace is confused about this until he realizes it means he must shed his old dragon skin. In other words, he has to repent. He has to confess the truth about himself.

He tries to do this, but it proves to be hard work. It takes a long time, but he peels off the hard, scaly dragon skin. When he goes to get into the water, he looks down at his foot and notices it's just as hard and scaly as it was before he started. In other words, there's another whole layer of dragon skin under the first layer. He tries again, but the same thing keeps happening, until finally he despairs. Then Aslan says to him, "You'll have to let *me* do it."

Here's how Eustace describes the experience:

> I was afraid of his claws, I can tell you, but I was pretty nearly desperate now. So I just lay flat down on my back to let him do it.
>
> The very first tear he made was so deep that I thought it had gone right into my heart. And when he began pulling the skin off, it hurt worse than anything I've ever felt. The only thing that made me able to bear it was just the pleasure of feeling the stuff peel off. You know—if you've ever picked the scab off a sore place. It hurts like billy-oh but it *is* such fun to see it coming away. . . .
>
> Well, he peeled the beastly stuff right off—just as I thought I'd done it myself the other three times, only they hadn't hurt—and there it was lying on the grass: only ever so much thicker, and darker, and more knobbly looking than the others had been. And there was I as smooth and soft as a peeled switch and smaller than I had been. Then he caught hold of me—I didn't like that much for I was very tender underneath now that I'd no skin on—and threw me

into the water. It smarted like anything but only for a moment. After that it became perfectly delicious and as soon as I started swimming and splashing I found that all the pain had gone from my arm. And then I saw why. I'd turned into a boy again.[28]

In your mind's eye, come to that pool now. Invite Jesus into the moment. Reflect on how great his love is for you, that he considers you so valuable that he would offer his life for yours.

Ask him, as Eustace did, to perform spiritual surgery on you. Ask him to remove all your defensiveness, denial, self-justification, and all the little tricks that keep you from seeing the truth about yourself. Tell God that you are willing to let him strip away these layers of old, dead dragon skin, even if it stings. Ask for clarity—to blame yourself neither too much nor too little. Ask for understanding. Ask him to purify your feelings and thoughts and give you the desire to live your life differently.

Do not leave this time of reflection without remembering God's *grace*. For Jesus himself said, "There is no greater love than to lay down one's life for one's friends."

If you're wondering who he meant by that, take a look in the mirror the next time you're near one.

CHAPTER 6

THE JOY OF JURY DUTY

THE GOLDEN RULE OF INTIMACY

When two people connect, when their beings intersect as closely as two bodies during intercourse, something is poured out of one and into the other that has the power to heal the soul of its deepest wounds and restore it to health. The one who receives experiences the joy of being healed. The one who gives knows the even greater joy of being used to heal. Something good is in the heart of each of God's children that is more powerful than everything bad. It's there, waiting to be released, to work its magic. But it rarely happens.

Larry Crabb, *Connecting*

It was 9:00 on a Monday morning and I was one of 150 unhappy campers sitting on plastic chairs crammed into a sterile basement room in the San Mateo County Courthouse, reporting for jury duty. We all had one thing in common: We wanted to be somewhere else.

Until Larry happened.

Larry works for the government, and however much we pay him, it's not enough. In a few short minutes, he won over the crowd of prospective jurors and infused us with a sense of honor and purpose. He began by saluting the elephant in the basement.

"I know you're all busy people. You have busy lives. You have a lot of things to do, and this is kind of an interruption. But I want to say thank you. I want to tell you, on behalf of the judges and our legal system and the county of San Mateo and, really, our nation, we're grateful for your service."

Although almost no one is happy about getting a summons to jury duty, Larry said, it's actually incredibly meaningful, and it's the foundation of a justice system in which people have a right to trial by a jury of their peers.

He told us a story about a ninety-five-year-old woman who was no longer able to drive, but who took three buses to get to the courthouse so she could serve. When she arrived, Larry asked her, "Did you call ahead like you're supposed to, to find out if you're even needed for jury duty?" She said, "I couldn't. I don't have one of those push-button phones." Turns out, she still had a rotary dial phone. (You can google it if you don't know what it is.)

Larry reminded us of the nobility of justice, and the long centuries of struggle for it, and how, even now, people around the world were fighting, and in some cases dying, for the right to exercise this privilege.

As he spoke, people stopped texting; they sat up straight; they nudged each other and seemed inspired.

By the time my number was called, I was so excited to serve that when the judge asked me whether I could pronounce someone guilty, I told him I was a pastor and that, according to the Bible, everybody was guilty. I said, "I could even pronounce *you* guilty!"

I wasn't selected to serve on a jury that time, but the point is that a room full of sullen, silent, phone-checking, self-important draftees had been transformed into a community of joyful patriots in a matter of minutes. When people left the courthouse that day, they were talking and laughing like old friends.

How did this happen?

It's called the "golden rule of intimacy."

THE GOLDEN RULE

The core secret to human connection is found in a single command given by the apostle Paul. If you follow this principle, you will never lack for intimate friendships. If you fail to follow it, you will never experience intimate relationships. It is at the heart of what every good parent instinctively does for a child. It is a fundamental need that allows children to develop the capacity to deal with reality—and even helps a child's brain develop in a healthy way.

This principle is so simple that even a child can master it, and so challenging that even some geniuses never quite get it.

What is the golden rule of intimacy? Here it is: "Rejoice with those who rejoice; mourn with those who mourn."[1]

Rejoicing and mourning are at the core of our emotional lives. What makes the miracle of human connection possible is our ability to discern another person's emotional state, empathize with it, and enter into it. People who can read us well—like Larry the Courthouse Officer—not only bond with us, but they also have the ability to lead us from a negative emotional state to a positive emotional state. That's pretty powerful.

Rejoicing generally involves small triumphs. Your boss was happy with a project you did at work. Somebody complimented you on how you looked. You thought the car was going to need repairs, but it spontaneously fixed itself. The Cubs won the World Series. (No, really—they did!) When you notice that someone is smiling a little more than usual, or is being a little more talkative or more optimistic, and you celebrate and joke and tease, you're connecting.

At the other end of the spectrum, mourning doesn't necessarily involve sackcloth and ashes. It's running late for work because traffic was bad. Or having an argument at home before you left. Or one of your children is doing poorly at school. Or you deleted a file you needed. Or you're disappointed in how a presentation went. Or the Indians lost the World Series. When you see someone looking downcast and withdrawn, and you reach out and show empathy, you're connecting. Just one person who notices and mourns with us can make a world of difference.

Even before we're able to sort a particular feeling into complex categories, such as envy or gratitude or frustration, our emotions trigger an automatic sensation that is either positive or negative. As soon as this happens, we seek out someone with whom we can share the experience.

Watch a mom with her baby. When the baby starts to cry, the mom will instinctively stick out her lower lip and make sad, comforting little noises. This is saying to the baby, "I understand you. I know inside myself how you feel inside yourself." In turn, the child "feels felt." And then something amazing and miraculous happens physiologically: The baby's brain changes just a little, and he or she calms down just a little. It's as if the mother has taken some of the baby's sorrow upon herself, and in the process has given the baby a little bit of the mother's peace.

"Feeling felt" is to the human soul what food is to the stomach, or air is to the lungs.

Feeling felt requires two gifts that we can give to one another: *knowing* and *acceptance*. If you know about my weakness or my woundedness, but you don't care, you won't be able to help me.

On the other hand, if you accept me as I am, but you don't know about my breaking heart, you won't be able to bring healing to my particular situation.

But if you know about my weakness—my sorrow or my pain—and yet accept me fully, the beauty of connection can happen.

A similar (but more fun) process happens when a baby smiles. The parent smiles back. When the baby gives a little gurgle, the parent responds with a little shimmy that says, "I can see you're happy, and I want you to know that I'm feeling happy just watching you be happy. We're doing the happy dance."

This process of connection involves what Daniel Goleman calls *attunement*—"attention that goes beyond momentary empathy to a full, sustained presence that facilitates rapport."[2] A baby laughs. The parent nods and smiles. The baby knows he or she is understood. And so we grow. And so we live. And so we love.

When we were very young, the development of our brains was utterly dependent on this process. Even now that we're older, it's still this attunement interaction that creates our sense of connection with another human being.

Intimacy is shared experience, and rejoicing and mourning are basic categories of our heart's experiences. The heart (figuratively) is the feeling part of us, the place where we feel joy enough to fly or pain enough to die. And there's a magic arithmetic in the sharing of our experiences: When we share joy, it increases. When we share pain, it decreases.

On the other hand, if we disregard Paul's golden rule of intimacy, we sow the seeds of human discord. When someone else rejoices and I mourn, the stage is set for envy, jealousy, ingratitude, dissatisfaction, and discontentment.

On the subject of jealousy, Anne Lamott says one of the hardest things about being a writer is that "some wonderful, dazzling successes are going to happen for some of the most awful, angry, undeserving writers you know—people who are, in other words, not you."[3] She wrote that in a book called *Bird by Bird*, which is brilliantly written and hilariously funny and has sold a gazillion copies and I'm so happy for her!

It is equally damaging when someone else mourns and I rejoice. The German word for this is *schadenfreude*, which means something like "malicious joy." In other words, I take pleasure in your misery. This attitude is addressed in the book of Proverbs: "Do not gloat when your enemy falls; when they stumble, do not let your heart rejoice."[4]

WHY JOY IS COMMANDED

Romans 12:15 is one of several places where Paul (among other Scripture writers) commands us to rejoice. It's not surprising, perhaps, that the Bible would say joy is *available* to us. But why *command* it?

I think it's because when we are joyful people, we end up giving a gift of joy to everyone we meet. In other words, our joy is not just about us. We all know that it enhances our lives to be around joyful people—whether at home, at work, at church, or wherever. Therefore, we owe it to the people in our lives to be as joyful and as happy as we can be. And because joy is naturally contagious, it follows that joyful people will experience more intimacy than joyless people.

When I was a kid and my dad was in a particularly good mood, he would wake up my siblings and me by singing. Now, my dad is not a natural singer, and he would deliberately mangle the song—"Good morning to yooooou"—so that he sounded like a moose with a bad sinus problem. But we all loved it because it meant Dad was happy. When you're a kid and your dad is in a good mood, something deep inside says, "It's going to be a good day."

Recently my parents, who are now in their eighties, moved after many decades in one house. My brother and sister and I were all there to be with them, and there was a whole lifetime of memories in the stuff my parents had.

One morning, my dad went out to get coffee for everybody, and when he came back in, he was singing. My sister, Barbie, who is in her sixties, still talks about how good it was just to hear my dad singing for joy.

Later that day, when I was driving to the airport, my mom, who's a very fun person, was jabbing me from the back seat, in a very playful way, about my driving. It doesn't sound like fun, but it actually was.

"We'd go faster, John," she advised me, "if you would drive in the carpool lane."

When I got into the carpool lane, she said, "We're going to miss our exit."

When I started to get out of the carpool lane, she said, "You can't cross the double yellow lines."

When I got back into the carpool lane, she said, "Now we're going to miss the exit for sure."

Finally, I crossed four lanes in one smooth move, and my mother said to my sister in the back seat, "Barbie, put your seat belt on right now."

I said, "Mother . . . ," and she uttered one of those classic mother lines: "I'm not saying a word."

She always says that.

Then it struck me: "If you're not saying a word, what are those little noises I hear coming out of your mouth? If you're saying, 'I'm not saying a word,' you must be saying words to say you're not saying a word. So you're refuting what you're saying while you're saying it, and you've been saying that your entire life. In fact, I know what I'm going to put on your tombstone when you die: 'Here lies Kathy Ortberg. Finally, she's not saying a word.'"

We all laughed so hard I missed the exit.

The point is, we treasure joyful moments because they somehow heal and connect us. What's more, our joy is not just about us. In fact, the research is quite clear on this: Joyful people are more compassionate in their actions than less joyful people. They are more financially generous than less joyful people. They develop more friendships and deeper friendships than less joyful people. They are more likely to stay married. They are more resilient in the face of hardship. They exhibit greater vitality and a zest for life.[5]

Nehemiah said, "The joy of the LORD is your strength."[6] This is literally, physically true. Where joy increases, energy increases, health increases, goodness increases, and virtue increases.

When we work, we have an obligation to be joyful in our workplace, because when we work joyfully, it enhances the work of everyone around us.

People who are skilled at intimacy look for opportunities to create joy for other people. For example, I work with a colleague named Linda, who is a great friend to both Nancy and me. Linda has the spiritual gift of teasing. Knowing that I love books, Linda once secretly placed a bunch of Danielle Steel romance novels on my office bookshelves—right next to all the Bible commentaries and theological works—and started a betting pool with several people to see how long it would take me to notice they were there.

To make it even more fun, whenever I needed a publicity photo, she made sure I was standing in front of those books. Someone more observant than I may have wondered why I would pose for a picture with books like *Passion's Promise* and *Season of Passion* right behind me. (*Answered Prayers, Amazing Grace,* and *Prodigal Son* would have made more sense.) Regrettably, Linda is not on staff anymore, but it was really fun while it lasted. (Just kidding. She is still a joy to work with.)

WHAT'S THE GOOD OF MOURNING?

Paul also commands us to mourn with those who mourn. He doesn't say, "Give advice to those who mourn." He doesn't say, "Remind those who mourn that they are supposed to triumph through the Resurrection, so their sadness must indicate a lack of faith." He doesn't say, "Explain to those who mourn that God always has a good reason for whatever happens, so they should just trust him." He doesn't say, "Fix those who mourn."

What he does say is that we are to "bear one another's burdens, and so fulfill the law of Christ."[7] Sorrow is one of those burdens. When we mourn with others, we share the burden of their sorrow. Nothing has changed. Nothing's been fixed. No problem has been solved—except this: They are no longer alone in their mourning. And that changes everything.

Philosopher Nicholas Wolterstorff notes how this advice is at odds with much of the wisdom of the ancient world when he writes, "The Stoics of antiquity said: Be calm. Disengage yourself. Neither laugh nor weep. Jesus says: Be open to the wounds of the world. Mourn humanity's mourning, weep over humanity's weeping, be wounded by humanity's wounds, be in agony over humanity's agony. But do so in the good cheer that a day of peace is coming."[8]

Weeping. One of the great mysteries of human existence is tears. Charles Darwin once described emotional tears as "purposeless." There was even a theory in the 1960s that humans evolved from aquatic apes and that tears helped us live in salt water.[9]

But it turns out that tears are one of God's most brilliant intimacy inventions. Tears activate intimacy. Tears show that we're vulnerable. In the words of poet Robert Herrick, "Tears are the noble language of the eye."[10] And the premier "crying" researcher of our time summarized tears like this: "We cry because we need other people."[11]

There once was a study done in which people were shown photos of someone crying. Some of the photos showed tears, and in others the tears had been digitally removed. It turned out that people were far more likely to want to reach out or express compassion when looking at photos that included tears.[12]

Other research has shown that people who rarely cry are actually less bonded to others. They have a tendency to withdraw. They describe their relationships as less connected.[13]

The Bible is full of tears. The word *tears* occurs about ninety times, with another thirty references to crying or weeping. Jeremiah cried so much over the fallenness of his country that he was known as "the weeping prophet." When the family of Lazarus was mourning his death, Jesus mourned with them. The shortest verse in all the Bible is one of the most poignant: "Jesus wept."[14]

The psalmist says: "You keep track of all my sorrows. You have collected all my tears in your bottle. You have recorded each one in your book."[15]

At one time, tear bottles—the technical name is *lachryma-tories*—were used to collect tears because they were considered precious. (In Persia, supposedly, when a sultan returned from war, he'd check his wives' tear bottles to see which wife had missed him and cried the most.) I bought a lachrymatory twenty years ago in Israel and kept it in my office, where it reminded me of the importance of mourning with those who came in weeping.

One of our staff members who has "the gift of tears" is named Phyllis. Her heart is so expressive in that way that her nickname is Puddles. For many years, she sat at our reception desk, and when people in sorrow called or dropped by, they would be "mourned with" by a master. Not long ago, Phyllis retired to care for her beloved husband of half a century, who had been diagnosed with Lou Gehrig's disease. I wasn't sure what to get her for a gift—until I looked on my shelf and saw the bottle of tears.

When people allow us to mourn with them, they become safe harbors for us. As nineteenth-century novelist Dinah Craik once wrote:

> Oh the comfort—the inexpressible comfort of feeling *safe* with a person—having neither to weigh thoughts nor measure words, but pouring them all right out, just as they are, chaff and grain together; certain that a faithful hand will take and sift them, keep what is worth keeping, and then with the breath of kindness, blow the rest away.[16]

Granted, sometimes it's easier for us to rejoice with God than to mourn with him.

Psychologist Paul Ekman, one of the consultants for the Disney/Pixar movie *Inside Out*, which is all about managing emotions, made a study of what he calls "display rules." These are often-unspoken guidelines about how much emotion we allow ourselves to display to others. For example, *minimizing* is keeping a poker face because I'm afraid my real emotions will get me in trouble. *Substituting* is when I exchange another emotion ("I'm fine") for my real emotion ("I feel like I'm dying inside").[17]

God has only one display rule: Bring your whole self to him—your sadness, your disappointment, your anger. In other words, bring your *real* self to him.

The book of Psalms is one of the most emotionally charged, emotionally aware, emotionally honest books in human literature. The psalmists don't tell their emotions to go sit in the corner. They hurl them at God.

Sadness? Look at this:

Now I'm flat on my face,
    feeling sorry for myself morning to night. . . .
I'm on my last legs; I've had it—
    my life is a vomit of groans.[18]

Who wants to hear your vomit of groans? God does. Don't try to make your sadness go away. Don't pretend it doesn't exist. Don't put it in charge of your life. Take it to God.

What about anger? Where do you take your anger? Check this out: In Psalm 137, which is a reflection on Israel's captivity in Babylon, the psalmist doesn't pray, "God bless the Babylonians because I want you to think I'm a really good guy." Instead, he ends his psalm like this: "Daughter Babylon, doomed to destruction, happy is the one who repays you according to what you have done to us. Happy is the one who seizes your infants and dashes them against the rocks."[19]

What?

Oh, you think God didn't know? You think God was

saying, "Man, you have a real anger problem. No more psalms for you"? Of course he knew. He always does. And he always will.

Naming an emotion honestly is the first step in healing that emotion inwardly. When we pray our honest feelings in God's presence, we have a place to stand before him. Remember, we are *not* our feelings. We *have* feelings, but our feelings don't have us. *God* has us.

LISTEN UP

Listening is the key to understanding who in the course of your day is mourning and who is rejoicing. Paul Coleman talks about the difference between "good listening" and "intimate listening." A good listener understands facts. An intimate listener understands feelings. A good listener can repeat what you said. An intimate listener can sense what you feel. When a listener "combines understanding with complete acceptance and a depth of caring," two inner worlds resonate with each other, and connection happens.[20]

Daniel Goleman tells a story about a friend of his, Terry Dobson, who, in the 1950s, was one of the first Americans to study aikido, the Japanese art of self-defense, in Tokyo.

One afternoon, Terry was riding home on the subway when a large, very drunk, and very angry man boarded the train and began terrorizing the other passengers. When the man took a swing at a woman holding a baby and sent an elderly couple scrambling for safety, Terry prepared to use his martial arts skills for the first time.

When Terry stood up to intervene, the drunk turned on him and shouted, "Aha! A foreigner! You need a lesson in Japanese manners!" But before the situation could get out of hand, an elderly Japanese passenger shouted, "Hey!" in "the cheery tone of someone who has suddenly come upon a fond friend." When the drunk turned to see who had called out to him, the old man "beckoned him over with a light wave of his hand" and engaged him in friendly conversation.

At first, the drunk continued his belligerent bellowing, but soon the warmth of the old man's demeanor began to break through as he talked about his wife, their garden, and how they enjoyed sitting on an old wooden bench drinking *sake* together in the evening.

"And I'm sure you have a wonderful wife," the old man said.

"My wife died . . ." the drunk said as he began to sob. He went on to tell the old man about the shame of losing his job and his home, as well.

Soon, the train came to Terry's stop. As he exited, he heard the old man invite the drunk to tell him all about his sorrows. The last thing he saw was the drunk man sprawled across the seat, with his head in the old man's lap.

"That," concludes Daniel Goleman, "is emotional brilliance."[21]

DIVINE INTIMACY

Psalms is a great prayer book, and the greatest "intimacy with God" book in all of human literature. Scholars who study the psalms have identified the two most common types: psalms of lament and psalms of celebration. And in this great and ancient book, we see that God rejoices and God mourns. And God invites us to join him.

Sometimes we do, and sometimes we don't.

In Matthew 11:16-17, Jesus tells a story about our response to his invitation.

To what can I compare this generation? They are like children sitting in the marketplaces and calling out to others:

> "We played the pipe for you,
>   and you did not dance;
> we sang a dirge,
>   and you did not mourn."

It's as if the gospel comes in both flavors: *sad* and *happy*. John the Baptist came speaking the language of sorrow and repentance—living in the desert, eating locusts, fasting, baptizing. He spoke of how God mourns over his fallen world. John was the dirge singer.

But people would not mourn.

Jesus came speaking the language of hope and joy—going to parties with sinners and restocking the wine supply at weddings. He told stories about feasts and fatted calves and buried treasures. Jesus was the pipe player.

But people would not rejoice.

For me, learning to rejoice with God was largely a matter of learning to connect the dots. Growing up, I experienced a lot of joy. And at church I was taught to think about God a lot. Still, I didn't make the connection between the joy I experienced in life with the God I heard about at church. In fact, the first question I can remember asking my parents about the church was, "Why is the preacher always mad at us?"

Rejoicing with God doesn't mean trying to make ourselves happy over a Bible verse or a church service. It's about taking something we're naturally happy about, remembering that "whatever is good and perfect is a gift coming down to us from God,"[22] and thanking him for that gift.

It could be something as simple as viewing a sunset, the ocean, a mountain, or a tree. It could be the taste of Swedish pancakes on a Sunday morning. It could be your favorite song, your favorite movie, a well-executed jump shot, or the sound of a bird singing. It could be congratulations from someone at work, a triumph for your child at school, or just the fact that your mind and body are working pretty well right now.

Often in the morning I'll write down five simple items for which I'm grateful that day. The years I lived in Rockford, growing up. Being the father of Laura, Mallory, and Johnny. Every new day is a new opportunity. The key is that I can't write down something I'm *supposed* to be grateful for. It has to be something that produces genuine feelings of gratitude at that moment—even if it's something that seems unspiritual. The taste of coffee. Getting on a scale and weighing less than I thought I would. Getting a notice from the IRS and paying less than I thought I would. The feel of Baxter the Dog curled up at my feet. I've been amazed to discover how the simple act of recording my gratitude can produce a greater sense of intimacy with God.

And joy.

And then the Cubs won the World Series.

And God rejoiced with us.

CHAPTER 7

WE SHOULD ALL BE COMMITTED

COMMITMENT AND INTIMACY: THE GREAT TENSION

It is the nature of love to bind itself.
G. K. CHESTERTON, *"A Defence of Rash Vows"*

WANNA HANG OUT?

Wanna go on a date?

Wanna go steady?

Wanna get engaged?

Will you marry me?

Intimacy and commitment go together like peas and carrots, like Bogey and Bacall, like Cheech and Chong. Along with a strong desire for intimacy comes a desire to bind ourselves to another—to our spouse, our children, and even to our friends.

Our days are marked, our identities are formed, and our intimate relationships are anchored by the commitments we make and keep:

"Can you keep a secret?"

"Would you do me a favor?"

"Want to have coffee on Thursday?"

"Want to be my friend?"

"Want to become a parent?"

"Want to commit to God?"

Commitment gives us what Lewis Smedes calls a "small island of certainty" in an uncertain world: "How strange it is, when you think about it, that a mere human being can take hold of the future and fasten one part of it down for another person. . . . I stretch myself into unpredictable days ahead and make one thing predictable for you: I will be there with you."[1]

Commitment is the foundation of intimacy, because without commitment there can be no trust, and without trust there can be no intimacy.

Because we are often unreliable, we will go to great lengths to try to get people to trust us. When we were kids, we often recited a familiar formula when we *really* wanted someone to believe us: "Cross my heart, hope to die, stick a needle in my eye." Who thought that one up? If I'm not telling the truth, may I violate the sign of the cross, may I perish, and may a needle be shoved into my eyeball.

I've written elsewhere about Henri Nouwen's fascination during the final year of his life with a group of trapeze artists called the Flying Rodleighs. Something about the grace and trust involved in the way they flew through the air together painted a picture for him of intimacy, joy, and safety in God's Kingdom.

Wanting to understand more about this myself, I signed up for a session at the Circus Center in San Francisco, where they teach classes on trapeze flying.[2]

I had been told I was on a waiting list, so I only intended to watch. But when the time came for the class and one of the other students saw how high above the ground the trapeze was, she suddenly remembered a previous appointment. So I got in. I was then introduced to Alan, who would be my catcher. (I immediately sized him up to see how strong he looked, how long his arms were, and whether he had sweaty hands.)

I remembered what the leader of the Rodleighs had told Henri Nouwen about the relationship between the two types of trapeze artists: the flyers and the catchers. Most people focus on and celebrate the flyers, because they do all the somersaults; but the catchers are the real heroes.

"The secret," Rodleigh said, "is that the flyer does nothing and the catcher does everything. When I fly to Joe, I have simply to stretch out my arms and hands and wait for him to catch me and pull me safely over the apron behind the catchbar."

"You do nothing!" I said, surprised.

"Nothing," Rodleigh repeated. . . . "A flyer must fly, and a catcher must catch, and the flyer must trust, with outstretched arms, that his catcher will be there for him."

When Rodleigh said this with so much conviction, the words of Jesus flashed through my mind: "Father into your hands I commend my Spirit." Dying is trusting in the catcher. To care for the dying is to say, "Don't be afraid. Remember that you are the beloved child of God. He will be there when you make your long jump. Don't try to grab him; he will grab you. Just stretch out your arms and hands and trust, trust, trust."[3]

When I'd read Nouwen's words in the quiet and safety of my study, they'd had a beauty that made me want to experience them. But when I climbed the ladder to the platform at the Circus Center, I didn't want to fly at all. I didn't want to obey their instructions. I didn't want to lean out over the platform. I didn't want to jump. I didn't want to stretch out my arms. I didn't want to let go of the bar.

Still, I trusted them just barely enough to do it all anyway.

And then those strong hands appeared from nowhere and grasped my outstretched arms. And I got caught.

And two became one.

Weddings, more than just about anything else in our culture, give us a glimpse of what commitment means. What makes a wedding a wedding isn't the cake, the clothes, the flowers, or the music. It's the *promise*. In a world of change and instability, a man and a woman give their solemn word that, from now on, there is one inviolable certainty we can all rely on. For better or for worse, for richer or for poorer, in sickness and in health—when you are young and sexy and the air is filled with scent of Eau du Sud, and when you are old, your teeth are gone, and the air is filled with the scent of Eau du Bengay—you can count on this promise. This is our sacred vow.

The reason that weddings require public witness is that it adds accountability to our promises. We're going on record. We're asking our community to mark this moment with us and to remind us to live up to our promise. That's why it used to be common to ask the question, "If anyone knows any reason why this man should not be married to this woman, speak now or forever hold your peace." Nowadays, the only weddings where you hear this question are in the movies—and then there's always some dramatic revelation, some reason why the wedding shouldn't happen, and the bride goes running out of the chapel in tears (at which point, her most intimate friends mourn with her).

When Nancy and I officiated at the wedding of one of our daughters a few years ago, I decided to ask the question. I had prearranged that my brother-in-law, Craig, would stand up and say in a booming voice, "Yes. I'm Laura's probation officer, she has violated her parole, and there are very serious reasons why this marriage should not happen."

I thought it was hilarious. Unfortunately, I hadn't thought to let the groom's family in on the joke. They had no idea who this probation officer was, so it wasn't *quite* as funny to them.

THE INTIMACY/COMMITMENT RATIO

Pastor Andy Stanley tells the story of a time he was teaching a group of high school students about preserving sexual intimacy (the ultimate physical expression of intimacy) for marriage (the ultimate expression of commitment). Later, a woman in her thirties who had also been at the meeting came and asked Andy a question: "That whole 'no sex till you're married'—that's for teenagers, right?" This woman was divorced and was now dating again, and she was asking sincerely. She had recently become a Christian and hadn't heard this idea before.

Pastors love these kinds of questions that put them on the spot, especially when a complete answer is more than just a sound bite. So Andy thought about it for a second and then asked her, "Has sex outside of marriage made your life better, or just more complicated?"[4]

This question struck a deep chord with her. When a relationship has intimacy without commitment, there's a greater potential for hurt.

On the other hand, couples sometimes end up in a relationship where they remain married to each other, but the fires of love burned out a long time ago. They have commitment, but no intimacy. This emptiness also creates hurt.

Psychologist Robert Sternberg proposed that marriage involves what he calls a triangle of love: *intimacy* (by which he means feelings of closeness, connectedness, and bondedness), *passion* (romance and physical attraction), and *commitment* (the decision to maintain that love).[5] These elements must be proportional. When intimacy exceeds commitment, there is potential for hurt. When commitment exceeds intimacy, there is disappointment for the heart. But when commitment, passion, and intimacy go hand in hand, relationships flourish.

THE COST OF COMMITMENT

We all want intimacy, and we know intimacy requires commitment; but here's the tension: Commitment comes with a price tag.

Sometimes, with one of our adult kids, we'll have a conversation that runs like this:

"Do you want to come over for dinner tonight?"

"Maybe. I don't know. We'll see."

Lurking under the surface, unspoken, is a haunting thought: *I might get a better offer—and if I'm already committed to you, I would miss out on that opportunity.*

Commitment can be frightening because it means the loss of options. After all, a commitment is a promise about the future, but things might change in the future. *What if I promise to marry you, but then I change? What if I promise to marry you, but then you change?* What if I promise to be your friend, but we have a fight, or I no longer feel close to you? What if I promise to follow God, but tomorrow I don't feel like following God? What if I'm not even sure there is a God?

Lewis Smedes identified three things we surrender when we commit ourselves to another person: our *freedom*, our *individuality*, and our *control*.[6] When we commit ourselves to someone, we're no longer the only ones in charge. Our time and our heart are no longer our own. Commitment builds an invisible fence around us, and we freely choose to honor its restrictions on our freedom. Once we've made a commitment, we're no longer just *me, myself, I*; we've become part of a *we*.

Commitment-phobes are afraid of missing out on something. They think, *As long as I'm not committed, I'm free to go for the gusto, free to see whomever I want, free to eat whatever I want, do whatever I choose, buy whatever looks good, say whatever seems useful, and experience anything I desire.* According to this way of thinking, avoiding commitment is the pathway to freedom.

Of course, commitment makers and keepers experience a kind of freedom that commitment avoiders will never know.

G. K. Chesterton once wrote an essay with the wonderful title, "A Defence of Rash Vows," in which he suggests that by making and keeping commitments, we transcend in some small way the limits of time and forge a lasting identity: "The man who makes a vow makes an appointment with himself at some distant time or place."[7]

In the act of commitment, I bind myself to that future moment. I'm not free to love another woman. I'm not free to follow another God. And yet somehow, that "not free" commitment leads to a deeper freedom than all the other options and escape clauses in a commitment-phobic world.

Chesterton calls escape from commitment "the reign of the cowards."[8] Having the courage to commit and trust makes possible an intimacy we would otherwise never know. It works like this: A commitment is made, and it's received by faith. As that promise is honored, faith is confirmed, and intimacy is deepened.

How do I know that Nancy is faithful to me? She promised. I trust her. It might be possible to put a Nancy Cam on her so that I could visually monitor her behavior 24/7, like the surveillance camera at a convenience store. But even if she offered to allow that (and trust me, she won't), I wouldn't do it. I'd rather trust her. The combination of commitment and trust makes possible a kind of intimacy that "knowing" never would.

The reason we're drawn to make commitments is that we are created in the image of a commitment-making, commitment-keeping God. Of all God's creation, only human beings can make a promise. Only human beings can make and keep a commitment. Only human beings can say, "I will meet you next Tuesday. I will serve on that team with you. I will keep that secret. I will be your friend. I will pray for you. I will have your back. You can count on me." Dogs can't make that promise. If they could, they would—and they would die to keep it—but they can't. Cats can't make that promise. If they could, they would. And then they would break it, and they would laugh in your face in their quiet cat way.

GOD'S COMMITMENT TO US

In the ancient world, if two parties wanted to enter into a formal relationship with one another, they did it through an agreement called a *covenant*. A covenant is a promise: I will do this; you will do that. We can trust each other. We are bound to each other.

To symbolize their commitment, the two parties would sacrifice an animal, cut it in half, and set the two halves on the ground—half the heifer here; half there. Half the goat here; half there. If you've ever heard someone order a "half-caf" at the coffee shop, now you know where that comes from. (Sorry. No more puns after this. Cross my heart. Unless a really good opportunity comes along.)

All the sights and smells of life and death were vividly present in the sealing of the covenant, and both parties expressed their commitment by walking between the two halves of the sacrifice and making a most solemn vow—sometimes called an oath of malediction: "May what happened to these animals happen to me if I do not keep my promise." (Kind of like "Cross my heart, hope to die, stick a needle in my eye." Except these guys were serious.)

When the Old Testament speaks of two people making a covenant, the phrase in Hebrew means to *cut* a covenant, referring precisely to this gruesome custom, through which God chose to teach human beings about making—and *keeping*—commitments.

We first see this practice in Genesis 15, when God makes a covenant with Abraham, and Abraham wants to know if he can trust God's promise. In an eerie scene, after Abraham has cut up the animals and set the pieces on the ground, he falls into a "deep sleep, and a thick and dreadful darkness came over him."[9] But here's the strangest part: He then sees a smoking firepot with a blazing torch—representing the person of God—do the covenant walk *alone* between the pieces of the sacrifice (whereas, normally, both parties would do it). In essence, God is saying that no matter what happens—even if it is humanity and not God who violates the covenant—God will bear the curse of the broken covenant himself. He would later fulfill this commitment when Christ died on the cross to redeem the covenant broken by us humans.

OUR COMMITMENT TO GOD

In 1 Kings 19, there's a wonderful picture of commitment in the story of a character named Elisha.

One day, an aging prophet named Elijah (I don't know why their names had to be so similar; I always get them confused) was thinking about retirement and needed a replacement:

> So Elijah went from there and found Elisha son of Shaphat. He was plowing with twelve yoke of oxen, and he himself was driving the twelfth pair. Elijah went up to him and threw his cloak around him. Elisha then left his oxen and ran after Elijah. "Let me kiss my father and mother goodbye," he said, "and then I will come with you."
>
> "Go back," Elijah replied. "What have I done to you?"[10]

This is a very dramatic moment. Elijah is an old man. He's standing in a field full of plowmen. He watches as eleven pairs of oxen go by. Then, removing his mantle, he walks over to the twelfth plowman, Elisha, and wraps the mantle around him.

The mantle is a symbol of Elijah's calling, of his office, of his life's work. So when he throws it onto Elisha, the meaning is clear: "Elisha, God has a job for you. Leave all of this and let's get started."

The telling of this story leaves out a lot of details that I would want to know if I were thinking about taking on a job like this. What's the health plan like? How many weeks of vacation will there be? If Elijah is going to train Elisha in how to be a prophet, does that mean there's some kind of prophet-sharing plan? (Sorry. That really good opportunity came along.)

We do know that Elisha has twelve teams of oxen at work. In that economy, it means Elisha is a person of staggering wealth. He has options. He's a golden boy. He can marry any girl in the village he wants. And now Elijah wants him to leave all of that to attach himself to a penniless preacher and face a life of opposition and danger and sacrifice? Seriously? What's he going to do if something better comes along?

Before he signs on the dotted line, Elisha makes a request: "Let me go kiss my mother and father good-bye, and then I will come with you."

This seems reasonable, but Elijah's response comes off as a little edgy: "Go back. What have I done to you?"

You can almost hear the wheels turning in Elijah's mind.

If he runs home to Mommy and Daddy, they'll remind him of the trust fund and the keys to the car and the vacation home. He's going to bail, and I'll probably never see him again.

But Elijah does something very important. He gives Elisha room to make the commitment himself.

"No skin off *my* nose. You decide."

Any good commitment that will have the strength to last must be freely offered. No pressure. No manipulation. No emotional appeals. The commitments we make must come from the core of who we are, or they will crumble when the pressure comes. And pressure *will* come.

When Elisha goes home, he does one last thing to confirm his commitment: He slaughters the two oxen he was driving, uses the wood from the plow for a fire to cook the meat, and hosts a farewell banquet for himself. "Then he set out to follow Elijah and became his servant."[11]

He burns the plow.

He kills the oxen.

He's all in. He expresses *physically* what he is offering personally and spiritually.

If you're really serious about keeping a commitment, one of the best things you can do is go public with it. Just like a wedding. And Elisha goes public big time. He decides to turn his sacrifice into a party, and he gives the meat to all the people. (Do you have any idea how many people you can feed with two oxen?)

Later, when Elijah leaves him and is taken up into heaven, Elisha says, "I can't go back. I burned the plow."

When a bunch of boys mock him and he calls a bear out to maul them, maybe he later thinks, *I'll never be a man of God. I'll never get this right.* But he knows, "I can't go back. I burned the plow."

When the king wants to kill him, when the enemies of Israel surround him, when a famine threatens to starve him and the people, when Israel rejects him so utterly that he weeps at his failure, there's one thing he knows for sure: "I can't go back. I burned the plow. That way of life is cut off from me. There is no retreat."

That's a plow-burning level of commitment.

In 1519, Hernán Cortés landed in Mexico with eleven ships, five hundred soldiers, and one hundred sailors, to pursue glory in the New World. When they came ashore in this unknown land, they were filled with uncertainty and fear. Some wanted to go back to Cuba, where they had sailed from, so Cortés gave an order to his men: "Burn the ships." In other words, "Going back isn't an option. We will succeed, or die trying. We will flourish, or we will perish, but we will not run away. We are committed. Burn the ships."[12]

This story is a favorite of business consultants and motivational speakers. But it's worth noting that although a story of unreserved commitment can inspire us, we are not called to glorify commitment merely for commitment's sake. Commitment to the wrong thing can do a lot of damage. If a football player has an overpowering commitment to win the Super Bowl, but a noncommitment to honoring his wife, that's not a good commitment. If a businessperson has an unquenchable commitment to his own success, but a quenchable commitment to his family, that's actually idolatry.

However, when we commit ourselves to a noble calling of God—when, as ordinary human beings, we say, "We're not going back. We have charbroiled the ox. We have kissed the trust fund good-bye. We have given up the keys. We have burned the plow"—God's power is released in our lives.

When Nancy and I got married, we had only one premarital session to cover money, sex, conflict, in-laws, parenting, goals, division of labor, expectations, etc. I don't recommend that. We could have used more.

At one point, our counselor asked us, "What will you do if you wake up one morning, and your feelings of love for each other are gone?"

Nancy immediately said, "I will honor my commitment."

Back then, that was the wrong answer for me. In my mind, we were so special and so magic, and I was so remarkable and unique, that the feelings of love would never go away. They might for ordinary people, but not for me. They would only grow more special and more magic every day. The idea that Nancy would ever have to stay with me out of commitment alone just seemed wrong—and I let her know that, by pouting.

But Nancy has kept loving me. How? She honors her commitment. That doesn't mean she's saying to herself, "I'm going to be a martyr. This is going to be so hard." And it doesn't mean she's saying, "What a noble human being I am to continue to endure someone as immature as you."

No, it's a thousand little commitments that are powered by God. It's saying, "I'll listen. I'll give. I'll fight honestly. I'll make up. I won't go surfing the Internet in places where I shouldn't. I won't go flirting in a bar. I won't escape with a bottle or with a screen. I made a promise for better or worse, for richer or poorer, in sickness and in health. I burned the plow. I'm all in."

MARITAL COMMITMENT

Psychologist Aaron Beck says that relational problems in marriage can be placed into one of two categories: Big Exits and Little Exits. Big Exits are the dramatic ones: divorce, betrayal, abandonment, infidelity. When couples get married, they promise not to take any Big Exits.

But more subtle problems can arise from what Beck calls Little Exits: avoiding conflict, escaping into television watching, investing more heavily in relationships with friends, or overworking. Little Exits might involve shopping, numbing ourselves with alcohol, living a parallel life with no real disclosure, or settling into a long rut of apathy and withdrawal.

Every Big Exit is preceded by a thousand Little Exits that have eroded the foundation of commitment. Just because we haven't taken a Big Exit doesn't mean we're keeping our commitments; it may just mean we're refusing to acknowledge the reality that we are living separate lives under one roof.

When we get married, we don't promise simply to avoid divorce. We promise to pursue intimacy—two-become-oneness. That means we can't afford exits—Big or Little.[13]

FAMILIAL COMMITMENT

Families are held together not by blood, but by commitment. When a husband and wife keep their promises to each other, those promises seep into the hearts of their children, as well. One researcher defines the family as "a group of people who are irrationally committed to each other's well-being."[14] That's why it's always such a joke to hear a company described as "one big family."

Here's how to tell if the company you work for is truly a family: Stop showing up for work, wait until you get a pink slip, and then go to your supervisor and say, "Hey, you can't fire me. I'm family."

Your supervisor will say, "No, you *used* to be family. Now you're fired."

In a real family, you can't get fired. As a parent, I'm connected to my children by unbreakable bonds. They might do something terrible. They might betray my values. They might deny God. They might break my heart. But we are bound by ties that cannot be severed. I will never stop loving them.

There have been times when I've realized that I wasn't truly *committed* to my family. I wanted the appearance and self-esteem of a committed person, but without actually burning the plow.

For instance, when Nancy and I got married, I said I was committed to an equal partnership. I said I was committed to being a servant. But after several years of marriage—about the time we had three preschool-age children—what I *did* didn't match up with what I *said*.

When Nancy asked me, "Are you 100 percent committed to a mutual partnership—sharing the workload, division of labor, doing dishes/washing clothes/cleaning rooms/giving baths/

fixing meals—are you really 100 percent committed to an equal-servanthood marriage?" my inner thought was, *Well, I'm not opposed to it. But did you have another percentage in mind?*

There's a difference between true commitment and saying, "I will comply if someone tells me what to do." William Law observed a long time ago: "[The follower of Jesus] does not ask what is *allowable* and *pardonable*, but what is *commendable* and *praiseworthy*."[15]

I've never conducted a job interview where the candidate asks, "How little can I do and keep my job?" Nor would I want that to be my level of commitment to my family.

It is in our commitments that we find ourselves. I am the one who committed myself to Nancy, Laura, Mallory, and Johnny, and to my father, mother, sister, and brother.

COMMITMENT TO OUR FRIENDS

In the twelfth century, a monk named Aelred of Rievaulx became so enamored of the power of friendship that he declared, "God is friendship." Quoting from the writings of Cicero, Aelred also said, "Those who banish friendship from life seem to pluck the sun from the universe, for we have no better, no more delightful blessing from God."[16]

One of the most famous friendships in history—between Jonathan and David—was built on commitment: "Jonathan made a covenant with the house of David, . . . and Jonathan had David reaffirm his oath out of love for him, because he loved him as he loved himself."[17]

We don't usually formalize friendship commitments in the same way as marriages. But if you poke around in the soil under what poet Samuel Taylor Coleridge called the "sheltering tree"[18] of friendship, you'll find a promise at the root.

People who are friendship-rich have a knack for commitment. They believe that lifelong friendships are both possible and desirable. They stay with their comrades through the dry spells: "There is a friend who sticks closer than a brother."[19]

A friend believes in you when you may not believe in yourself. A friend sees in you what you may not see in yourself. A friend enjoys being with you, honors your triumphs, and celebrates your birthday. A friend promises to remain loyal. Your colleagues may be with you when it suits them, but friends are born for adversity.[20]

I've known my good friend Rick for almost thirty-eight years. The first year of our friendship, I wanted to celebrate his birthday, so along with a few friends, I planned to kidnap him from his job at a counseling center in a seedy section of Pasadena. We even put nylon stockings over our heads to make it dramatic.

Near the end of the workday, we waited outside his building, but after half an hour, he hadn't come outside, so I went in to see what was going on. What we didn't know was that four business owners in the area had called the police to report a group of criminal-looking types who were hanging out in a crime-ridden part of Pasadena with nylon stockings over their heads.

The next thing we knew, five squad cars came screaming into the parking lot, with tires squealing, doors flying open, and officers taking cover with guns drawn. Overhead, a police helicopter provided aerial support.

"If you move we will shoot," the officers said to my friends, who were still outside. Inside the safety of the clinic, I had to decide between loyalty to my friends and preserving my own (pretty much) jail-free record. It was not a hard decision.

A few weeks ago, I sat around a table with twenty or so

others to celebrate Rick's birthday once again. There were no arrests this time, but there *were* thirty-seven years of memories to give thanks for. Friends commit to celebrating. They also don't let their friends get taken out by the SWAT team.

A true friend also helps us grow toward becoming our best selves. Aristotle once said that friendship is "training in virtue."[21] Friends endeavor to be the kind of people who are capable of keeping their commitments. Aelred advised us to test people's virtue and character quite carefully before entering into a deep friendship with them.[22] Political theorist Hannah Arendt suggests that the very commitments we're afraid might restrict us end up defining us: "Without being bound to the fulfillment of our promises, we would never be able to keep our identities; we would be condemned to wander helplessly and without direction in the darkness of each [person's] lonely heart."[23]

WHEN WE BREAK A COMMITMENT

When a personality assessment called the Enneagram told me that my shadow side involves deceiving others, I decided to work on making a commitment to honesty. I've never thought of myself as deceitful, but I decided to regularly ask myself, "Have I been honest?"

On the first day of my honesty commitment, I was driving on a long trip, with my wife and one of my daughters asleep in the car. I was trying to memorize a sermon, and I had a transcript of the sermon on my lap so I could occasionally refer to it. Mostly, I was looking at the road, but I would glance down quickly from time to time. When I got to the end of a page, I switched pages.

One such time, my daughter startled me by saying, "Dad,

what are you doing? Are you reading while you're driving?" It turns out she had stayed awake, which she never does in the car.

"No," I said.

"Well, then why did you put the top page on the bottom of the stack?"

All I could think of was, *Why are you awake? You're not supposed to be awake. You're grounded. I don't care if you are thirty years old!*

So here I am—it's January 1, I'm committed to a year of honesty, and I'm already lying to my family about a sermon about honesty.

Here's the deal: When I blow a commitment on January 1, I start again on January 2. When I fail a vow I made at 10:00, I start again at 10:01. Why? Because of grace. Because God is a commitment-keeping God, and at the cost of the cross where Jesus died, he keeps his commitments to us—even when we fail, even when we fall down, even when we don't keep our commitments to him.

COMMITMENT AND INTIMACY WITH GOD

Sometimes Christian speakers or writers will give emotionally charged appeals for commitment: "Are you 100 percent, sold out, no-matter-what, nothing-held-back committed to Jesus?" Pretty soon commitment becomes a competitive sport. I start to compare myself to others who are less committed. I sing songs about how devoted I am and get emotionally moved by reflecting on how deeply submitted I feel to God right now (even though I may have been sinning right and left a minute ago and will be again a minute from now).

When alcoholics join AA, it becomes a commitment that

defines their identity and guides their lives. But it never looks heroic to them; it just looks like a lifeline to sanity and survival. A good commitment works that way.

Someone once asked Dallas Willard, "If a person wants to grow spiritually, where should they start? Read the Bible? Pray more? Go to church?" Dallas's answer was completely disarming—and unexpected. He said, "Do the next right thing you know you ought to do. Now when you try that, you may wind up going to church, because you're going to need some help. Nothing will drive you into the Kingdom of God like trying to do the next thing that is right . . . because you *will* need help, and you *will* get it, because that's where God is."[24]

So today, from one moment to the next—as the thought enters your mind—do the next right thing you know you ought to do:

- Work with diligence and cheerfulness.
- Encourage someone next to you.
- Include a playful phrase in an e-mail to brighten somebody's day.
- Notice what the expression on another person's face is telling you about his or her heart.
- Apologize.
- When you're late for a meeting because you didn't allow enough time to get there, refuse to blame it on the traffic.
- Let someone merge in front of you on the freeway.
- Be patient with a difficult person.
- Don't blow up at your kids.

Sometimes doing the next right thing seems impossible, even when it's not. Once, after hearing Dallas Willard give a talk about "doing the next right thing," a man approached Dallas and said, "I have a rebellious son, and I can't help blowing up at him." Dallas told him to simply promise his wife that the next time he blew up at his son, he would contribute $5,000 to his wife's favorite charity.[25]

Often, "doing the next right thing" will demand a power not currently available to us. Just like with an alcoholic who decides that the "next right thing" is *not* to take a drink, willpower alone will not get this done. Success will require a new way of life in which we will need to access strength from a Power greater than ourselves.

The beauty of "do the next right thing" is that it often reveals that we're *unable* to do the next right thing. That realization drives us to seek God—and we will find him. But first we must be honest about our *intentions*.

When I lived in Chicago, I decided I wanted to get my body into better shape.

Then I met Doug, a professional trainer and body builder, and we started working out together. It was amazing. I felt like a member of a different and far inferior species. Nancy used to ask, "Can I come and watch you and Doug work out?"

"I can't make it today," I'd tell her. "It's just gonna be Doug."

"That'd be okay," she'd assure me.

At one point, I told him, "I'd like to look like you."

And he asked me, "Are you all in?"

"What do you mean?" I asked.

"You don't just drift into this," he explained. "I will lift weights until my muscles ache. I push myself so hard sometimes that I feel like I'm on fire. Some mornings, I hurt so much I can't bend down to tie my shoes. I monitor every calorie I put in my body. I wake myself up at night to ingest protein when it can best be absorbed. Mostly it takes the courage to face the pain—searing pain. Are you all in?"

Turns out, I wasn't. I was only partly in. I was okay with not looking all the way like Doug. I have a life. I'm more an admirer than a disciple.

Now, here is our friend Jesus. He's looking for disciples, people who will surrender their lives—money and reputation and achievements (which we cannot keep)—for a transformed character in a glorious Kingdom that we cannot lose.

It's not a bad thing to be an admirer of his. But he's looking for disciples. He promises to be there for us when we do well, and to be there for us when we don't. Cross his heart. Hope to die.

At the end of his essay defending rash vows, G. K. Chesterton writes one of the best sentences in English literature: "All around us is the city of small sins, abounding in backways and retreats, but surely, sooner or later, the towering flame will rise from the harbour announcing that the reign of the cowards is over, and a man is burning his ships."[26]

Are you ready to be all in—with your wife, your friends, your family—with Jesus?

Burn the plow. Burn the ships.

CHAPTER 8

SOMETHING THERE IS THAT DOESN'T LOVE A WALL

INTIMACY AND BARRIERS

They slipped briskly into an intimacy from which they never recovered.
F. Scott Fitzgerald, *This Side of Paradise*

In 1991, in the tiny town of New Berlin in upstate New York, the Chase Memorial Nursing Home was a place of despair. It housed eighty severely disabled elderly residents, many of whom had dementia. They were disconnected from their families, from the staff, from each other, and from the world. They were dying from what a new doctor there—Bill Thomas—called the Three Plagues of nursing home existence: *boredom*, *loneliness*, and *helplessness*.[1]

Bill was a doctor with the drive of a salesman and the personality of a game show host, and he decided that what the residents needed wasn't more *protection*, but more *connection* to life. He met with the nursing home director and the staff leadership to propose bringing green plants into all the rooms.

"Okay," they said.

"How about a dog?" he asked.

There were safety code issues. "But maybe so, yeah."

"Let's try two dogs," he said.

"It's against code," they repeated.

"Let's just put it down on paper," he said.

Dr. Bill was not seeing much enthusiasm in response, but he thought he was on a roll. "How about cats?"

"You want dogs *and* cats?" they asked.

"Some people aren't dog lovers," he reasoned. "How about two cats on both floors?"

"So, we're going to propose to the health department to allow two dogs and four cats?"

"Perfect," Bill said, beaming. "And we need more sounds of life around this place. You know what would be best? The sound of birds singing."

"How many birds are you talking to create this birdsong?" the staff inquired.

Bill thought a moment, then said, "Let's put down one hundred."

"One hundred birds? In this place!?" they exclaimed. "You must be out of your mind! Have you ever lived in a house that has two dogs and four cats and one hundred birds?"

"No," Bill said, smiling. "But wouldn't it be worth trying?"

Eventually, Dr. Bill wore them down and they ordered the birds. The hundred parakeets all arrived on the same day. But the birdcages hadn't come yet, so the delivery man released the birds into the nursing home's beauty salon.

It was total pandemonium. Feathers were flying everywhere, and many of the elderly residents gathered to watch through the salon's window. "They laughed their butts off," said Dr. Bill. It was a kind of "glorious chaos."

Sounds kind of like the beginning of Genesis.

Atul Gawande, who tells this wonderful story in his book, *Being Mortal*, says that "the effect on residents soon became impossible to ignore: the residents began to wake up and come to life. 'People who we had believed weren't able to speak started speaking,' [Dr. Bill] said. 'People who had been completely withdrawn and nonambulatory started coming to the nurses' station and saying, "I'll take the dog for a walk."'"[2]

Not only was new life injected into the daily routine of the nursing home, but the residents also stopped dying so much. The mortality rate dropped by 15 percent, and total drug costs plummeted to less than half of what they were at a comparative facility.[3]

Gawande identifies a phrase that social scientists often use to describe the condition of elderly people who no longer live with family: "intimacy at a distance."[4] He notes that in previous centuries, old age commanded so much respect and status that people actually lied about being *older* than they were; now we lie the other way around.[5]

Researchers came to study Chase Memorial Nursing Home. They saw the impact the new policies were making, but they couldn't explain it. Dr. Bill thought he could: People need a reason to live. People need a sense of *belonging*. We have an innate desire to be a part of something larger than ourselves. When we are connected to life and to each other, we thrive. When we are disconnected, we die.

He called this experiment the Eden Alternative.[6] As in Garden of Eden. As in the glorious chaos that human beings were assigned to care for. As in "It's not good for the man to be alone."

What if God is not so invisible, not so silent after all? What if the warble of every songbird, the bark of every dog, the light of every sunrise, the teeming life in every square inch of soil, and the tick of every precious second is God's way of saying, "Here is your invitation to join me in the love and care for all things"?

Eden was a picture of intimate life. The man and the woman walked with God during the cool of the day (intimate friendship with the Divine). They were "naked and not ashamed" (intimate love for one another). They studied and named the animals (intimate connection with creation). They tended the Garden (intimate engagement with their work).

With the Fall came the loss of Eden and the loss of intimacy. And we've been getting in our own way ever since. We have lived on the wrong side of what Milton called "the verdurous wall of Paradise."[7]

Our world is a world of walls. There is the Great Wall of China—built over centuries, stretching thousands of miles, and so labor-intensive that as many as four hundred thousand laborers died building it—and many are buried inside it.[8] There's also the Iron Curtain, the Bamboo Curtain, the Berlin Wall, and gated communities. But the hardest walls to scale are the walls of the human heart.

THE WALL OF EGO

The most inviolable wall in human existence is actually a curtain. It separates people who sit in first class on an airplane from the riffraff in the back. These two classes of people live two different lives. There is no intimacy between them.

If you're sitting in first class, a flight attendant will bring you a moist towelette to refresh your face, without your even asking. If you're in coach, your facial sweat is your own problem. If you're in first class—again, without your even asking—a flight attendant will bring you a bowl of warmed-up nuts and a free glass of wine, and maybe even slippers. In coach, you make do with whatever you brought aboard.

Normally I fly coach. When I do, I often find myself thinking, *Those arrogant people up there in first class, they ought to be back here with us. We the people . . . that's where the action is. That's where goodness is. They ought to be with us.*

Every once in a while, through some fortuitous circumstance, I end up flying first class. Then I find myself thinking, *Those poor slobs back there in coach. They must not function at as high a level as I do. They're probably just not as smart as my friends and me up here in first class.*

Here's what I've never seen: I've never seen anyone from first class stand up, rip the curtain in two, and say, "I'm breaking down the dividing wall of hostility. From now on, we will eat the same food and drink from the same cup, for we are all one."

Then there was the time I had to make a decision about which side of the wall I'd be on. I was on a flight with my wife. It was a Sunday afternoon. A flight attendant approached our row and said to me, "Mr. Ortberg, we were way undersold, and we actually have an upgrade for you. You can go sit in first class."

But they only had one seat . . . for me.

To make things worse, earlier that day I had preached on Acts 20:35, the passage where Paul quotes Jesus as saying, "It is more blessed to give than to receive." I had talked about how giving is the greater blessing.

So I turned to my wife and said, "Nancy, would you like my upgrade? Or would you prefer the greater blessing? Because I don't want to get in the way of that." It turned out she was just fine with the lesser blessing.

In all my relationships, even with those closest to me, I

keep running into a wall put up by what Immanuel Kant called "the dear self"[9]—that is, acting based on self-love, rather than purely from duty (which Kant believed was the only action that had moral worth).[10]

There's a poem I love by Robert Frost, called "Mending Wall." It's written in the voice of a farmer who, every spring, walks the perimeter of his property, along with his neighbor, who stays on the other side of the wall that separates them. As they gather and replace the stones that have fallen out of the wall over the winter, the farmer observes a strange force at work in the universe—as if creation itself keeps trying to remove the barrier between the two neighbors.

"Something there is that doesn't love a wall . . ."

As the two men work together, the farmer wonders aloud whether the wall is really necessary. His neighbor responds reflexively, "Good fences make good neighbours."

"Spring is the mischief in me," the farmer muses, "and I wonder if I could put a notion in his head: '*Why* do they make good neighbours? . . . Before I built a wall I'd ask to know what I was walling in or walling out, and to whom I was like to give offence. Something there is that doesn't love a wall, that wants it down.'"[11]

My ego blinds me to walls. My ego whispers that I'm entitled to my life of privilege. It blinds me to the humanity of the kids across the counter at McDonald's, the person who takes my money at the gas station, the Vietnamese woman at Supercuts who cuts my hair.

Brené Brown writes of being on her cell phone one time as she received a drink order in the drive-through lane at a fast-food restaurant. She apologized as soon as she could get off the phone: "I'm so sorry. The phone rang right when I was pulling up and I thought it was my son's school."

The woman who was serving her got tears in her eyes and said, "Thank you so much. You have no idea how humiliating it is sometimes. They don't even see us."[12]

A friend of mine who works in the food-service industry used to dread Sundays because church people, she says, were some of the most demanding and least generous customers. One church even created a website called SundaysAreTheWorst.com after a pastor (a pastor!) not only snubbed a waitress, but wrote on the bill: "I give God 10 percent; why do you get 18 percent?"[13]

Ego keeps me inside the walls of my tribe, my comfort zone. But here's the thing: Intimacy goes up when walls come down.

In *When Helping Hurts*, Brian Fikkert describes how the people in his Sunday school class decided to get outside the walls of their Presbyterian church and start tearing down walls of separation in their community. They went into an under-resourced, mostly African American neighborhood, and they started asking people, "What do you do well?" Then they started doing an asset mapping exercise, because so often that doesn't happen in under-resourced areas. Not "How can we help you?" but "What are your strengths here?"

> Each member of the class individually went door-to-door, saying to people, "Hello, I am from Community Presbyterian Church, the church just around the corner. We are conducting a survey today to find out what gifts God has placed in this community. What skills and abilities do you have?"
>
> The truth is that I wanted to die. Racial tensions are still very present in our city, so I knew there would be at least some social discomfort for both the African-American residents of this housing project

and for me. Furthermore, my height can be quite startling and intimidating, adding awkwardness to virtually all first encounters. And finally, the words I was supposed to repeat sounded totally hokey to me. "Hello, I am from Community Presbyterian Church, the church just . . ." Yuck! I would rather be selling Girl Scout cookies. I had a bad attitude about this exercise and wished I had chosen to attend the Sunday school class that was examining the finer points of Presbyterianism. But alas, I had chosen this class, so off I dutifully marched and knocked on the first door.

The thirty-something African-American woman who cracked open the door slightly was about 5'2", giving her a wonderful view of my belly. She looked up at me the way one would look at one's first sight of a Martian. I tried not to flinch and launched into my sales pitch, "Hello, I am from Community Presbyterian Church, the church . . ."

She said, "What?!" looking even more incredulous than before. . . .

I swallowed hard and repeated, "What skills do you have? What are you good at doing?"

She repeated, "What?!" And then I repeated my questions again, asking God to add jewels to my crown for going through all of this. . . .

"Well, I guess I can cook."

Suddenly, a voice from the dark unknown behind the lady shouted out, "She can cook chitlins like there is no tomorrow!"

Another voice yelled, "Yeah, ain't nobody can cook as good as she can!"

Slowly a smile spread across her face and she said, "Yes, I think I can cook."

Next thing I knew, I found myself sitting in the living room with about six African Americans gathered around. I live in the South. This does not happen easily. Not sure what to do, I reverted to script, "Hello, I am from Community Presbyterian Church . . ." They took it from there.

"This is Joe, he can fix bikes. . . . And this here is Mac. How is your car running? If you ever have trouble with your car, bring it right here to Mac." . . . They went on and on, bragging about one another to me. . . .

We started a process of empowerment by asking a simple question: what gifts do you have? When one is feeling marginalized, such a question can be nothing short of revolutionary."[14]

Something there is that doesn't love a wall.

THE WALL OF TECHNOLOGY

Let's start with this disclaimer: Technology is fabulous. For most of human history, most people couldn't read; and even if they could, they didn't have access to their own Bible. Now, thanks to advances in technology:

- We can read the Bible anytime anywhere.
- We can read the noblest thoughts of the greatest minds.
- We can listen to the greatest music ever composed.
- We can talk to people anywhere in the world—and even look them in the eye.

- We can look up information that entire libraries cannot contain.
- We can solve an infinite number of calculations.
- We can be guided, turn by turn, to any location on the planet, without a map.
- We can order a ride, measure our heart rate, monitor our finances, and check up on our kids, all without getting up from the recliner.

Our term "technology" comes from two Greek words found in the New Testament (*techne* and *logia*). These words are closely related to terms used to describe Jesus: *tekton* and *logos*.

Tekton is the word for craftsman. Jesus crafted the universe. When he became human he was actually called a tekton: "Isn't this the carpenter [tekton]? Isn't this Mary's son?"[15] Jesus was a techie.

Logos is Greek for "reason" or "word"; it speaks to our divinely given ability to understand and discover. "In the beginning was the Logos, and the Logos was with God, and the Logos was God."[16]

We marvel at technology because it's an expression of what God commanded when he made people in his image and told them to exercise dominion in Eden. Exercising dominion was intended to be an extension of our connection to God, to each other, and to creation: *In the beginning was the Tweet, and the Tweet was with God; and the Tweet was God, and the Tweet became flesh and twittered awhile among us.*

But it turns out the same technology that promises to help us be more connected than ever is—in some ways—making people more disconnected than ever.

On average, children eight and older are in front of screens more than seven hours a day.[17]According to a 2012 Pew survey, only 35 percent of kids between the ages of twelve and seven-teen said they "regularly socialized face-to-face," but 63 per-cent "said they communicated mostly via text messages and averaged 167 texts a day."[18] A study at Indiana University–Fort Wayne found that 89 percent of the subjects experienced phantom pocket vibration syndrome—thinking their cell phone is vibrating when it's really not.[19]

We think we're *using* our cell phones, but after a while we *need* them. Instead of their serving us, we're serving them. Ask yourself:

- Do you sleep with your cell phone on your nightstand or in your bed?
- Do your friends or family complain about your attending to a screen too much?
- Do you check your phone first thing in the morning and last thing at night?
- Do you feel bummed when you forget to bring your cell phone into the bathroom?
- Have you practiced the art of secretly texting while maintaining eye contact?
- Do you check your cell phone at business meetings, intimate dinners, or during sermons?

If you answered yes to most (or all) of these, you may have a tech addiction. The good/bad news is, you're not alone.

Because intimacy involves *shared experience*, it also requires *presence*. And presence doesn't mean simply having my body in the same room with yours. It requires sustained, focused *attention*. It demands eye contact. It demands that we look up from our screens and put down our devices.

In 2015, Brandie Johnson, a mother of young twin boys,

decided to conduct a little experiment: She took an hour one morning to unplug and simply watch her boys play. She also decided to keep score: If the boys ever looked over to see if she was watching them, she'd make a mark on a piece of paper. She ended up with twenty-eight marks. Here's her report, as posted on Facebook:

> As I sat quietly in the corner of the room I tallied how many times they looked at me for various reasons: to see if I saw their cool tricks, to seek approval or disapproval for what they were doing, and to watch my reactions. I couldn't help but wonder if I was on some sort of technology what message would I have been sending? 28 times my angels would have wondered if the World Wide Web was more important than them. 28 times my boys would have not received the attention most adults are searching for. 28 times my loves would have questioned if they were alone emotionally. 28 times my kids would have been reassured that who you are online is what really matters. In a world where we are accepted as who people perceive us to be and not who we really are, in a world where validation comes from how many followers or likes we have, in a world where quality time with loved ones is being replaced by isolation and text messages from the other room, I beg you to be different. Please put down your technology and spend some time with your family & loved ones. The next generation of children is counting on us to teach them how to be adults, don't be too busy on social media, you never know who is watching and what message you are sending.[20]

The website where I first read about this experiment ended with an ironic invitation: *"Please send this to all your friends on Facebook."* It just shows how invisible an addiction to technology can become.

MIT researcher Sherry Turkle identifies three "gratifying fantasies" that technology offers but can't fulfill:

- That we can put our attention wherever we want it to be
- That we will always be heard
- That we will never have to be alone.[21]

When I read those "fantasies," it strikes me that the reason we're so drawn to always being connected is that we are *made* to be connected. And maybe those dreams aren't so unfulfillable after all. Centuries ago, it was expressed like this:

You have searched me, LORD,
    and you know me.
You know when I sit and when I rise;
    you perceive my thoughts from afar.[22]

No matter where my attention may be, I have God's attention.

Before a word is on my tongue
    you, LORD, know it completely.[23]

I am always heard.

If I go up to the heavens, you are there;
    if I make my bed in the depths, you are there.
If I rise on the wings of the dawn,
    if I settle on the far side of the sea,

even there your hand will guide me,
    your right hand will hold me fast.[24]

I am never alone.

I have attention everywhere, I am always heard, and I am never alone. Only God can connect the human soul in the ways we most deeply desire.

We have an infinite need for connection, and God has an infinite capacity to connect.

Something there is that doesn't love a wall.

THE WALL OF HOSTILITY

John Gottman is a leading researcher on relationships and intimacy. He is able to predict the likelihood that a couple will stay together, versus getting divorced, at more than a 90 percent accuracy level—after fifteen minutes of conversation![25] How does he do it?

Simple. He looks for the presence of what he calls the "Four Horsemen of the Apocalypse" (referring to the four riders mentioned in Revelation 6:1-8, representing *conquest, war, famine,* and *death*).[26]

In a relationship, the first apocalyptic horseman is *criticism.* Criticism is different from a complaint. Every relationship will have its complaints—which are simply statements of problems and often are the first step in problem-solving. Criticism is a complaint with a barb on the end. We can turn any complaint into criticism by adding the phrase, "What's your problem?"

If we have a critical spirit and have a disagreement with our spouse, instead of going into problem-solving mode, we will interpret the disagreement as an indication of the other person's irremediable character flaws. We will magnify our spouse's negative traits and frequently comment on them. We will minimize and rarely acknowledge his or her positive qualities.

Sarcasm becomes an ingrained habit when we are critical. We can't make requests without slipping in a verbal jab: "Would you mind taking some time out from your television watching to help your fatherless son with his homework?"

The second horseman identified by Gottman—which he says is the worst of the four—is *contempt*. Contempt is a devaluing expression that may manifest itself through a look, a rolling of the eyes, or a tone of voice. Contempt says, "You are an irritation to me." It often involves verbal put-downs, a refusal to listen, or the deliberate infliction of pain.

As human beings, we are acutely sensitive to contempt. In fact, people who are contemptuous of each other are more susceptible to infectious illnesses, such as colds and flu. On the other hand, studies have shown that people with a common cold recover one day sooner than others, and shed less mucous, when they visit a doctor who is empathic.[27] It's literally true—empathy makes people less snotty.

The third horseman is *defensiveness*. We get defensive when we cannot admit we have done something wrong. We rationalize. We minimize. We evade. We deflect.

The fourth horseman is *stonewalling*. Here, we may go away without leaving the room. We avoid eye contact. We look at the floor. We withdraw. We go silent.

A friend of mine told me that when his wife starts to argue with him, he literally thinks about the rope-a-dope strategy that Muhammad Ali used against George Foreman: "I'll retreat to a corner of the ring and let you metaphorically punch yourself out until you're tired."

Something there is that doesn't love a wall.

THE WALL OF COMPARISON

When King Saul was so depressed he could hardly function, the one person who could bring him out of his funk was a young lyre player named David. Saul came to love David. And when David defeated Saul's biggest enemy, Goliath, it seemed their friendship was sealed.

But David turned out to be such a great warrior that, after battles, we're told, "The women came out from all the towns of Israel to meet King Saul with singing and dancing, with joyful songs and with timbrels and lyres. As they danced, they sang: 'Saul has slain his thousands, and David his tens of thousands.' Saul was very angry; this refrain displeased him greatly."[28]

Why did it displease him? Well, for one thing it's a really lame song. Rumor has it they sang it to the tune of "It's a Small World (After All)."

Saul has slain his thousands after all.
  David has slain his tens of thousands after all.
Saul has slain his thousands after all.
  David has slain his tens of thousands after all.

And they would just keep going. "Sing it again!" That would drive anybody crazy.

But the real problem was comparison. Saul compared himself to David and decided that David was more successful, and more loved, and therefore was a threat to the king's happiness. Imagine the conversation he had with his friends:

"Why are you so angry, Saul?"

"I'm offended. They have credited David with tens of thousands but me with only thousands."

"Are you kidding me, Saul? Who's 'they'?"

"Well, everyone."

"Saul, what do you care what everybody thinks? You're the king. You're the man. David works for you. If he wins, you win."

"What more can he get but my kingdom?"

When you're jealous, it's always because something precious is at stake—usually your kingdom. Better to find a kingdom that isn't yours and isn't at stake.

Another word for jealousy is envy. Envy is when I compare my life to somebody else's life and feel sad as a result.

A number of studies have found that people become more depressed and anxious the more time they spend on social media. We see pictures of people having dinner together at some great restaurant, and they're all laughing, and we wonder, *Why didn't they invite me?*

I compare your Facebook life with my real life—which almost always leads to discouragement. It turns out people are selective in what they post. We use technology to project an image of our lives that really isn't true.

Remember when families would send out Christmas newsletters? And it always seemed that their kids were all neurosurgeons and their dogs got into Harvard? Well, now we don't have to wait for Christmas to get discouraged. We simply have to check our Instagram feed, and all of a sudden we're flooded with evidence of our comparative inferiority:

She got married?

They got to go *there* on vacation? *I've* never been there.

Her job is *that* successful?

He's having *that* much fun?

Their kids got into *that* college?

There's a great quote by Frederick Buechner that says, "Envy is the consuming desire to have everybody else as unsuccessful as you are."[29]

Someone should post *that* on Facebook.

Of course, it's one thing to take out our frustrations on social media. It's another thing to take them out on God. The movie *Amadeus* is a great example of this. It tells the story of a court musician named Antonio Salieri, whose life is destroyed by envy. He compares his musical ability—which is merely outstanding—with Mozart's, which is genius. Salieri becomes convinced that God has done him wrong, and he prays this prayer:

> From now on we are enemies, You and I. Because You choose for Your instrument a boastful, lustful, smutty, infantile boy and give me for reward only the ability to recognize the Incarnation. Because You are unjust, unfair, unkind, I will block You, I swear it.[30]

In reality, Salieri had enormous privilege in his life. He lived at court. His gifts put him in the top one-tenth of one percent in the world. He could have been Mozart's friend and sponsor. Instead he became his enemy.

The movie is titled after Mozart's middle name, Amadeus, which means "friend of God." It ends with Salieri in an insane asylum, telling a priest how God has cheated him: "I will speak for you, Father. I speak for all mediocrities in the world. I am their champion. I am their patron saint."[31] He is finally wheeled through the yard of the asylum, saying to all the inmates, "Mediocrities everywhere, I absolve you."[32]

Hard to create intimacy with that attitude.

THE WALL OF PSEUDO-INTIMACY

Two couples are sitting at different tables in a restaurant. One couple is clearly on a date. They are carefully groomed and dressed. You can smell the perfume and cologne two tables away. Careful to make sure that no silence lasts too long, they laugh and gesture, tell stories, and ask about each other's food. Internally, they are always thinking about what they might say next.

The other couple is clearly married. All you can smell is the food. They are dressed for comfort and not fashion. Their comments to each other are briefer, they have less eye contact, and sometimes they gaze into space for minutes at a time. Are they experiencing the comfort and ease of years of intimacy, or have they settled for a mind-numbing rut of pathetic boredom?

You can't tell from watching.

The true indicators of stagnation are *inside* the relationship. Inevitably, the high-adrenaline rush of early infatuation will wear off. There is a good reason why this is so, and it's not a failure of love. Much of the emotion generated early in a relationship is based on the intensity of uncertainty. We wonder, *Does she really love me?* and feel a rush of relief when the answer is yes. That adrenaline rush is the same reason we ride roller coasters and watch scary movies. In a good relationship, when commitment is deep and known, the adrenaline rush goes away—which is a good thing.

When Nancy and I lived in the Midwest, she used to wear an outfit that included sweatpants and loafers. One time when we met for lunch, and she'd worn the outfit once too often, I told her, "Look, you either wear sweatpants with tennis shoes, or loafers with jeans. But if you keep wearing sweatpants and loafers, I will have to take you back to the wife store."

The truth is, I actually love the variations in how Nancy dresses—sometimes glamming up and sometimes cozying down. But intimacy is not the same as being comfortable.

Slugs are comfortable. To know whether a relationship has slipped into stagnant territory, we ask questions like these:

- Are we still growing?
- Are we still learning new things about each other?
- Are we challenging each other to become our best selves?
- Do we go out of our way to give gifts?
- Do we experience gratitude or take too much for granted?

Scott Peck identifies one of the great dangers in human relationships as "pseudo-community." In pseudo-community, people are nice to each other, well-mannered, pleasantly agreeable. They tell little white lies to smooth things over and avoid conflict. They pretend. They quit noticing. "It is an inviting but illegitimate shortcut to nowhere."[33]

The only way out of this is to enter into chaos.[34] Real community requires having the courage to say what I actually think, even though I don't know how the other person will respond, and even though that not knowing scares me.

Entering into chaos is like diving into a cold pool. But when we speak truth to our friends or children or spouse or parents, we have the opportunity to know one another at a deeper and truer level. And then growth can happen.

Intimacy is always a balance of chaos and comfort.

Kind of like sweatpants and loafers.

THE WALL OF TOO MUCH TO DO

One of the biggest walls to intimacy is spelled O-V-E-R-W-H-E-L-M-E-D.

I am overwhelmed because I feel I have to do the perfect job and have the perfect career so I don't disappoint people. I am overwhelmed because I want to be a really good son to my parents, and a really good brother to my siblings, and a really good husband to my wife, and a really good father to my children, and I fall short.

I want to pastor people well, and I feel guilty for moving too quickly through the church hallways. I want to lead well, and I feel inadequate because of my failures. I want to have time when my friends call me during the day so that irritation and hurry don't leak out of my voice, which I know they do.

I want to make sure our investments are in order. I want to update our will from thirty years ago so all our money doesn't go to our first child. (Just checking to see if any of you kids are actually reading this.)

I want to take vacations that create lasting memories with my family. I want to get better at preaching. I want to read great books I haven't even cracked open yet.

And it's not just that I *want* to do these things; I feel as if I *should*. I can find myself feeling guilty about any one of them.

And yet it's not the achievements we will remember, but the intimate moments of our lives.

When Nancy and I found out she was pregnant with our first child, we wanted to find a memorable way to let my parents know. We arranged a special meal at our favorite restaurant, and had the waitstaff bring out a special order under a covered dish. When my parents opened it, they found a pair of baby booties inside.

The illusion I live with is that I can get around to loving the life that wears those little booties whenever I have enough time. The reality is that those little feet grow very quickly, and if I'm going to love them, I must find time to do it *today*.

Even the phrase "find time" is not quite right.

God doesn't ask us to do what he doesn't give us time for.

Hurry is the enemy of intimacy.

Pressure is the enemy of intimacy.

Stress is the enemy of intimacy.

As the old saying goes, "If the devil can't make you sin, he'll make you busy."

Relationships are not efficient. People are not efficient. People take time. So how do we pursue intimacy?

Writer Anne Lamott tells about the time her ten-year-old brother was feeling overwhelmed by a report on birds he needed to write. He'd had three months to write it, but he kept putting it off. Finally, it was the day before it was due:

> We were out at our family cabin in Bolinas, and he was at the kitchen table close to tears, surrounded by binder paper and pencils and unopened books on birds, immobilized by the hugeness of the task ahead. Then my father sat down beside him, put his arm around my brother's shoulder, and said, "Bird by bird, buddy. Just take it bird by bird."[35]

A late-night conversation.

A phone call with a friend.

A retreat with some college buddies.

A visit to a nursing home.

Going to the Stanford Theater to see an old movie.

Pausing to ask a coworker about his or her spouse, who's in the hospital.

Or not.

Welcome to the wall called Too Much to Do.

There's never enough time.

There's always enough time.

BE STILL

The connection we yearn for most isn't technological; it's spiritual. It's not with the Internet; it's with God. Sometimes, in order to connect with God, we need to disconnect from everything else.

One of the most important commands in the Bible is this one: "Be still, and know that I am God."[36] I would submit that "being still" is harder today than ever before.

In a series of studies published in *Science*, researchers gave subjects a choice: sit alone with your thoughts for six to fifteen minutes, or give yourself an electric shock. *One-fourth* of the women—and *two-thirds* of the men—chose the shock. One man shocked himself *190 times* in fifteen minutes. Some people would rather punish themselves with electric pain than be still.[37]

But if we're never willing to be still, we'll never know that God is God.

If we're never willing to be still, we'll never really pray.

If we're never willing to be still, we'll never know real peace.

A few weeks ago, I tried a "tech Sabbath." At sundown on Friday night, I turned off my computer, turned off my cell phone, turned off the TV, and went cold turkey for twenty-four hours. No calls, no texts, no tweets, no e-mails, no posts, no blogs. I took a long walk. I had some long conversations with people I love. I read for no reason but the love of reading. I prayed. I played the piano. It was wonderful.

If the thought of being without your cell phone for an

entire weekend is too much for you, maybe you could start with this simple meditation based on Psalm 46:10 instead. Beginning with the entire sentence, reread the psalm, removing a word or two at a time:

> Be still and know that I am God.
> Be still and know that I am.
> Be still and know.
> Be still.
> Be.

In the Old Testament, God gives a wonderful instruction to a group of Levites: "They were also to stand every morning to thank and praise the LORD. They were to do the same in the evening."[38]

What if the first and last words of your day belonged to God instead of to your in-box?

The secret of our "connected selves" is that we were made to live in unceasing connection with God. Think of those twin boys busily playing while their mom watched and waited for them to look up. At some level, every human being is asking, "Is anyone watching? Anyone listening?" Well, God's paper is filled with a trillion marks.

"I am," he says.

In the early days of the Internet, it was amazing to be able to access it. You had to dial up. It took forever. You had to pay. Now you can go to a coffee shop or hotel or library and get unlimited, uninterrupted, instantaneous free Internet access.

That little word *access* is one the apostle Paul loved: "Through [Jesus] we . . . have access to the Father by one Spirit."[39]

You are always seen.

You are always heard.
You are never alone.
You have access to the Father.
It's the Eden alternative.
Something there is that doesn't love a wall.

CHAPTER 9

NAKED AND UNAFRAID

THE PARADOX OF VULNERABILITY AND AUTHORITY

There is a crack . . . in everything. That's how the light gets in.
LEONARD COHEN, *"Anthem"*

IT WAS THE MOST unforgettable speaking moment I've ever had. We were hosting a conference that drew church leaders from around the country. The place was packed. I had been asked at the last minute to do a reading of Psalm 150.

"You gotta read it with exuberant enthusiasm," said my friend Nancy Beach, who was directing the service.

To kick off the service, there was a hip-hop number that involved a kind of liturgical break dance. Brought down the house. My job was to bridge to an even louder and more joyful song, so I started reading fast and loud and kept getting more exuberant.

Praise the LORD

Praise God in his sanctuary;
    praise him in his mighty heavens.

Praise him for his acts of power;
    praise him for his surpassing greatness.

After this rousing introduction, the psalm is basically a list of instruments. (It's the last of 150 psalms, so by that time the psalmist had to stretch his material.)

Praise him with the sounding of the trumpet,
    praise him with the harp and lyre,
praise him with timbrel and dancing,
    praise him with the strings and pipe,
praise him with the clash of cymbals,
    praise him with resounding cymbals.

By now, I'm shouting. If they want energy, I'll give them energy.

Then I have a slight verbal tic on the next line.

Let everything that has breasts . . .

Pause.

Did I just say what I think I just said?

The house erupts.

Yep.

I stand naked on the stage, waiting for the people to stop laughing, trying to figure out what to say next. Maybe I could tell them this is from *The Message* and blame it all on Eugene Peterson.

They never stopped laughing.

I finally just walked off the stage.

I never did finish the psalm.

It's a funny thing. My job involves trying to help people live more closely connected to God by teaching under the authority of Scripture with as much diligence and skill as I can muster. And yet what I will always be remembered for is my Freudian-slip reading of Psalm 150.

STRONG AND WEAK

Now let me tell you about the most important friendship moment I've ever had.

The best friend I made in graduate school is my friend Rick. I admired him from the first time I met him. He could do so many things so well. He was a better athlete than I was, he knew how to dress better, women naturally liked him, and he was a much better therapist than I was. I was also pretty sure he was a better husband. Once in the early days of both our marriages, he came over to our apartment and asked Nancy if he could borrow an iron because he needed to iron his shirt. When Nancy gave it to him, he said he had to rush off because he was stir-frying an elaborate recipe for dinner that required constant vigilance. When I got home, I found out the husband bar had been reset at a much higher level.

After Rick and I had been friends for about a decade, I decided I would like to try an exercise in intimacy I had never tried before—to confess to him everything I could think of that needed confessing. I had just finished writing what folks in AA call "a fearless moral inventory." When it was done, I met with Rick and read through everything I had written down—details of lying, and jealousy, and lust, and anger, and pride, and woundedness. Some of them were matter-of-fact for me, but some were so mortifying that I couldn't look at him while I was reading them; all I could do was focus on the paper.

It was his response that slew me.

I hadn't really thought about what he might say when I was finished. I was too caught up in my own sense of shame, and in what I knew would be his lessened opinion of me.

He asked me to look up at him, and then he spoke the sentence I'll never forget: "John, I've never loved you more than I love you right now."

Well, if that's *how it works, let me see if I can't think up some more bad stuff.*

In his book *Strong and Weak*, Andy Crouch writes that most of us think of *authority* and *vulnerability* as two points on a single continuum.[1] (Crouch speaks about them in terms of *flourishing*, but I want to consider them in terms of *intimacy*). We think of ourselves as either high-capacity or highly fragile.

We often think our goal should be maximizing our authority and minimizing our vulnerability. However, Crouch argues that this is not the best way to picture how God intends for us to live. Actually, God created human beings to have both great authority *and* great vulnerability.

God created humanity in his own image. He told them they were to "rule over the fish in the sea and the birds in the sky . . . and over all the creatures that move along the ground."[2] But he also created human beings to be utterly dependent on him. Susceptible to temptation. Naked.

We could picture this as a two-by-two chart.

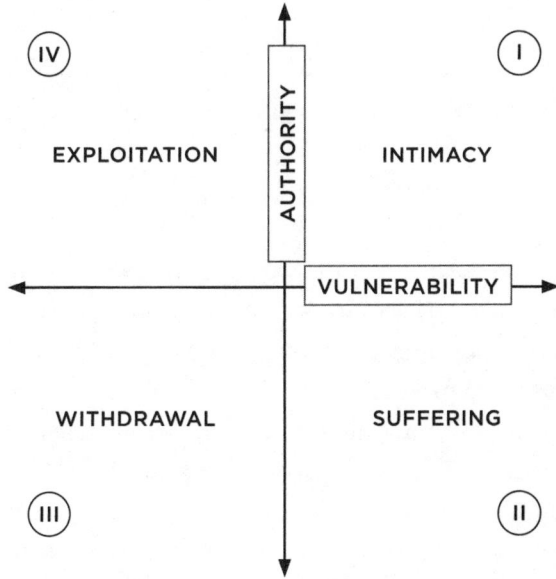

Authority, Crouch says, might be defined as "the capacity for meaningful action."[3] Teachers have it in the classroom; surgeons in the operating room; judges in the courtroom. When we have authority, all we need to do is command, or ask, or even imply, and it will be done.

I walk into my office and books have been straightened and meetings arranged. Why? I have authority.

I go into my children's rooms and beds have been made and clothes put away. Why? I have authority.

I come home and there are slippers by the La-Z-Boy and iced tea on the tray. Why? I've walked into the wrong house.

King David marvels that human beings are so tiny compared to the scale of the universe:

Yet you have made them a little lower than the angels. . . .
You made them rulers over the works of your hands;
  you put everything under their feet.[4]

But we're not made just to have authority. We're also made to
be vulnerable. "Adam and his wife were both naked, and they
felt no shame."[5]

Naked is a vulnerable word.

Of all the creatures in the world, only human beings
can be naked. By adulthood, every other creature
naturally possesses whatever fur, scales, or hide are
necessary to protect it from its environment. No other
creature—even naked mole rats or Mr. Bigglesworth,
the hairless feline sidekick of Mike Myers's movie
villain Dr. Evil—shows any sign, in its natural state,
of feeling incomplete in the way that human beings
consistently do.[6]

That's why little kids love to come up with jokes like,
"Why can't two elephants swim together? They only have one
pair of trunks."

Our lives begin and end in vulnerability. Vulnerability, says
Andy Crouch, might be thought of as "*exposure to meaningful
risk.*"[7] And we live with the knowledge that one day, our bodies will give out on us. As Wallace Stegner memorably put it,
"Seen in geological perspective, we are fossils in the making,
to be buried and eventually exposed again for the puzzlement
of creatures of later eras."[8]

We see the ultimate combination of vulnerability and
authority in Jesus. On the one hand, he was born a helpless
infant—like every other child—and laid in a manger by his

parents, a poor couple who soon had to flee from King Herod. He was hungry, tired, and thirsty; he bled, he wept, and he ended his life nailed to a cross.

And yet, while he walked the earth, he did wonders that no one had ever done; he taught in ways that affected the course of history like no one else; he told his followers that their mission was to call every single person in the world to become one of his disciples. (It's often called the Great Commission; when you consider its staggering audacity, you might call it the Great Presumption.) His final recorded statement on earth includes this claim: "All authority in heaven and on earth has been given to me."[9]

Ultimate vulnerability. Ultimate authority. Which enables him to offer us ultimate intimacy.

Intimacy flows out of Jesus' vulnerability because he suffered like us, was tempted like us, felt pain like us. Intimacy flows out of his authority because now nothing "will be able to separate us from the love of God that is in Christ Jesus our Lord."[10]

INTIMACY IS BUILT ON BOTH AUTHORITY AND VULNERABILITY

Old Testament scholar Walter Brueggemann notes that "bone of my bones and flesh of my flesh"—the words used by the first man in recognizing the first woman—"are used together to speak about a person in his total relation to another."[11]

Intimacy thrives on the paradox between *bone* (hard, rigid, strong, powerful, and mighty) and *flesh* (soft, pliable, frail, weak, and vulnerable).

Bone and flesh.

Strength and weakness.

Authority and vulnerability.

Brueggemann further explains the relationship between these two contrasting concepts.

> Our two words [*bone* and *flesh*], which conventionally
> appear in English as physical properties of the
> body, need to be rendered in ways that speak of the
> functioning of the whole organism. . . . Together
> they mean something different from what either
> might mean separately. Because they are antithetical,
> it is most likely that they mean to state two extreme
> possibilities and include everything in between
> them, thus all physical-psychological dimensions of
> interaction from A to Z.[12]

The previous diagram (on page 161) above shows the range of possible combinations of authority and vulnerability. When either one is weak or missing—or worse yet, when both are—relationships are marked by suffering, exploitation, or withdrawal. When both are present and strong, intimacy can grow.

One of the stories in the Bible in which we can most clearly trace the pain of lost intimacy and the struggle with authority and vulnerability is the saga of Jacob and Esau. The first time we meet the twin brothers, they are fighting each other in the womb:

> When her time to give birth came, sure enough, there
> were twins in her womb. The first came out reddish,
> as if snugly wrapped in a hairy blanket; they named
> him Esau (Hairy). His brother followed, his fist
> clutched tight to Esau's heel; they named him Jacob
> (Heel).[13]

Why were they fighting? Apparently, little fetal Jacob looked at little fetal Esau and said, "He's closer to the exit than I am and will get out first. He'll be the heir, Dad's favorite. He will have authority and I will be vulnerable. Simple solution: I will grab his heel and pull him behind me, and then I'll be #1 and he'll be #2."

But Jacob was too weak. He failed to be born first. He was a little fetal failure. And failure would haunt him for a long time. Until it *saved* him.

While the two boys were growing up, every time Esau walked into the room, Jacob saw their father's eyes light up. Every time Jacob walked in and his dad saw it wasn't Esau, Jacob could see the disappointment on his dad's face.

Before long, "Not Esau" became Jacob's identity. Sometimes this happens to you and me:

I'm the one my _____ doesn't love.

father
mother
spouse
child
boyfriend/girlfriend

Jacob's sense of authority was very low. His sense of vulnerability was very high. He lived in quadrant II: Suffering.

But Jacob had an ally. His mother, Rebekah, loved him best and concocted a plan for Jacob to steal his father's blessing by pretending to be Esau. When he objected that he might get caught, Rebekah responded, "Let the curse fall on me. Just do what I say."[14]

Rebekah knew she had a much stronger will than her

husband, Isaac. Rebekah was in quadrant IV: Exploitation (high authority, low vulnerability).

It's often tempting to manage our relationships by trying to live in quadrant IV.

Andy Crouch writes of one way to think about this. Imagine you walk into a room crowded with people—most of whom you don't know—and you have to talk to them. How do you cope?

For churchgoers who are introverts, the worst part of a church service is the thirty seconds when they have to greet people. I know of people who sit out in the lobby just to avoid that. Ultra-extroverts, on the other hand, *love* the meet-and-greet times: "Hundreds of new friends just waiting to get to know me!" (You know who you are. The rest of us know who you are too. We envy you and find you truly bizarre.)[15]

Think about when you were young and you went off to school or to a party and felt like an outsider. Now imagine you could give yourself a glass full of something, and the more you drank, the less discomfort you'd feel. It would be like liquid authority.

When you begin to use alcohol to manage vulnerability, you are moving toward quadrant IV. For the moment, it feels really good. The problem is, over time the feeling wears off, and it takes more and more alcohol to produce the same effect. Eventually, it will rob you of authority and lead you into suffering.

Quadrant IV is the quadrant of the very first temptation. The serpent says to Eve:

"You will be like God" (high authority).

"You won't die!"[16] (no vulnerability).

Instead the opposite happens:

They become unlike God (low authority).

They will surely die (high vulnerability).

Sin promises authority without vulnerability; it leads to vulnerability without authority.

Rebekah tells Jacob he can wear Esau's clothes, and she puts goat hair on his skin so he can smell like Esau and feel like Esau. Isaac's eyesight is so bad that Jacob doesn't even have to look like Esau. All he has to do is talk like Esau and act like Esau and everything will be just fine. It's like a scene from a movie.

He went to his father and said, "My father."

"Yes, my son," he answered. "Who is it?"

Jacob said to his father, "I am Esau your firstborn."[17]

Not just "I am Esau," but "I'm Esau, your firstborn—you know: #1 in your heart, your favorite."

Isaac's blind eyes light up. Jacob learns that if you can't get what you want by being who you are, maybe you can get what you want by pretending to be who you're not.

For Brené Brown, one of the biggest surprises in her research was the discovery that "belonging" and "fitting in" are not the same thing. *Belonging* is being accepted for *you*. *Fitting in* is being accepted for trying to be who you're not.[18]

If I belong, I get to be me.

If I have to fit in, I can't be me.

When I first moved to California, a friend invited me to tag along as he stood outside big Hollywood banquets and award shows to collect autographs from movie stars. We noticed how lax the security became fifteen minutes or so after each event started. So I got a ten-dollar tuxedo from a Pasadena thrift shop and we would sneak into these events. I got pictures with Jimmy Stewart, chatted with Cary Grant; once, I pointed Elizabeth Taylor up to the podium to speak. I fit in. But I didn't belong. I was always afraid of being discovered, of getting thrown out of Eden.

Sometimes, being a Christian kid was more about pretending and fitting in than belonging, and I got pretty good at it.

I pretended I was better than I was.

I pretended I was happier than I was.

I pretended to agree with people when I really didn't.

I pretended I didn't want to drink, even though I really did want to drink (but I was afraid of getting caught).

I pretended I was really mature and sophisticated—into learning and activities and sports and not really crazy about girls. Truth was, I would have sold my grandmother to go out with a cute girl. (And my grandmother meant the world to me.)

When you're fitting in instead of belonging, you're always afraid someone will find out that you're wearing a used tuxedo and you weren't invited.

Sometimes, if I'm fearful in a relationship, I'll try to misuse vulnerability in order to avoid conflict or manage my fear. I abdicate the authority God has given me.

We have a five-year-old yellow lab named Baxter, after Richard Baxter, the seventeenth-century Puritan author of *The Reformed Pastor*—or maybe it was after Ron Burgundy's gentleman dog ("like a miniature Buddha covered in hair!") that ate a whole wheel of cheese in the movie *Anchorman*.

Baxter looks like he possesses authority; he's large and athletic and growls at strange noises. But as soon as anyone walks in the door, he rolls over and exposes his jugular. "No threat here. Please love me. I'm desperate."

The Manson family could come in carrying knives and clubs, and Baxter would still roll over. "Wanna rub my belly?"

I know people like that.

Years ago, I took Baxter to a trainer. At the end of the first session, the trainer gave me some pointers. "When you're giving a command to your dog, never crouch down and look at him at eye level. Always loom over him. If your dog signals that he wants to go out by scratching at the back door, never let him out directly. Make him obey some command of yours first. Always remember that you are reinforcing your authority in every interaction."

I know people like that too.

Sometimes you're the trainer, and sometimes you're Baxter. But true intimacy grows only when both people in a relationship are living in genuine authority *and* vulnerability with each other.

THE GIFT OF VULNERABILITY

Back to Jacob and Esau. The signature event at the center of Jacob's life is the strange story of his wrestling with God. Is it really God he wrestles with, or an angel? The text doesn't say. Why does God make Jacob struggle for his blessing? The text doesn't say. All we know is that his longing for God's blessing is fierce. When the struggle is over, Jacob is left with a limp that—as far as we know—never went away. He wanted a blessing, and he got a limp. Or maybe the limp *was* his blessing.

When Jacob went to see the brother he had wronged, we're told that "Esau ran to meet Jacob and embraced him."[19] We're not told that Jacob ran to Esau. Why not? Because he limped.

It may be that Jacob's limp did more to soften Esau's heart and prepare the way for the restoration of intimacy than his successes and wealth ever could.

Vulnerable comes from the Latin word *vulnerare*, which means "to hurt or wound." Perhaps Jacob's limp was his gift.

But it's a gift that nobody wants.

Brené Brown starts her book *Daring Greatly* with the story of a visit to her therapist that exposed her love/hate (mostly hate) relationship with vulnerability:

> I looked right at her and said, "I frickin' hate vulnerability." I figured she's a therapist—I'm sure she's had tougher cases. Plus, the sooner she knows what she's dealing with, the faster we can get this whole therapy thing wrapped up. "I hate uncertainty. I hate not knowing. I can't stand opening myself to getting hurt or being disappointed. It's excruciating. Vulnerability is complicated. *And* it's excruciating. Do you know what I mean?"
>
> Diana nods, "Yes, I know vulnerability. I know it well. It's an exquisite emotion." Then she looks up and kind of smiles, as if she's picturing something really beautiful. . . .
>
> "I said it was *excruciating*, not *exquisite*," I point out. . . . "I hate how it makes me feel."
>
> "What does it feel like?"
>
> "Like I'm coming out of my skin. Like I need to fix whatever's happening and make it better."
>
> "And if you can't?"
>
> "Then I feel like punching someone in the face."
>
> "And do you?"
>
> "No. Of course not."

"So what do you do?"

"Clean the house. Eat peanut butter. Blame people. Make everything around me perfect. Control whatever I can—whatever's not nailed down."[20]

Brené lists the circumstances that make her feel most vulnerable—anxiety or uncertainty, being criticized or doing something that is uncomfortable, experiencing scary things, feeling like things are too good and might get jinxed—while her therapist responds with a series of increasingly annoying empathic head nods designed to elicit even more vulnerability. Finally, Brené blurts out: "Can I get to exquisite without having to feel really vulnerable in the process?"[21]

No. Not possible. Thanks for playing.

Henry Cloud points out that it's no coincidence that God placed our tear ducts in our eyes. They could have been in some less conspicuous place—in our armpits, maybe, or between our toes. But God placed them in our eyes. He wants our tears to be out front, right where we don't want them, right where other people can see them.[22] We are vulnerable not by accident, but by design.

What is your limp? Maybe it's a divorce. Or a business failure. Or a disability. Or your body type. Or your education. Or your anger. Maybe it's a series of failed relationships. Maybe it's an addiction. Maybe it's a prison record. Maybe it's a history of abuse—given or received. Maybe it's cowardice. Maybe it's panic attacks or emotional illness. Maybe it's your aloneness.

What if it never goes away?

What if God wants to use it?

It's a strange truth that I admire vulnerability in other people, but I don't want to have to be vulnerable myself.

Madeleine L'Engle writes, "When we were children, we used to think that when we were grown-up we would no longer be vulnerable. But to grow up is to accept vulnerability. . . . To be alive is to be vulnerable."[23]

We are drawn to people who embrace their vulnerability. When someone once accused the famously homely Abraham Lincoln of being two-faced, he immediately responded, "If I had another face, do you think I'd wear this one?"[24]

At a conference one time where I heard Anne Lamott speak, she looked at the monitor as she stepped to the podium, saw the image of herself and her scraggly dreadlocks, and sighed in despair, "Oh God . . . my hair."

After that opening, she had us all eating out of her hand.

Intimacy is sparked, and a team becomes a family, when a leader is willing to say:

I'm sorry.

I was wrong.

I don't know.

I need help.

I'm depressed.

In her book *The Wounding and Healing of Desire*, Wendy Farley reaffirms the notion that we are vulnerable by design. In reflecting on the vulnerability of mothers and babies, and what their interactions can teach us about God, she writes, "Intimacy arising out of delight allows the infant's pain to impress itself on the mother as if it were her own pain."[25]

We are born into utter dependence. A mother experiences the desire to relieve her baby's suffering much like her desire to relieve her own suffering. It's as if she has doubled her capacity to suffer—along with her capacity for delight.

What does this tell us about God, who said, "Can a mother

forget the baby at her breast? . . . Though she may forget, I will not forget you!"[26]

We begin our lives inside the body of another, in uncertainty and risk. God chose to take the same risk—and experience the same intimacy—by sending Jesus into the world as a baby.

In *The Power and Vulnerability of Love*, Elizabeth Gandolfo writes, "The incarnate life of divine love begins in a pool of blood. . . . The blood-borne origins of the Incarnation remind us that the invulnerable nature of divine love becomes not only possible, but also *vulnerable* in the crimson waters of Mary's womb. Nearly one in four pregnancies end in miscarriage. So much could have gone wrong . . . Mary did not have to do an anxiety-filled Google search on 'miscarriage' to know this."[27]

Jesus is most present in the most vulnerable. As he said, "Whatever you did for one of the least of these brothers and sisters of mine, you did for me."[28]

THE BLESSING OF VULNERABILITY

In the story of Jacob and Esau, Jacob is not the only vulnerable one. Earlier, after he had stolen the birthright and run away from his brother, he traveled to his ancestral homeland and worked for his uncle Laban. Laban had two daughters. The younger one, Rachel, "had a lovely figure and was beautiful."[29] Her older sister, Leah, had "weak eyes."[30]

Jacob falls in love with Rachel. He agrees to work seven years to marry her. But apparently he got lost on his way to the bridal suite, because we're told, "When morning came, there was Leah!"[31]

Just like Jacob grew up being "not Esau," Leah's identity was intertwined with being "not Rachel." Rachel was the pretty one, the one all the boys wanted to talk to. Nobody who went trolling for hot babes landed on Leah's profile.

Imagine growing up in a culture where your worth as a woman was defined by your physical appearance. (Hard to fathom, right?) Body image, body type, your face, your skin, your race, your age, or other external characteristics that have nothing to do with your soul would determine whether you get fawned over or ignored.

Marriage is excruciatingly vulnerable. Sex can be excruciatingly vulnerable. Not having the right body or the right face makes us vulnerable.

Not long ago, I went to the doctor to get photodynamic treatment for precancerous cells on my face. It makes your face completely red and bumpy, like a pizza. For the next several days, I had to explain the situation to everyone I talked to. They'd all scrutinize my face and then say, "You don't look so bad."

For the most part, I don't think a lot about my looks, but after several days of "You don't look so bad," it did start to get to me. Try greeting people that way this week.

How do you find intimacy in a culture where getting married and having children is the only dream a girl is raised to know? Now imagine having a father who believes that the only way he can marry you off is to fool your sister's fiancé into sleeping with you by mistake.

"When morning came, there was Leah!"

Imagine the pain behind those words. Leah wakes up on the first morning of her married life. She wonders what Jacob will say. Maybe he will be kind. Maybe he will be tender. Maybe he will understand the pain of having to pretend to be who you're not, in order to belong.

But he doesn't. "His love for Rachel was greater than his

love for Leah."[32] Enough so that he was willing to work for Laban for another seven years in order to marry Rachel.

At this point, the main character of the story enters the scene for the first time in the chapter, and he has an answer for overlooked, under-loved Leah: "When the LORD saw that Leah was not loved, he enabled her to conceive."[33] In a culture where a woman's perceived value was tied to her ability to produce children, God blesses Leah almost beyond measure. And here the story becomes incredibly poignant.

"Leah became pregnant and gave birth to a son. She named him Reuben, for she said, 'It is because the LORD has seen my misery. Surely my husband will love me now.'"[34]

She thinks, *Maybe now Jacob's eyes will light up for me the way they do for Rachel. Maybe he'll hold me and whisper things to me. Maybe this baby will fix our relationship.*

But it doesn't.

She has a second son, whom she names Simeon: "Because the LORD heard that I am not loved, he gave me this one too."[35]

And then a third son, named Levi: "Now at last my husband will become attached to me, because I have borne him three sons."[36]

And a fourth, named Judah.

After Judah was born, Leah stopped having children (though years later she would add two more boys and a girl to her brood). Maybe she gave up hoping that Jacob would ever love her like he loved Rachel. Maybe she decided to find a better source for the love she needed to fill the hole in her heart.

But even if Jacob never changed his mind about Leah, she knew that God saw her and cared about her.

If you're feeling unloved; if you haven't been healed; if you aren't strong; if you think you're not pretty; if you think you're not smart; if you feel like a failure; if you think you're all alone—the Lord sees. The Lord cares. The Lord knows.

But just because God sees doesn't mean the rest of the story will be smooth sailing.

"When Rachel saw that she was not bearing Jacob any children, she became jealous of her sister. So she said to Jacob, 'Give me children, or I'll die!'"[37] And Rachel is the favorite wife!

When there's a hole in your heart, somebody else's success just makes you feel worse about yourself. The writer wants us to see how absurd this can get.

Leah and Rachel engage in what author Kent Hughes calls "Birth Wars!" to see who can have the most kids.[38] And both women offer their maids to Jacob to increase their chances of winning.

Then Leah's son Reuben finds some mandrakes and gives them to his mother. In the ancient world, mandrakes were thought of as an aphrodisiac—like oysters or green M&M's. That's why they're in the story. They also came with a little warning: Seek immediate medical help if the mandrake's effects last longer than four hours.

When Rachel hears about the mandrakes, she asks Leah for some of them. But Leah says, "Wasn't it enough that you took away my husband? Will you take my son's mandrakes too?"[39]

So Rachel cuts a deal: "He can sleep with you tonight in return for your son's mandrakes."[40]

Leah slept with Jacob that night (the Bible doesn't shy away from telling it like it is), and she became pregnant and bore him a fifth son.

Really? And Jacob is one of the patriarchs? And the twelve

tribes of Israel are the result of Birth Wars? There isn't a single person in the entire saga who comes off like a hero.

Maybe that's the point. Intimacy is for limpers. For rejects. For pretenders. For people who try to fit in because they're afraid they don't belong. It's not a story about unbroken people. It's a story about broken people and the love that heals them.

THE HOPE OF VULNERABILITY

Researchers say that babies learn how to "fake cry" by the time they are six months old, to get attention when nothing is wrong.[41] Think about that. Before you even learned how to use words, you learned how to lie.

Back when my kids were small, I noticed some boogers on the headboard as I was tucking one of them in one night.

"Where did these come from?" I asked.

"A birdie did it."

Ask a stupid question . . .

I'm happy to report that this child soon outgrew this phase—becoming a *much* more competent liar.

The point is, we learn early to lie, to pretend, to misrepresent what's going on inside. But in order to achieve intimacy, we must be willing to expose our weaknesses, our insecurities, our true selves.

Many of us may not want that level of intimacy, writes Kent Dunnington, "for that would entail not only our humiliation but also a vulnerability to others in which many of us have no interest. We are afraid that if we confessed our sins, other people might make claims on our lives by insisting on praying for us and asking us how we are doing. Most of us are not sure we want church to be that involved."[42]

Not long ago, I met a man named Doug Mazza, who was the top American executive at Suzuki and then was recruited to be the head of American Hyundai. Doug has a lot of reasons to be self-confident. But Doug also has a son named Ryan, who was born with profound disabilities. His skull was misfused, so the growth of his brain pushed both eyes out of their sockets. He lives in a wheelchair, he is blind, and he has never spoken. He is utterly vulnerable. He has no apparent authority. And through Ryan, Doug became aware of his own profound vulnerability.

After a successful career in the automotive industry, Doug left Hyundai and later became president and COO of a ministry called Joni and Friends that seeks to love the 600 million human beings living with disabilities. Doug travels the world to help them. He said that he considers himself a "junior partner" with his son Ryan.

Ryan's great vulnerability has blessed Doug, Doug's great authority has blessed Ryan, and now a community flourishes where great authority and great vulnerability dance together.

Ryan will never speak, but he can hear. Doug often reads the Bible to his son, and when he does, Ryan smiles.

Reflect for a moment on the vulnerability of Jesus. Remember the story of his birth, and reflect on what it means that God was inside a woman's womb for nine months. In the words of Elizabeth Gandolfo, "God Almighty (!) became a little, tiny, wrinkly, red, squalling, peeing, pooping, drooling, and desperately hungry human creature."[43]

Remember that Jesus hungered and thirsted and wept and slept and bled. Think about the vulnerability of Jesus when he was betrayed—and as he was tried, beaten, and crucified.

The word *excruciating* comes from the Latin *excruciare*,

which derives from *cruciare*, to crucify. It means unbearably painful or extremely agonizing.

In the beginning, in Eden, human vulnerability was exquisite.

Then came the Fall, and hiding, and shame. And it became excruciating.

Then Jesus entered into our vulnerability, so that one day it might become exquisite again.

That is our hope.

CHAPTER 10

THE DEEP DOWN DARK

THE INTIMACY THAT COMES FROM SUFFERING

It is said of God that no one can behold his face and live. I always thought this meant that no one could see his splendor and live. A friend said perhaps it meant that no one could see his sorrow and live. Or perhaps his sorrow is splendor.

NICHOLAS WOLTERSTORFF, *Lament for a Son*

IN *DEEP DOWN DARK*, Héctor Tobar tells the story of thirty-three Chilean miners who were trapped two thousand feet below the surface for sixty-nine days.[1] It was in all the headlines. They had to live in the dark, with almost no food, cut off from the rest of the world. They began to lose weight. They didn't know if they would ever see daylight again. One newspaper in Santiago put their odds of survival at 2 percent.

Many of the miners, face to face with imminent death, took stock of their lives and realized they had a lot of regrets. Somebody asked José Henríquez, who was known to be a religious man, if he would pray for everyone.

He did.

As he got down on his knees, some of the other men joined

him, and he began to talk to God: "We aren't the best men, Lord, but have pity on us."

You'd think that might be a little offensive—"Who's he talking about, not the best of men?"—but somehow, in the deep down dark, nobody objected. Because they knew it was true.

So Henríquez went on, and actually got more specific: "Víctor Segovia knows that he drinks too much. Víctor Zamora is too quick to anger. Pedro Cortez thinks about the poor father he's been to his young daughter . . ."

Again, nobody objected. In fact, this was the beginning of something special, something unanticipated—*intimacy*. Somehow, in the deep down dark, buried under the earth, with death staring them in the face, the men discovered a new sense of fellowship. They actually began to meet every day for their one meal—a spoonful of tuna, maybe a cookie, a little water—and then José Henríquez or Osman Araya would give a short sermon, and the men would get on their knees and pray.

"God, forgive me for the violence of my voice before my wife and my son."

"God, forgive me for abusing the temple of my body with drugs."

Amazingly enough, these prayers spontaneously grew into times when the miners apologized for their wrongdoings toward each other and practiced mutual confession.

"I'm sorry I raised my voice."

"I'm sorry I didn't help get the water."

Intimacy is shared experience. Suffering, by definition, means experiencing something we do not want to experience— such as pain, loss, disappointment, or despair. And yet, this group of hardened miners found that in shared suffering—as they cared for one another—they formed a bond that never would have grown between them *without* the suffering. When they were cut off from the pursuit of pleasure, money, and alcohol, they saw the folly of living for those things.

Meanwhile, a group of people above the surface had begun to drill down through the earth to try to save them. The leader of the drilling crew said they should pray for the hole they were about to dig.

"Let's put all our trust in the skinny guy," he said (referring to "the skinny guy" on the cross).

As they bowed their heads, one of the team members said, "Hey, boss, let's hold hands as we pray." And eight burly, Chilean drill operators held hands and asked Jesus for help. A rescue effort was born, and people from all over the world began trying to help, or give, or pray for the men to be saved.

Unfortunately, the happiest part of the story is also the saddest.

The drill cuts a narrow hole through the rock. The miners get food and supplies and iPads; they know that eventually they'll be rescued; they find out they're becoming famous and they might get rich.

And then the confessing stops.

The praying stops.

The lure of money and fame undoes the transformative community that had developed in their shared suffering.

They were at their best when life was at its worst.

GOD MEETS PEOPLE IN SUFFERING

The Deep Down Dark is the place where you know you can't make it on your own. The Deep Down Dark is the place where you realize you need God.

The doctor tells you it's malignant.

Your beloved daughter runs away and you don't know where she is, and hardly know *who* she is, and don't know if she'll ever come home again.

He tells you he's leaving you.

She tells you she doesn't love you.

He tells you he's never loved you.

Your job is gone.

Your money is gone.

Your drinking is out of control.

You wake up anxious every morning.

Leaving the house takes heroic effort.

You are the victim of deep unfairness.

This is the Deep Down Dark.

Suffering does not automatically lead to great intimacy. David Brooks, writing about how suffering transformed the famous Catholic activist and writer Dorothy Day, says, "For most of us, there is nothing intrinsically noble about suffering. Just as failure is sometimes just failure (and not your path to becoming the next Steve Jobs), suffering is sometimes just destructive."[2] But sometimes—not always—something strangely redemptive happens.

In Nazi Germany, Dietrich Bonhoeffer formed a small group of pastoral students to receive spiritual training in an underground school. They found a fellowship, an intimacy together in their need and vulnerability that they had never known when life was easy.

I've heard countless stories of someone who binges for the thousandth time, loses his job, loses his family, and finally goes to AA because he knows that on his own he's going to die. He finds a community there he never found when he was still clinging to control.

"Suffering, like love, shatters the illusion of self-mastery," writes David Brooks. "Recovering from suffering is not like recovering from a disease. Many people don't come out healed; they come out different. . . . Instead of recoiling from the sorts of loving commitments that often lead to suffering, they throw themselves more deeply into them."[3]

After the horrific shootings at Mother Emanuel Church in Charleston, South Carolina, I flew there with one of my daughters to attend the service on Sunday. For more than two hours, a church that was packed to overflowing sang and read and wept and prayed and protested and worshiped to try to find solace together.

I have never attended a service with more grief.

I have never attended a service with more anger.

I have never attended a service with deeper love or fiercer joy.

I do not understand it. But I witnessed it.

God meets people in their suffering.

One of the survivors at Mother Emanuel church was a woman named Felicia Sanders, who was covered with so much blood that the shooter thought she was dead. Her son, Tywanza, was shot and did not survive. *Time* ran a cover story about the power of forgiveness that was expressed by the victims in the aftermath of acts of unspeakable racial terrorism and cruelty. According to the story, "Felicia Sanders asked the FBI for one thing: the return of two Bibles. The FBI said they were not recoverable. She insisted. So the investigators sent her Bible and Tywanza's Bible to the Bureau's high-tech labs in Quantico, Virginia, where they were cleaned as thoroughly as possible, leaf by leaf. Sanders has them now. The pages are pink with blood that will never wash away. But she can still make out the words."[4]

ARE YOU ABLE TO DETECT AND ENTER INTO THE SUFFERING OF ANOTHER?

Some people have a gift for empathy. They can instantly perceive the slightest hint of suffering in a fellow human being. Others wouldn't recognize abject misery if it hit them squarely in the face.

In *The Developing Mind*, Daniel Siegel tells the story of "a frustrated wife [who] looked at her confused husband and said, 'You never understand what I am talking about. All you know is what you have learned in books. You couldn't read my face if your life depended on it!' To this challenge, the man responded, 'I can tell from what you say that you're probably not happy with me. But, you know, there are two kinds of people in this world: those who are too needy, and those who aren't.' The wife got up and left the room."[5]

The story of Joseph in the Bible, however, is an amazing example of someone who learns empathy through suffering. When Joseph was a young man, he was his father's favorite. We're told repeatedly of how his brothers resented him, but Joseph was unaware of their pain and suffering.

Then he goes through a long journey of suffering into the Deep Down Dark himself. He is betrayed by his brothers. He's sold into slavery. He loses his home. He's unjustly accused of corruption. He's unfairly condemned. He is locked up in a foreign prison, along with two attendants to the king.

"[Joseph] asked Pharaoh's officials who were in custody with him in his master's house, 'Why do you look so sad today?'"[6]

Some people perceive misery; some don't.

There are forty-three muscles in the human face. According to a popular urban myth, it takes fewer muscles to smile than to frown; but the reality is, no one knows. What we do know is that the face has so many muscles in order to make it the most valuable and unique conveyer of the heart in the universe.

Daniel Siegel observes, "We are . . . hard-wired to express emotional states through the face."[7]

When it comes to the heart, our faces often communicate what's going on inside far more powerfully and poignantly than words. Words such as *sad* or *angry* have a limited range; but our faces have the capacity to indicate an almost infinite number and intensity of feelings.

Parents study their baby's face like a meteorologist looking at a weather map. Lovers cannot get enough of gazing into each other's eyes. Good friends are able to immediately spot signs of joy or sadness or concern in the faces of their friends— subtle signs that other people would miss.

To love someone is to study his or her face.

In the Fellowship of the Deep Down Dark, Joseph has learned the art of empathy. Many years later, when he is reunited with his brothers, one response is overwhelming:

He turned away from them and began to weep.[8]

Deeply moved at the sight of his brother, Joseph hurried out and looked for a place to weep. He went into his private room and wept there.[9]

Joseph . . . made himself known to his brothers. And he wept so loudly that the Egyptians heard him, and Pharaoh's household heard about it.[10]

Then he threw his arms around his brother Benjamin and wept, and Benjamin embraced him, weeping. And he kissed all his brothers and wept over them.[11]

Joseph threw himself on his father and wept over him and kissed him.[12]

They sent word to Joseph, saying, "Your father left these instructions before he died: 'This is what you are to say to Joseph: I ask you to forgive your brothers the sins and the wrongs they committed in treating you so badly.' Now please forgive the sins of the servants of the God of your father." When their message came to him, Joseph wept.[13]

Joseph is the biggest crybaby in the Bible. How ironic that, although in our day we often take tears as a sign of weakness, in the first book of the Bible, tears characterize the man who has climbed to the highest position of leadership and influence.

In suffering, Joseph found the capacity for intimacy that success and grandiosity would never have given him.

This is the gift of the Fellowship of the Deep Down Dark.

DO I GRUMBLE OR DO I GROAN? THE LANGUAGE OF THE DEEP DOWN DARK

The Bible uses two main words to describe people's response to suffering: *groaning* and *grumbling*.

Let's start with the first: "The Israelites groaned in their slavery and cried out, and their cry for help . . . went up to God. God heard their groaning . . . and was concerned about them."[14]

Their groaning registers with God, who says: "Moreover, I have heard the groaning of the Israelites, whom the Egyptians are enslaving, and I have remembered my covenant."[15]

Groaning is enshrined in the sacred literature. David groans so much he's got groan-fatigue.

> My soul is in deep anguish.
>> How long, LORD, how long? . . .
> I am worn out from my groaning.[16]

Groaning is actually commanded in Ezekiel—which is not a book that gets read a lot at weddings.

> Therefore groan, son of man! Groan before them with broken heart and bitter grief.[17]

Grumbling happens as often as groaning, but it doesn't garner the same response.

> The people grumbled against Moses, saying, "What are we to drink?"[18]

Moses reminded the people later on:

> You grumbled in your tents and said, "The LORD hates us; so he brought us out of Egypt . . . to destroy us."[19]

Grumbling is also discussed in the Psalms:

> They grumbled in their tents
> and did not obey the LORD.[20]

But whereas groaning is commanded, grumbling is forbidden.

> Do everything without grumbling or arguing.[21]

In fact, grumbling got some people into serious trouble:

> Do not grumble, as some of them did—and were
> killed by the destroying angel.[22]

God commends groaning but forbids grumbling. What's the difference? In a nutshell it's this: Groaning is complaining *to* God; grumbling is complaining *about* God. Groaning happens to God's face. Grumbling happens behind God's back.

In the Bible, the place where people groan is on their knees—where they've been driven by sorrow, suffering, and adversity. The place where people grumble is in their tents—where they think they are in private and are free to exaggerate, blame, play the victim, and excuse their own lack of obedience.

This difference between grumbling and groaning has a similar effect on intimacy, whether with God or with people: Groaning in suffering builds intimacy. Grumbling destroys intimacy.

Grumbling is also contagious. People with a negative grumbling spirit will inevitably look for other grumblers to join them. In one study, researchers had two people sit in chairs and look at each other and not say a word. If one of them was in a negative mood, at the end of the five minutes the other person would have grown significantly more negative, just from sitting near the first negative person. In grumbling I exaggerate my suffering to justify a negative attitude.

When I flew home from the memorial service at Mother Emanuel, I got in at 1:00 in the morning, and I was grumbling in my spirit about that. Then my phone went missing and I grumbled about that, too. (I had just gotten a brand-new cell phone after dropping my old phone in the toilet. I'm the one who dropped it, but I grumbled as if it were the toilet's fault.)

So it's 1:00 in the morning, every passenger is off the plane by now, and the flight attendant comes over to me.

"Maybe it's in your computer bag?"

"Don't you think that's the first place I looked?"

I had been through every pocket. I had crawled on the floor across the aisle and back. The flight attendant had lifted out the seat. I went into the restroom to see if it was in the toilet (because I often keep my phone there). As I went back to my seat, it occurred to me: The guy in the seat next to me had looked suspicious. *I'll bet he took it off the armrest while I was sleeping.*

The flight attendant said, "Ninety percent of the time, it ends up being buried in the computer bag."

I said, "You know, friend, I checked every inch." (Anytime you call a complete stranger *friend*, you don't really mean it.) I opened up the side pocket of my bag to show her how thorough I'd been, and she pointed into it and said, "What's that phone-looking object right there?"

Apparently, while I had my back turned, my prodigal phone had come home. But I was not joyful. I did not say, "Let's slay the fatted calf, for this phone of mine was lost and has been found." In fact, I don't think I said anything.

Suppose one of those ancient Israelites from Moses' group of grumblers was magically transported to modern times so I could talk to him at that moment. He'd probably say to me, "You got to be part of a national event that could stretch and challenge you in ways we could only imagine, then return to a home, a spouse, children, and a job you love. And look at how you got there! You walked through a door in the side of a giant cylinder, sat down in a chair, and when you stood up, you had flown through the air and traveled farther than I did in my entire lifetime. And you got to eat and drink while you were flying. And now you're grumbling because a stranger was kind enough to help you find this thin, little box you can use to talk or write to anyone anywhere in the world and look up more information than even existed when I was alive. And you think *I'm* ungrateful?"

Who asked him?

Sometimes I think that if there's just one verse that's not in the Bible but should be, it would be 1 Trepidations 1:1: "'Suck it up,' sayeth the Lord."

In grumbling, I make my irritations and inconveniences known to everyone around me. But in groaning, I speak directly to God about what troubles me. I hold nothing back.

At the same time, in groaning we view suffering in a larger context of others who have suffered. In the Bible, groaning includes an awareness of our own sin—which is why psalms of lament often include confession. Groaning includes the call to be my best self, and the honest struggle to cling to God when it's difficult. Groaning is God-centered, even when God seems absent.

In human relationships, if there's a problem between us, groaning means I commit to talk to *you* about *us,* not talk *about* you to somebody else.

SUFFERING BUILDS INTIMACY WHEN WE HONOR DIFFERENCES

Dr. Deborah Tannen writes of how women and men will often speak about their troubles differently, and if these differences are not understood and respected, it can lead to a loss of intimacy, in marriages and cross-gender friendships.[23]

Women often bond over such "troubles talk." The disclosure of a problem by one woman will often lead to the disclosure of another problem by the other woman. They will experience a sense of solidarity. The conversation is not about solving the problem—in fact, if the problem were solved, they would need to find another problem to talk about. The conversation is the point; the problem is a means to an end.

Men, on the other hand, build their sense of self-esteem when they are able to demonstrate competence to other men. In male culture, identifying a problem is often an admission of incompetence, so men tend not to do it. If a man does raise a problem, good taste requires the other man to either offer a solution or change the subject.

When talking with each other, men tend to speak much less about troubles than women would. After I've been with my friend Rick, Nancy might ask me how he's doing—what's happening with the crisis in one of his kids' lives (if there happens to be one), or how he's responding to having a limb amputated. Then I have to pretend that I noticed he'd had a limb amputated. I often find myself wondering, "What *did* we talk about?"

It's no wonder men and women get frustrated with each other. But with understanding, we can enter each other's world and respond in ways that foster, rather than diminish, intimacy.

SUFFERING CAN INCREASE INTIMACY WHEN WE LEARN HOW TO RESPOND

David Brooks writes about how Dorothy Day learned "what sensitive people do when other people are in trauma. . . . In the first place, they just show up. They provide a ministry of presence."[24]

In the book of Job, Job's friends sat with him in silence for seven days when he'd suffered a great loss. Their words would later get them into trouble, but in their silence they were at their best.

Sensitive people learn not to compare. Each instance of suffering is unique; each sufferer responds in unique ways, and comparison is not helpful.

Sensitive people do practical things. They watch the kids. They bring a meal. They clean the house. They run an errand. I have stood next to many grieving people at funerals, and the comment most often heard from other mourners is also the most useless: "If I can do anything, please call me." Helpful people never say that, because they know how hollow it rings. Someone who wants to help doesn't wait to be called.

Sensitive people don't try to comfort prematurely. They don't pretend to have answers. They don't seek to lessen the pain with an explanation. They allow the dignity of suffering.

Sensitive people watch for surprising moments of gratitude.

I remember talking to someone who was dying of cancer, with a prognosis as severe as it could be. We chatted for a bit, and then I asked: "How are you doing?"

With no trace of irony or sarcasm, she said, "I'm so fortunate. I have hardly any pain, which I would have expected. And I'm surrounded by family that loves me."

There are two ways to suffer, somebody once wrote. I can suffer *from* something, or I can suffer *with* someone.

As a victim of adversity, I suffer *from* illness, or injury, or mosquitoes. But I suffer *with* someone when I choose to take that person's suffering onto myself as an act of intimacy, a shared experience.

A mother suffers *with* a sick child, a son suffers *with* a sick parent, and a companion grieves *with* a widowed friend. Suffering *with* is an act of tremendous intimacy.

Paul says that when we suffer *with* victims of hurt or poverty or loss, we are suffering *with* Jesus, who became human to suffer *with* all of us, to share all human suffering. As Lewis Smedes observes, "When we do suffer with someone else, even a little, we may be sure we are moving on the wave of God. We are doing what God does."[25]

SUFFERING CAN INCREASE INTIMACY WHEN WE GIVE THE GIFT OF PATIENCE

There is a world of difference between sharing the experience of suffering and endorsing despair.

One of my favorite pictures of this comes from my friend Dan Allender. He tells the story about a time he went with his wife and his son, Andrew (who was ten at the time), to speak at a conference in Montana. Having seen the movie *A River Runs Through It* once too often, he decided to take his son fly-fishing. I'll let him tell the story:

> The first day we were there, I didn't have to teach, so about 8:00 p.m. I went into the water with a float tube and all my gear. I was so excited! It was dusk and the mountains and water and sunset were beautiful, but I couldn't help but notice that there were many birds flying around me. I'm really not an outdoorsy-type person, and I don't know much about ornithology, but still, the presence of these birds surprised me. I guess I thought they would be in bed by then. But they were fully awake, flying very rapidly as they went right over me, up and around me.
>
> Suddenly I realized they weren't birds. They were bats! And I am terrified of bats. I started using my rod

as a tool to create what I would call a kind of No-Fly Zone.

You know how you always hear that you cannot hit a bat? Well, it's not true. I hit a bat, and it dropped into the water. When it surfaced, it started toward me, so I whacked it again . . . and again. I kept hitting at it and finally—this is horrifying to admit—I drowned one of God's creatures.

By this time, I was completely panicked. I wanted out of there, but as it happened, a fish that had been created from the foundation of the earth for this very moment came and took my fly! You might think that would be exciting. But I didn't want to catch a fish; I just wanted out of that water.

Up to this point in my life, all I had ever caught were trout. But as I pulled this fish up, it became clear this was no trout. It was a big, ugly, gray fish, and its huge mouth was opened very wide. I was startled. I don't like to touch fish, but I had to get that big fish off the hook. I had kind of a meltdown. I wanted out of the water so badly that I began swinging the fish. In fact, I swung that fish so hard that eventually I ripped off its lips, which sent it hurtling back into the water.

As I got out of the water, I noticed a figure sitting on a chair about fifty feet away, near the end of the dock. As I walked by this man, he reached up, grabbed my arm, and pulled me down close to his face.

"Son," he said, "I've been fishing for over fifty years. I want you to know I have never seen the likes of this. I just wanted to thank you."

For the rest of the conference, I did my best to avoid this man.

Throughout the week, I took my son fishing for a couple hours right after lunch. For three days straight, we caught nothing.

On the third day, the man I had been avoiding approached me and said, "I see you've been taking your son out to catch fish."

"Yes, sir, I have."

"Also noticed you haven't caught anything."

"Yes, sir."

"Do you know that fish don't usually bite between 1:00 and 3:30?"

"No, sir, I didn't know that."

"Do you want your boy to catch a fish?"

"Absolutely. Yes."

"Then what I want you to do is be out here at 5:30 tomorrow morning."

The next morning, Andrew and I went out at 5:30. By 7:45, we hadn't caught a thing.

I had told my wife we'd be back at 8:00, so I said to Andrew, "We gotta go in." Inside, I was ticked at God that he could divide the Red Sea but he wouldn't provide my son with one lousy fish.

Andrew looked at me plaintively and very quietly said, "Please, Dad. Just one more time?"

Inside, I was raging, but I sensed the Spirit of God say to me, *Do you want to kill hope in your son?* I looked at Andrew and said, "You can cast five more times."

The first cast went out. Then the second. And the third. With each cast I prayed, "Oh, Lord, please let him have a fish!" By the fourth cast, I was back to thinking, *Why should I hope?*

I began to pull on the oars as Andrew threw his line out for the fifth time. All of a sudden he was yelling, "Dad! Stop!"

I turned around and saw that his pole was bent over. For the next five or six minutes, he fought to bring in his fish. When we finally got the fish into the boat, it turned out to be a big northern pike.

It was a phenomenal moment—probably one of the most important moments in my life as a father. As we neared the shore, Andrew said, "Dad, we have a God, don't we?"

"Yeah. Yeah, we do."

After another moment, Andrew said, "Dad, I know God's name."

"What do you mean, Andrew?"

"God's name is 'the God of the fifth cast.'"[26]

Often in relationships, suffering can lead to impatience. When Nancy's father died, she had all the grief of a daughter who had lost her dad. In addition to that, we had three children who were four years old or younger. In my expectations about division of labor, expression of grief, physical intimacy, or the need for space, I simply did not adequately understand the Deep Down Dark that was inside Nancy's soul.

Knowing that we serve "the God of the fifth cast" is what gives us the patience to sit quietly during times of suffering.

When a husband or wife is diagnosed with cancer, about half the time the couple will still not have discussed their emotional reactions with each other a week later. Often each is afraid of upsetting the other. Sometimes they try to cheer each other up by expressing false optimism. But false optimism never builds true intimacy. Intimacy grows only when we tell each other our real feelings, and put our hope in the God of the fifth cast.

THE GOD OF GROANING . . . AND HOPE

Philosopher Nicholas Wolterstorff lost his twenty-five-year-old son, Eric, in a mountain-climbing accident. Wolterstorff's book *Lament for a Son* is the anguished cry of a shattered father's heart. In it, he does not find a God who *explains* suffering, but he finds a God who *enters* our suffering.

"GOD IS LOVE. That is why he suffers. . . . God is suffering love. So suffering is down at the center of things, deep down where the meaning is. . . . The tears of God are the meaning of history."[27]

Here is what you need to know about God and groaning. One of the most remarkable passages in human literature says: "Creation was subjected to futility. . . . The whole creation has been groaning together in the pains of childbirth until now."[28]

Creation itself groans. Groaning goes deeper than words. This raw response to suffering and pain goes to the heart of our vulnerability.

When our daughter Laura was a year old, we took her in for an immunization. I held her while the doctor shoved a giant needle into that tiny, smooth-skinned arm. Laura's eyes got big and filled with tears, her lip trembled, and she let out a wail, as if to say, "Daddy, every day of my life, you have protected me from pain—until now. Why have you done this to me?"

I said to her, "Oh, honey, I know, I know. . . . This was Mommy's idea."

Sometimes when we suffer, the pain is so savage, so shattering, that all we can do is cry out—a raw cry, like an animal would make. If you've ever been there for that, you never forget it.

"Not only the creation, but we ourselves, who have the firstfruits of the Spirit, groan inwardly. . . . Likewise, the Spirit helps us in our weakness."[29]

How does the Holy Spirit do this? Not by making our lives easier. Not by making our hearts tougher. Not by making our suffering shorter. But by direct intercession.

"The Spirit helps us in our weakness. For we do not know what to pray for as we ought, but the Spirit himself intercedes for us with groanings too deep for words."[30]

God himself will know, experience, bear, and give voice to your worst anguish, pain, shame, and suffering. The God of the Bible is the God who groans.

In the Fellowship of the Deep Down Dark, hope is nonperishable. When those Chilean miners were trapped beneath the surface, they came together at noon each day for their one tiny meal and to confess and pray. They listened to "el Pastor" tell stories from the Bible. Know what their favorite story was? Jonah and the whale. They said it was kind of like they were living out that story. If God could rescue Jonah, God could rescue them. They loved that story because it gave them hope.

It's a strange thing about hope that if you want to keep it, you have to give it away. When you give hope to others in love, you receive it most yourself.

In merely human community, we often traffic in false hopes. We encourage each other by saying, "I think you'll get what you want. I think circumstances will turn out well."

Our hope must go deeper than that.

One day, a little community formed around a teacher who

promised them great joy; yet he was also known as "a man of sorrows . . . acquainted with grief."[31] He said that people who suffered—the poor, the meek, those who mourn—were actually the community of the blessed.[32]

Then this same man was executed on a cross. He ended his life (seemingly) as an emaciated, disappointed failure.

On the cross, he was utterly alone. And yet, somehow, we were with him. Somehow, people have met him at the cross, or through the cross, in ways they never would have met him anywhere else.

On the cross, he chose to *share* in the experiences that most isolate us—guilt, pain, hopelessness, and death. And the mysterious result is that we no longer have to be alone—or afraid—in those moments.

His body was taken down from the cross and laid in a tomb. In a hole in the ground, with death staring him in the face, the Father of heaven came to his crucified Son, and the Fellowship of the Deep Down Dark had its first meeting. Jesus "descended into hell."[33] And if you can find Jesus there, you're likely to run into him anywhere.

A few days later came the first resurrection day. And another one is coming. That's our hope. Jesus, who died for our sins and was raised from the dead, will one day return to gather his own to himself. For the past two thousand years, his community has had only one hope they bet the farm on: Jesus, who died on the cross for our sins, was raised from the dead. And one day, we will be too.

We're betting it all on the skinny guy.

CHAPTER 11

THIS TIME IT'S PERSONAL

DEALING WITH ACCEPTANCE AND REJECTION

Having been embraced by God, we must make space for others in ourselves and invite them in.
MIROSLAV VOLF, *Exclusion and Embrace*

Accept one another, then, just as Christ has accepted you.
ROMANS 15:7

ONE OF THE PEOPLE who attends the church where I work is named Jia Jiang. Born in China, he came to the US as an exchange student at sixteen, not knowing a soul. He was assigned to a host family in rural Louisiana, where he felt vulnerable and alone. He had hoped for a host family that would accept him, but they turned out to be a family of criminals. Jia slept in the bedroom of a son who had been convicted of murder. Within a few weeks, his new family had stolen all his money.

Welcome to America.

Jia was reassigned to a different family, and this one attended an Assemblies of God church. "It was an exciting church," he once told me. "Not like ours."

He remembers them singing and dancing and fainting, and

at times he had no idea what they were saying. But he understood love, and they loved him, and he met God there.

Jia made it through school, and eventually got married and decided to start his own company. But his requests for funding were turned down.

This rejection did to Jia what none of his other trials could do—it paralyzed him. Rejection is different from failure, Jia realized. Failure happens to your plans. Rejection happens to *you*. It's personal. It makes you withdraw. It keeps you from making the "invitations to connect" that enable intimacy. Fear of rejection will keep people from taking all sorts of risks:

- asking someone out for a date
- making friends
- sharing confidences
- giving trust
- getting married
- joining a small group

Jia realized that if he didn't learn to deal with rejection, it would cripple his life. He heard about a kind of treatment called "rejection therapy," in which participants make outrageous requests—ones they *know* will be rejected—so that hearing the word *no* gradually loses its power and they discover how to survive rejection.

Jia began his "one hundred days of rejection" by asking a stranger to loan him one hundred dollars.

"No."

On day two, he went into a fast-food place and asked for a burger refill.

"What?"

"Can I get a burger refill?"

"No."

Another time, he went into the grooming area at PetSmart and asked, "Could I get a haircut like a German shepherd?"

"No."

He filmed these experiences so he could play them back and learn from them. Not only that, but he decided to post them online so that other people could witness his humiliation.[1] By the dozens—and then hundreds—people began to follow his strange journey of rejection.

As Jia watched himself on video and reflected on how God loved him whether people said *yes* or *no* to his requests, he began to realize that it wasn't *rejection* that paralyzed him; it was his *fear* of rejection.

No is just an answer. But it can sting when it touches our fear or something else highly personal:

- I must not be good enough.
- I'm not attractive enough or smart enough or persuasive enough.
- People will find out I'm a fake.
- I don't have the right people skills.
- I'll always be an outsider.

Then came the doughnut that changed Jia's life.

He walked into a Krispy Kreme Doughnut shop one day and asked for a "specialty doughnut": five doughnuts linked together to look like the Olympic symbol.

Instead of saying *no*, the woman behind the counter asked him how soon he needed it. Jia didn't know what to say. He wasn't prepared for anything but rejection.

"Uh, maybe fifteen minutes?"

The employee put her hand on her chin, trying to visualize

the request. Then she got out a piece of paper to sketch what the Olympic doughnuts might look like.

"Wait here," she said.

A short while later, wonder of wonders, she brought him five interlocking, multi-colored, made-to-order Olympic ring doughnuts.

He didn't know what to say.

"What do I owe you?" Jia asked.

"Don't you worry about it," she said. "That one is on me."

Seriously?

Yes.

Jia was prepared for rejection. He wasn't ready for someone to go out of her way to do him a favor.

When he posted the doughnut video, it went viral. He got e-mails from people around the world who were inspired to battle their fear of rejection. Interview requests came in, ranging from MSNBC to Fox News. The week after the video went viral, Krispy Kreme stock rose from $7.23 to $9.32. Jia was tagged the "Rejection Whisperer."[2]

One weekend, after Jia told the story at our church, I decided that, as a matter of integrity, I should try a little rejection therapy myself. So I wrote the Krispy Kreme people and asked if they would give six thousand free doughnuts to our church.

They said yes. And they did.

Sacramental doughnuts.

THE FEAR, REJECTION, SHAME LOOP

In their book *Thanks for the Feedback*, Douglas Stone and Sheila Heen note that we face rejection all the time. Each year . . .

- Almost 2 million teenagers will get SAT scores, and many of them will deal with rejection letters from colleges they hoped would accept them.
- At least 40 million people will size each other up for love online—and most will be found wanting.
- More than 500,000 entrepreneurs will open their doors for the first time, and almost 600,000 will close their doors for the last time.
- A quarter-million weddings will be called off, and 877,000 spouses will file for divorce.[3]

We try out for teams we don't make; we apply for jobs we don't get; we pitch projects we can't sell. We don't wear clothes we love because we're afraid we'll look silly; we don't offer to use gifts God has given us because we're afraid we'll get turned down.

From birth, our survival depends on being accepted. We experience this when our presence is welcomed; when our cries for help are heard and responded to; when our happiness brings delight to another. Because this acceptance is literally a matter of life or death, we are exquisitely attuned to signs of rejection.

Children are born with a need to connect. When they feel afraid or alone or threatened, they naturally look to their mom or dad for love and assurance. Normally, if they're separated from their parents, they experience delight when they see them again. They run to them, cuddle with them, and receive strength from them.

But for some children, this hunger for connection meets frequent rejection, with heartbreaking results. When they've been separated from their parents and the parents return, these kids seem to pay no attention. They don't run toward their parents; they don't show delight. They don't seem to even notice. But inside their bodies, a small earthquake is going on. Their pulse accelerates. Their blood pressure rises. It's as if they have trained their bodies not to show their longing for connection because they can no longer stand the pain of rejection. They do this without being conscious of it, without being taught, and without effort.

When condemnation embeds itself deeply enough in the human psyche, it becomes shame. Shame is actually self-condemnation—the internalization of rejection. As Lewis Smedes puts it, "Shame is a very heavy feeling."[4] Guilt causes us to feel bad about *what we've done*; shame causes us to feel bad about *who we are*. Shame—at least the toxic kind—causes us to feel that we will never be acceptable. It touches the very core of our identity.

In my sophomore year of high school, I played in the conference tennis tournament. I had missed most of the season with mononucleosis, and now was in the process of losing my first match. At one point, I double-faulted and the coach yelled at me across the tennis complex loud enough for everyone to hear. I glared over at him, feeling exposed and ashamed. After the match, with the entire team gathered around him, he vented his anger at me and then slapped me hard across the face.

Nowadays, that sort of thing would invite a lawsuit, I suppose, but at the time I didn't question his right to do it. I didn't tell anyone about it. I was too ashamed that it had happened. The sting to my face lasted only a moment—the deeper hurt was in my mind and spirit. *Weak. Failure. Loser.*

"When we condemn another," writes Dallas Willard, "we communicate that he or she is, in some deep and just possibly irredeemable way, bad—bad as a whole, and to be rejected.

In our eyes, the condemned is among the discards of human life."[5]

You must look perfect.

You must be the perfect wife and mom and friend and career success.

You must please everybody.

You must be strong and successful and a winner.

You must not be that boy who loses and gets slapped.

"Shame," says pioneer researcher Gershen Kaufman, "is without parallel a sickness of the soul . . . a violation of our essential dignity."[6]

The good news is that there *is* healing. But it only comes from finding an acceptance greater than our greatest rejection.

JESUS: THE GREAT REJECTION THERAPIST

Let's look at a story about the most rejected character in the Bible.

In John 4:5-6, we're told that Jesus "came to a town in Samaria called Sychar, near the plot of ground Jacob had given to his son Joseph. Jacob's well was there, and Jesus, tired as he was from the journey, sat down by the well. It was about noon."

The first lesson about shame is found here in a tiny detail: Jesus was tired.

Usually, leaders take pride in having more energy than anyone else on the team. "The speed of the leader is the speed of the team," they say. Sometimes, leaders will use their superior drive and persistence to motivate or even shame their followers. Not Jesus.

When John recorded this story, he was an old man. But he still remembered that Jesus was the only one of the whole group so tired he had to sit and rest. How did the disciples know Jesus was tired? Most likely because he said, "Hey, guys, I'm tired. You go ahead. I'll wait here and rest."

Shame wants to hide. Not Jesus. He knew he had nothing to be ashamed of. He felt no pressure to defend his identity as the Messiah by pretending to be energized. He was the weak one of the group. And he was okay with that. This isn't a story about Superhero Jesus. This is a story about Tired Jesus.

But wait—there's more.

God uses Jesus' tiredness. God uses his weakness. Because Jesus is tired—because he stays behind—he has a conversation that changes things for a whole bunch of people.

"It was about noon . . . [and] a Samaritan woman came to draw water."[7]

In the ancient world (and still today in many parts of the world), water-gathering was women's work. If a family had the means, they'd have a servant girl do it. If they were poor, they had to do it themselves. But it would be the woman who would go—usually early in the morning or around sunset, and often as a social activity, with the women of the village all going together. (The practice of talking around the water cooler has deep roots.)

A Samaritan woman approaches a well. A man is sitting on its ledge. He is a rabbi. She knows what will happen. As she draws near, he will withdraw—twenty or so paces away. He won't look at her. She'll get her water and leave.

Except the strangest thing happens: As she approaches the well, he doesn't move. He doesn't look away. Instead, he says to her, "Will you give me a drink?"[8]

This, you will remember from an earlier chapter, is an "invitation to connect." Without this simple request, this ice-breaker, the rest of the story wouldn't happen.

The Samaritan woman says, "You are a Jew and I am a Samaritan woman. How can you ask me for a drink?"[9]

This was an outrageous request, as the text makes clear—"for Jews do not associate with Samaritans."[10] Jesus is *asking* to be rejected. He might as well have asked for Olympic-ring doughnuts!

Here's where things get interesting.

Hebrew scholar Robert Alter writes that the setting actually makes this a much more loaded story than you might realize.

In ancient literature, certain settings are used for certain stories where everyone knows what to expect.

It's like if you're watching an old Western, you know there's going to be a villain who has excellent fast-twitch muscles, and a hero who's even faster.

If the movie is set in a deserted campground where a bunch of teenagers hear muffled screams coming from the boathouse and walk toward it in the dark and someone says, "Hey, where's Jimmy? He was here a minute ago"—you know Jimmy is not going to have many more lines.

In the ancient world, with no singles bars or online dating, boy-meets-girl stories happened at wells.

That's where Isaac's wife, Rebekah, was found.[11]

That's where Jacob met Rachel.[12]

That's where Moses met Zipporah.[13]

Everybody reading this story in John's Gospel knows it's a boy-meets-girl story. Except it's in the wrong place (Samaria), at the wrong time (noon), with the wrong girl (a Samaritan serial divorcée), and the wrong boy (Jesus).

In those days, a man rarely spoke to a woman in public— even his own wife. A single man—and especially a rabbi— would *never* speak to or touch a woman, especially if she were a Samaritan, of whom it was said: "Samaritan women are deemed menstruants [i.e., unclean] from their cradle."[14]

But Jesus had a way of embracing Samaritans:

- A "good Samaritan" is the hero in one of his stories.[15]
- Of the ten lepers he heals in Luke 17:11-19, the Samaritan is the only one to come back and thank him.
- When James and John suggest asking God to nuke an unwelcoming Samaritan village, Jesus protects the Samaritans and rebukes his own disciples.[16]
- His chronic failure (in the eyes of the Jews) to reject the Samaritans led to a rumor: "Aren't we right in saying that you are a Samaritan and demon-possessed?"[17] (By the way, this was considered the ultimate insult—kind of like in the movie *The Sandlot* when eleven-year-old boys taunt each other with: "You play ball like a girl.")

Jesus engages the Samaritan woman in a theological conversation. He tells her that God has a kind of spiritual water that alone can quench the deep thirst of her rejected soul:

The woman said to him, "Sir, give me this water so that I won't get thirsty and have to keep coming here to draw water."

He told her, "Go, call your husband and come back."

"I have no husband," she replied.

Jesus said to her, "You are right when you say you have no husband. The fact is, you have had five husbands, and the man you now have is not your husband. What you have just said is quite true."[18]

"I have no husband." This is true, but a little evasive. In that culture, women were not able to sue for divorce. So this is a woman who has been rejected over and over. Five times she has gotten married, hoping that this time it will work. Five times she has seen the signs of things falling apart. Five times she has heard a man say, "I don't want you anymore." And if she's currently with a man who is not her husband, most likely it is in the form of a quasi-slave relationship, where sexual relations would be part of his prerogative.

Others look at her and say: "She can't keep a man. She can get 'em, but she can't keep 'em."

Now we know why she came to the well at noon. She'd rather face the pain of searing heat than the pain of judgment and rejection.

Rejection hurts.

Literally.

In fact, according to a study published by the National Academy of Sciences, the part of our sensorimotor system that registers physical pain is the same as that which registers the pain of rejection.[19]

Jesus notes the truth about the woman's marital history, but he does it without condemning her. There is a great chasm between discerning truth and condemning someone. A good dentist discerns the truth about my cavity but doesn't condemn me for it.

Condemnation is not simply an observation about my condition; it is observation combined with malice: "You haven't been flossing often enough—now your teeth are rotting. Nice going!"

In identifying the truth about the woman's history, Jesus names her shame. And yet, instead of becoming defensive or hiding from him, she engages him in conversation—the longest conversation with Jesus recorded in the Gospels.

Eventually, Jesus' disciples returned "and were surprised to find him talking with a woman. But no one asked, 'What do you want?' or 'Why are you talking with her?'"[20]

The disciples don't say a word to her. Their experience tells them that she is to be rejected, that she is "other." But their experience also tells them Jesus has a strange way of not rejecting people they think he should reject.

On huge cattle ranches in Australia, I'm told, there are two ways to keep the cattle together. One is to build a fence. The other is to dig a well. Wells also have a way of bringing people together.

The rabbis in Jesus' day talked about "building a fence around the law." If the law said don't commit adultery, they'd extend the rule further out to create a safer boundary: Don't touch a woman; don't even talk to her.

Rejection builds fences. Acceptance digs wells. Jesus said that he himself is a well of living water: "If you knew the gift of God and who it is that asks you for a drink, you would have asked him and he would have given you living water."[21]

The point is, the Samaritan woman is the poster girl for shame:

- wrong gender
- wrong ethnicity
- wrong religion
- wrong moral track record
- wrong relational status
- rejected by her husbands
- rejected by her peers

And then she meets a boy at a well. This woman, who has been to the well once too often goes once more. And she is so moved by her connection with Jesus that she hardly even notices the fact that the disciples are not talking to her.

Jesus tells her to return home and get just one person: her (not-legal) husband.

But as she's going back to town, she says to herself, "You know what? I could do more than tell just one person. I could tell the whole village. I could make an outrageous request. I could ask everybody in the town to come listen to Jesus. What's the worst that could happen? They could say no. They could reject me. That's no problem. I have this living water. I've met Jesus."

She doesn't even take the water jar back with her. This is a woman who came to the well with a bucket and went home with the well.

> Leaving her water jar, the woman went back to the town and said to the people, "Come, see a man who told me everything I ever did. Could this be the Messiah?"[22]

This is the first sermon ever preached in the movement started by Jesus. It is brief ("come and see"), compelling, enthusiastic, vulnerable ("he told me everything I ever did"), Jesus-centered, and incredibly effective—and it's delivered by a five-times-married, shacked-up-with-a-live-in, not-enough-money-for-a-servant-to-fetch-the-water Samaritan woman.

And instead of universal rejection, she gets a giant *yes.*

> Many of the Samaritans from that town believed in
> him because of the woman's testimony, "He told me

everything I ever did." So when the Samaritans came
to [Jesus], they urged him to stay with them, and he
stayed two days.[23]

I imagine this woman bringing everybody in town to Jesus.
Of course, that includes all of her exes. I wonder what that
conversation was like.

"Hey, Jesus, here are husband number one and
husband number two. They don't get along with each
other at all, so you're going to have to work with them
on the 'Love your enemies' and 'Turn the other cheek'
things.

"Then, Jesus, here's husband number three. I don't
know what I was thinking when I got married to this
one. Total rebound husband, kind of a loser. I'm sure
you can do something with him.

"I tried to get husband number four to come, but
he's still really mad at me. He won't even talk to me,
but I'm going to keep working on him. I'm going to
get him here.

"As for husband number five . . . to tell you the
truth, I'm kind of not over husband number five yet,
so you're going to have to talk to him, because my
heart is a little bit tender on that one.

"Oh, and here's number six. I'm not married to
him yet. I told him about that verse in the Bible: 'If
you want it, you have to put a ring on it.' I think it's
in the book of Beyoncé, or something like that. I told
him, 'We're going to have to go through premarital
counseling.' I'm thinking of starting a divorce recovery

ministry just with my ex-spouses and their ex-spouses. Would that be okay?"

God has an amazing way of taking our biggest mistakes, our biggest wounds, our biggest scars, and our biggest hurts and using them to enable us to do ministry and become messengers for Jesus with people we never thought we could reach because he's Jesus.

We need an acceptance that's bigger than our rejections. In this story, the Samaritan woman gradually discovers *who* is accepting her.

At the beginning, as she approaches the well, all this woman sees is a Jewish man. Then a slightly crazy and pretentious Jewish man. Then a prophet. Then the Messiah. And finally, one of the greatest titles in all the Gospels: "Savior of the world."[24]

There's an ancient description of this encounter, attributed to Ephrem the Syrian, that I have always loved.

> First she caught sight of a thirsty man, then a Jew,
> then a Rabbi, afterwards a prophet, last of all the
> Messiah.
>
> She tried to get the better of the thirsty man, she
> showed dislike of the Jew, she heckled the Rabbi, she
> was swept off her feet by the prophet, and she adored
> the Christ.[25]

OUR ONLY HOPE

So how do we heal from shame? Lewis Smedes notes three conventional responses:

- Lowering our ideals to the level of our abilities
- Making ourselves acceptable enough to satisfy the ideals we already have
- Persuading ourselves that we're just fine the way we are.

But none of these methods work. We cannot "dilute our ideals whenever we find them a bother"; our hearts know better.

We cannot make ourselves acceptable; "the star moral achievers among us are often the most burdened by a feeling of their unworthiness."

We can't convince our consciences we're fine; it's our conscience that nags us in the first place.

The only answer, says Smedes, is "a spiritual experience of grace. . . . The experience of being accepted is the beginning of healing for the feeling of being unacceptable."[26]

In acceptance, I can allow my *false* self, with all its posing and hiding, to come into the light.

I can allow my *actual* self—with my real history, choices, victories, and shame—to be known and loved by the one who made me.

And I can allow my *true* self—the self that God created me to be—to be born.

I cannot offer myself enough acceptance to overcome the power of self-rejection. Freedom comes from being accepted in the grace of all-knowing love.

The apostle John puts it like this: "See what great love the Father has lavished on us, that we should be called children of God! And that is what we are! . . . And what we will be has not yet been made known."[27]

The Cross was Rome's ultimate expression of rejection of a would-be Messiah. For Jesus, the Cross also epitomized his rejection by all those in the crowd who were yelling for him to be crucified.

From a broader perspective, the Cross is the ultimate symbol of humanity's rejection of God.

For the most rejected person in the Bible was not the Samaritan woman. It was Jesus.

He was "despised and rejected by mankind."[28] He knows all about the pain of our rejection—yours and mine. At the Cross, our rejection of God and God's acceptance of us miraculously come together.

The great story of the Bible is this: God makes world, God loses world, God gets world back.

Meet him at the well.

CHAPTER 12

HOUSTON, WE HAVE A PROBLEM

INTIMACY RUPTURE AND REPAIR

One great splitting of the whole universe into two halves is made by each of us; and . . . those names are "me" and "not-me."
WILLIAM JAMES, *The Principles of Psychology*

In families no crimes are beyond forgiveness.
PAT CONROY, *The Prince of Tides*

ONE DAY, OUR TINY DAUGHTER got very mad. She squinted her little eyes, looked up with great irritation, and said, "I hit you." Nancy and I had to explain to her that we didn't handle anger that way. So the next time she was angry, she bared her teeth and said, "I bite you." She had only three teeth at the time, so she looked hilarious. It was hard not to laugh as we explained that we also had a no-biting policy.

Then she made her hand into a little gun, pointed her index finger, and said, "I shoot you—*pssh pssh*." No dice on that one either. From there, she graduated to, "I squish you," and she would take two little fingers and give you a pinch.

We thought we'd nixed that one until one day she came out of her baby brother's room and was startled to see us. She looked up, grinned a guilty cherubic grin, and said, "We don't squish the baby, do we?"

That was thirty years ago, and I think she still squishes people every once in a while.

If hitting and biting and shooting and squishing are out of bounds, how do we keep conflict and anger from destroying intimacy? Is there a secret weapon? Turns out there is. Here's what it looks like from Harvard psychiatrist William Betcher's perspective:

Jean has a tendency to be bossy, a trait she picked up from her dad, Harold. She can't help telling people how to do things. When her old boyfriend would confront her on her bossiness, she would inevitably get defensive and argumentative, even though deep down she knew it was true. One of the first things she noticed in her relationship with John, to whom she is now married, was that he handled the situation quite differently.

She can still remember the first time she tried to tell him how to go about something: John was helping her cook a meal . . . peeling the carrots. Jean decided that he was doing the job all wrong and started to tell him how he *should* do it. John turned to her and leaned back against the counter with a sort of whimsical, knowing look on his face, and said, "Yes, *Harold.*" He drew the words out and said them in an exaggerated, joking way. Jean thought this lighthearted reference to the origin of her bossiness was very funny. Instead of getting defensive, she . . . began to imitate her father all the more—putting on his accent and pretending to look out over a pair of eyeglasses as her father often did. . . .

Since then, John's expression, "Yes, Harold," has become a signal to Jean that she is tending to become bossy, a characteristic that has greatly decreased since it has been addressed in a nonthreatening way.[1]

John's ability to signal to Jean that he wants to remain connected with her in the moment of conflict is sometimes called a "repair attempt." Like old cars, relationships inevitably throw gaskets and leak oil every once in a while. Little ruptures happen regularly. The key isn't to avoid ruptures, or even to solve the problems that irritate us. The key to maintaining intimacy is *how we talk about* our problems.

People in damaged relationships sometimes wonder: Is it really possible to have honest conflict and still remain connected?

Yes, Harold.

WHY RUPTURES HAPPEN

Ironically, the same thing that gets in the way of intimate friendships and intimate family connections—the fact that we are different from one another—is also what makes intimacy possible. We have different temperaments and different values. We have different likes, dislikes, interests, and aptitudes. We have different backgrounds—perhaps different genders or ethnicities. We may come from a cultural background that values task-orientation, direct communication, and individualism, or from a culture that values relationship-orientation, indirect communication, and belonging.

With all our differences, it can be tempting to think, *I'd like you more if you were more like me,* but often our differences are what draw us toward one another and become "grist for the mill" of a great—and intimate—relationship.

A therapist friend of mine asks people in troubled relationships this question: "Of all the things in life you can agree or disagree on—from political ideas, passions, and religion to money, parenting, sex, and TV shows—on a scale from 0 to 100, what percentage of the time do you disagree?" He asks each partner to write down a number to get their honest estimates. He told me that in the most difficult case he's ever had, both partners said they disagreed with each other 80 percent of the time. (In fact, the only thing my friend could remember them ever agreeing about was how much they disagreed!)

Differences mean that conflict is inevitable. Often friendships, as well as marriages, have an early phase that is relatively conflict-free. Sooner or later, though, reality sets in.

For one young man, serving his wife-to-be was a privilege during the courtship days. He carried her books home from school. During college, he carried her treasures up to her dorm room. On their honeymoon, he carried all the luggage. When they moved into their apartment, he carried her across the threshold. Then he developed a back problem. Six months later, when she said, "I'd like to try this sofa in the living room," he said, "Well, don't move it now; wait until my show comes on, and I'll switch to the La-Z-Boy."

That is a *rupture.*

Ruptures happen when the sense of connection in a relationship is broken—like when an electrical pathway is short-circuited. Everyone knows what a rupture feels like:

- I feel emotions toward you that are more negative than positive.

- My words toward you are strained or heated.
- I am less likely to look at you.
- Instead of wanting to serve you or help you, I'm more likely to want you to feel pain.
- Instead of giving you the benefit of the doubt, I'm likely to interpret what you do or say in a negative light.

People who are skilled in intimacy develop the ability to monitor potential ruptures the way seismologists can detect shifts in the earth's crust on the Richter scale. If I'm clueless in a relationship, the other person may feel estranged from me without my even knowing it, and I'm likely to blunder into even more damage. At the other end of the spectrum, if I'm hypersensitive, constantly monitoring the other person's face and voice and actions for any sign of disagreement, I place a load of anxiety on the relationship that will stifle its freedom.

Intimacy does not mean having a relationship without conflict. Intimacy does not mean having a relationship without any ruptures. Every relationship experiences ruptures from time to time. What determines ongoing intimacy is what happens next.

THE NATURE OF REPAIR

A *repair attempt* is "any statement or action . . . that prevents negativity from escalating out of control."[2] It doesn't have to be dramatic or groveling. It can even be something silly. For instance, maybe in the middle of an argument, she sticks out her lower lip like Shirley Temple doing a pout face, puts her hands on her hips, and stomps on the ground. It's a way of saying, "I disagree with you about this, but *we* are still okay, because we're laughing."

Sally was arguing with her boss, who had been coming late to team meetings that Sally led. Sally was frustrated because this was wasting other people's time. Her boss suggested she should talk about something that didn't require his presence till he got there.

"What do you think I've been doing all this time?" she asked.

He quickly realized he'd made a mistake. He didn't know what was going on in his department, and he'd discounted Sally's intelligence. This could have triggered a major escalation. Instead, he made his hand into a little gun, pointed his index finger at his head, and pulled the trigger—a gesture that said to Sally, "Sorry. Of course I should have known you'd do that." They both laughed, and were ready to work on solving the problem together.

One way of measuring the health of a relationship is how quickly a couple moves to repair the connection when they experience a rupture. The all-time record may be a note that writer Charlie Shedd says his wife once left him when they'd been arguing about something:

> *Dear Charlie,*
> *I hate you.*
> *Love, Martha*[3]

One of the most remarkable and emotionally brilliant commands of the Old Testament is this one: "Don't secretly hate your neighbor. If you have something against him, get it out into the open; otherwise you are an accomplice in his guilt."[4]

The antidote to secret hate is open repair.

Once I got home after a long Sunday and sat down on the couch, and Nancy said, "Why don't you choose a movie for us to watch?"

I said, "Okay, but I want input from you, because I want us both to enjoy it."

"I want you to choose," she said.

I chose. We watched. It was great. It was a classic. When it was over, Nancy said, "I saw it years ago—and it was as bad as I remembered."

That kind of bugged me.

I woke up the next morning, and it still kind of bugged me. So I brought it up with Nancy.

There was a lag time of twelve hours from identifying the problem to discussing the problem, from rupture to repair. By now, you know that I'm Scandinavian, with a spiritual gift of pouting (which is incredibly healthy), so a mere twelve hours is like emotional warp speed for me.

Here's the thing: I didn't want to bring it up, because it was embarrassing. I wasn't sure if I was being too sensitive or not. And it was so small—about a two on a scale of one to ten. Not a huge deal. But if you're not careful, over time all those twos start to add up, and before you know it, your relationship is in trouble to the nth degree.

When a marriage ends, it often ends with hatred in the heart. Sometimes people ending a marriage don't just say, "I don't love you"; they say, "I don't think I *ever* loved you." What's more, they often don't even know how they got to that point.

It didn't happen by accident. There were a thousand little ruptures that never got repaired. A thousand crucial conversations that never happened. A thousand moments that were just a one or a two on the scale, and got glossed over.

It's not worth fighting about.

I know exactly what she (or he) is going to say.

I don't want to expend the energy.

Before you know it, all those ones and twos turn into fours and fives—and then into nines and tens—and the love is gone.

Love doesn't magically disappear, but it can slip away when a couple chooses not to fight for it over and over and over.

When I think about moving from rupture to repair, I find it helpful to visualize a few simple symbols. They keep me from doing deeper damage and move me in the direction of reestablishing connection.

STOP

The first symbol is a *stop* sign. Anytime I feel my emotions flooding and my pulse racing, it's time to stop and shift my internal gears. It works like this: If you make a fist with your hand, you'll get a quick picture of your brain. Your fist and fingers represent the cerebral cortex, the thinking part of your brain that is reasonable and does math problems and learns French and figures out how to access Netflix. (Think Alex Trebek, host of *Jeopardy!*) The thumb underneath represents what might be called the *reactive* brain—the part of the brain that is instinctive and deals with emergencies. (Think The Hulk, or the cast of a reality show.)

When we're calm, our cerebral cortex does most of our thinking for us; but when anger takes over, we shift into the reactive brain. It's sometimes called the "bird brain," partly because a bird's brain has a relatively small cortex and a proportionately larger reactive brain. And, it turns out, birds don't do much thinking. They are not effective at reasoning. The bird brain is 100 percent self-protective. It does flight or fight, period. God gave humans that part of our brain for emergencies. But if we're reacting from our bird brain, we cannot have a productive conversation. It doesn't matter how smart we are.

I say things in the bird brain that I would never say otherwise. In the bird brain, I'm Jack Nicholson going postal on the witness stand in *A Few Good Men*. I'm so mad, I'm saying the very words that will send me to prison, but in the moment all I want is to see that miserable Tom Cruise squirm.

Red-hot anger produces what might be called the Jim Carrey Effect: As I get madder and madder, I get dumber and dumber. The only solution is to stop, and switch to a setting where I can safely ride out the surge of adrenaline.

One of the first scientific studies of anger (conducted in 1899) elicited this response from a twenty-three-year-old male:

> Once when I was about 13, in an angry fit, I walked out of the house vowing I would never return. It was a beautiful summer day, and I walked far along lovely lanes, till gradually the stillness and beauty calmed and soothed me, and after some hours I returned repentant and almost melted. Since then when angry, I do this if I can, and find it the best cure.[5]

Going off to be alone while cooling down remains one of the best anger-management strategies around, though, as Daniel Goleman notes, "a large proportion of men translate this into going for a drive—a finding that gives one pause when driving."[6]

The book of James says, "My dear brothers and sisters, take note of this: Everyone should be quick to listen, slow to speak and slow to become angry."[7]

ASK

The second symbol is a *question mark*. After I stop long enough to get out of my bird brain and back into my cerebral cortex, I ask myself two questions: "Why am I angry?" and "What do I want?"

Here's why it's important to understand *why* I'm angry: Anger is usually a secondary emotion with roots in our previous experience—often the result of being hurt, frustrated, or afraid. So if I want to deal constructively with my anger, I first need to step back and ask what lies underneath it. Otherwise, I'm just dealing with the surface emotion, not the root cause.

What do the roots look like?

If you ask out someone you're attracted to and he or she says, "I'm not going out with you because I just don't find you attractive," the root of your anger is likely *hurt*.

If you get caught in a traffic jam on your way to something you urgently want to be on time for—an interview for your dream job, a date with your soul mate, or church with your absolute favorite pastor—and then if you get a flat tire, the police pull you over for a random vehicle inspection, and your mother calls to ask you how to access Netflix, you may think you're angry, but underneath your anger is *frustration*.

If it's pitch dark, and suddenly there's a loud, thumping noise downstairs that sounds as if someone with a large club has broken into your house, and your wife tells you that you need to go downstairs because "you're the man"—plus she doesn't have her makeup on—you may think you're mad, but underneath your anger is *fear*.

Understanding what you're feeling is the key to figuring out how to respond.

The second question, "What do I want?" is what helps us

get out of our bird brains and back under the control of the cerebral cortex. When my emotions have escalated too high, my only focus is on how I can win the argument—or worse, how I can inflict pain on the other person. I forget to ask, "What's the deeper goal, and how can I pursue it in a way that builds intimacy instead of destroying it?"

When Tim Keller started Redeemer Presbyterian Church in New York City, he knew he would have to work disproportionately long hours for about the first three years. He promised his wife, Kathy, that he would cut back after that. But when three years had passed, he did not cut back. Even when Kathy reminded him of his promise, he kept working just as many hours as ever.

"Just a couple more months," he kept saying as the months continued to roll by—until finally Kathy reached a breaking point.

One day [when] I came home from work . . . I noticed that the door to our apartment's balcony was open. Just as I was taking off my jacket I heard a smashing noise coming from the balcony. In another couple of seconds I heard another one. I walked out on to the balcony and to my surprise saw Kathy sitting on the floor. She had a hammer, and next to her was a stack of our wedding china. On the ground were the shards of two smashed saucers.

"What are you doing?" I asked.

She looked up and said, "You aren't listening to me. You don't realize that if you keep working these hours you are going to destroy this family. I don't know how to get through to you. You aren't seeing how serious this is. This is what you are doing." And she brought the hammer down on the third saucer. It splintered into pieces.[8]

In the Old Testament, the prophets often dramatically acted out messages of justice when words alone failed to penetrate the people's defenses. They held plumb lines, married prostitutes, or stopped changing their underwear. Performance art.

Apparently, Kathy Keller was a prophet—and now she had her husband's full and undivided attention. As Tim describes it, "I sat down trembling. I thought she had snapped. 'I'm listening, I'm listening,' I said."[9]

As they talked things through, Tim says, "her arguments were the same as they had been for months, but I realized how deluded I had been. There would never be a convenient time to cut back. . . . I had to do something."[10]

When he finally listened and understood what his wife was saying, he apologized and repented. More important, he changed his behavior.

After things had calmed down a little bit, Tim asked Kathy what had made her lose it to such an extent that she would sacrifice the china he knew she loved so much.

"When I first came out here I thought you were having an emotional meltdown. How did you get control of yourself so fast?"

With a grin she answered, "It was no meltdown. Do you see those three saucers I smashed?" I nodded. "I have no cups for them. The cups have broken over the years. I had three saucers to spare. I'm glad you sat down before I had to break any more!"[11]

This is not to recommend crockery breakage as a communication technique. But it *is* worth asking: Is there any conversation you need to have—with your spouse, a friend, or a family member—that you've been putting off? What is it that you really want in that relationship? And how about the other person? What does he or she want in your relationship?

Often when we sense frustration in another person, we lean away from asking about it. We hope it will somehow resolve itself. But anger that is rooted in frustration rarely just goes away. It needs to be dealt with. And a word to the wise: Don't wait until it's crockery-breaking time.

CAUTION

The third symbol is a *caution* sign. This sign indicates that you are entering a potential hazard zone. You need to proceed with care. This is especially important in regard to how you bring up sensitive topics.

When people are writing a speech or presentation, they tend to put more time and thought into the introduction than any other part of the message. They know it's a key moment that sets the tone for the entire talk. In fact, people often remember the beginning of a talk longer than any other part.

When we enter into conflict, we too often put the *least* amount of thought into how to start the conversation. We wait until we hit the boiling point, and then we lead with a verbal jab or an uppercut, and it causes the entire conversation to go sideways.

"Why can't you *ever* be on time?"

"Are you planning on watching TV all day?"

"You apparently didn't put one of the new cover sheets on your report. Did you *see* the memo about this?"[12]

"You are *just* like your mother."

Having an ear for repair attempts is important, not just because it reduces emotional tension, but also because the right words spoken in the right way lower the stress level, which keeps our hearts from racing and protects us from feeling flooded. It gives us a better chance to actually *think* about what we want to say.

Why is this important?

According to one study, 96 percent of the time it's possible to predict the outcome of a fifteen-minute conversation based on what happens in the first three minutes.[13]

In other words, a conflict tends to end the way it begins.

The Bible puts it like this: "A soft answer turns away wrath."[14] "Soft" here doesn't mean vague, evasive, appeasing, or weak. It means I'm mindful of my posture, my face, and my voice so that my response will *open up* communication and not shut it down. It means setting and preserving a tone to let you know that my goal is to *deepen* intimacy and not damage it.

If we start with defensiveness, criticism, and blame, we'll probably end up there. If we start with grace, courage, and honesty, we'll probably end up *there*.

The end is in the beginning.

YIELD

The final symbol is a *yield* sign. In a healthy relationship, yielding doesn't mean pretending to agree with the other person when we really don't. Nor does it mean always giving in and letting others have their way. It means slowing down enough to recognize and acknowledge what the other person is experiencing in the conversation.

For example, Keith and Hope are having conflict about sex.

They have different levels of desire. They also have two young boys. Hope says, "Keith, I feel like you follow me around the house all the time just waiting in case I'll say yes."

Keith immediately explodes. "I feel like I have to, because the window of opportunity is so narrow. If I'm not watching you all the time, the moment might pass, and I'm afraid I'll miss it! It's like last night . . . I asked you, and you said no!"

"I told you—I had a headache!" she explodes in response.

"You're always talking about how good women are at multitasking," he counters. "Can't you have a headache and sex at the same time?"

In any relationship, the person who has the lowest level of need holds the power. Whether it's the need for sexual intimacy, words of affection, or time together, there is an inverse relationship between love and power.

Let's look at this conversation a different way.

Keith realizes this is a draining season of life for his wife, and he wants her to understand the vulnerability he feels under the surface of this conflict.

Keith starts by quieting his frustration. He explains, "When we're in bed, and I reach out for you, and you don't respond, I feel lonely and unwanted."

Hope softens. She hadn't realized that. Keith had never told her. When Keith reveals his hurt, it touches her heart in a way that pressure and anger never will.

Stop. Ask. Proceed with caution. Yield. When you ignore the signs, wrecks happen.

EXERCISE GRATITUDE MORE THAN IRRITATION

The apostle Paul once wrote, "I thank my God every time I remember you. In all my prayers for all of you, I always pray with joy."[15] However, if we're in a distressed relationship, we might actually write a letter that sounds quite different from Paul's letter: "I complain to God every time I remember you. In all my prayers, I always pray, 'God, why can't you change her?' 'Why can't you make him different?' 'Why can't I have some normal, healthy people in my life?'"

Comedian George Carlin did a routine in which he identified the two kinds of drivers in the world: *maniacs* (anyone who drove faster than he did) and *idiots* (anyone who drove slower). In a distressed relationship, I start viewing the other person from a George Carlin state of mind.

Harvard researcher Shawn Achor once spoke with a tax auditor who was very depressed. As they were talking about why, the auditor mentioned that one day during a break at work, he had created an Excel spreadsheet listing all the mistakes his wife had made during the past six weeks.[16] (I am not making this up.) I can only imagine his wife's (probably now his ex-wife's) response when she found out her husband had done a "flaw audit" on her.

Now, we may not have a flaw audit spreadsheet on a computer somewhere, but we have one in our minds, don't we? *Every mistake you make, I know, and that's what I remember. And I complain to God every time I remember.*

Paul makes a remarkable claim in a letter to the church in Corinth: Love "keeps no record of wrongs."[17] It doesn't rehearse them. It doesn't magnify them. It doesn't dwell on them. In fact, Paul does the opposite: He conducts a *gratitude* audit—dwelling on "whatever is true, whatever is noble, whatever is right, whatever is pure, whatever is lovely, whatever is admirable . . . excellent or praiseworthy."[18]

Imagine your spouse's response to that!

THE BEAUTY OF REPAIR

Joseph Ellis's Pulitzer Prize–winning book, *Founding Brothers*, tells of one of the great friendships in American history between two radically different personalities: Thomas Jefferson and John Adams.

> Adams, the short, stout, candid-to-a-fault New Englander; Jefferson, the tall, slender, elegantly elusive Virginian; Adams, the highly combustible, ever combative, mile-a-minute talker, whose favorite form of conversation was an argument; Jefferson, the always cool and self-contained enigma, who regarded debate and argument as violations of the natural harmonies he heard inside his own head. . . . They were the odd couple of the American Revolution.[19]

For two decades they expressed great affection for one another. John's wife, Abigail, even said that Jefferson was the only man in whom her husband could fully confide. When Jefferson's wife died, Adams was his consoler.

Then they were separated by political differences and rivalry. By the time Jefferson defeated Adams's bid for a second presidential term, he had hired a journalist to discredit Adams's reputation. Abigail spoke for her husband when she wrote to Jefferson that his actions "have my utter abhorrence and detestation, for they were the blackest calumny and foulest falsehoods."

For over a decade, no word passed between Jefferson and Adams. Then, as old men, through the help of a mutual friend, they began to reconnect and then to delight in one another. They both died on the same day—the Fourth of July—fifty years to the day after independence. Adams's last words were "Thomas Jefferson still lives."[20]

The point is, there are few phrases in the world more powerful than "I'm sorry. Please forgive me."

Dear Tom,
I forgive you.
Love, John

AWAY, AGAINST, TOWARD

Lewis Smedes writes in *Forgive and Forget*:

> There is an old, old story about a tailor who leaves his prayers and, on the way out of the synagogue, meets a rabbi.
>
> "Well, and what have you been doing in the synagogue, Lev Ashram?" the rabbi asks.
>
> "I was saying prayers, rabbi."
>
> "Fine, and did you confess your sins?"
>
> "Yes, rabbi, I confessed my little sins."
>
> "Your little sins?"
>
> "Yes, I confessed that I sometimes cut my cloth on the short side, that I cheat on a yard of wool by a couple of inches."
>
> "You said that to God, Lev Ashram?"
>
> "Yes, rabbi, and more. I said, 'Lord, I cheat on pieces of cloth; you let little babies die. But I am going to make you a deal. You forgive me my little sins and I'll forgive you your big ones.'"[21]

Bargaining with God or offering him our forgiveness is not the right approach, of course. Over and over, the writers of

Scripture assure us that "God is light; in him there is no darkness at all."[22] Still, we often live with what Philip Yancey calls "disappointment with God," which ruptures our intimacy with him.[23]

Messages, books, and blogs about dealing with our disappointment are always widely popular. The Bible itself is full of such statements, and we need to read them honestly.

Even people who don't believe in God are troubled by the question of why life is as painful as it is. C. S. Lewis says of his younger years as an atheist, "At this time [I was] living . . . in a whirl of contradictions. I maintained that God did not exist. I was also very angry with God for not existing."[24]

Sometimes I wonder whether God has a book on his nightstand titled *Disappointment with People*. We might think that's a possible subtitle for the Bible.

We catch little glimpses of it in the Scriptures:

> The LORD saw how great the wickedness of the
> human race had become. . . . The LORD regretted
> that he had made human beings on the earth, and his
> heart was deeply troubled.[25]

Here's an even sadder thought of a book that might be in the divine library: *Disappointment with John Ortberg*. And yet, when I'm mean to one of my children, arrogant toward my peers, deceptive toward my wife, demeaning to women, closed-hearted toward the poor, dismissive of those who are different from me—how could God *not* be disappointed?

Each time I sin, I am in effect "dis-appointing" God—that is, rejecting his divine appointment to reign for good in my life. I dis-appoint God so that I can appoint myself to be God in his place. Every act of sin is a rupture in the cosmic *shalom*.

When a relationship is ruptured, both sides have three choices: move away, move against, or move toward. To move toward is to seek repair and reconciliation, even at considerable cost.

When our relationship with God was ruptured in the Garden of Eden, God chose to *move toward* humanity to seek repair and restoration.

This move was called the Incarnation. It's almost as if God began writing a new book—"In the beginning was the Word"—filled with stories of a lot of people who thought they were big disappointments to God (only to find out that Jesus was crazy about them), and a few people who were certain that God was crazy about them (yet who found themselves disappointed with Jesus).

The story begins in a manger and seems to end on a cross. Jesus begins to heal our experiences of disappointment with God by intimately sharing in them: "My God, my God, why have you forsaken me?"[26] The next chapter begins with an empty tomb, and the rest is still being written.

God has been moving toward us from the very beginning. The question is, which way will *we* move?

CHAPTER 13

WHO WILL CRY AT YOUR FUNERAL?

THE POINT OF INTIMACY

We are put on earth a little space that we may learn to bear the beams of love.
WILLIAM BLAKE, *"The Little Black Boy"*

PATRICK MORLEY WRITES ABOUT the nagging sense he had that he was not getting life right.[1] As he started to become successful in his work, people who used to ignore him began to court him. He was invited to join organizations, speak at events, and meet with important people. There was almost always money behind the offers—and the decisions about where to devote his time. People now wanted his time because he had something to offer them.

He felt connected because so many people wanted a piece of him. But they were superficial relationships based on his utility to others, not significant friendships of genuine intimacy.

At the same time, the people who needed him the most—particularly his children—were getting the least of him.

For a time, he mistook the quantity of his network for the quality of his relational life.

"We've arrived!" he said to his wife one day.

"Yes, but at the wrong place," she replied.[2]

Then this thought occurred to them: "'Why not prioritize everything we do on the basis of who's going to be crying at our funeral?' . . . Why should you and I give ourselves to people who don't love us, at the expense of those who do?"[3]

In *The Entrepreneur Roller Coaster*, Darren Hardy mentions a *Newsweek* article about funerals that said only about ten people will cry at the average funeral. Hardy writes, "I was floored. . . . You mean I can work hard all my life trying to do good and please others, and in the end only ten people will care enough to cry?"[4]

According to the same article, Hardy says, the number one factor that determines whether someone will attend your graveside ceremony is . . . wait for it . . . *the weather*. If it's raining, half the people will decide they have somewhere else to be. That realization, writes Hardy, was "all it took for me to stop caring what others thought of me."[5]

Herod the Great thought about who would cry at his funeral. He was the greatest builder and most powerful ruler of that century in Palestine. But he was not a master of intimacy. He had ten wives, and the only one he truly loved he suspected of wanting his throne, so he had her killed. He also had her mother killed. And he had three of his own sons killed. He wanted to be remembered, so he gave his offspring names like Herod Antipas, Herod Philip, and Herodias—which is kind of like George Foreman naming his sons George Jr, George III, George IV, George V, and George VI.

But as Herod lay dying, he realized that *no one* would cry at his funeral. According to the ancient historian Josephus,

Herod "commanded that all the principal men of the entire Jewish nation . . . should be called to him," and imprisoned in the hippodrome at Jericho.[6] Herod then left orders with his sister and brother-in-law that, on the day he died, these prominent Jews were to be executed—thereby guaranteeing there would be crying on the day of Herod's funeral.

WILL THEY OR WON'T THEY?

So, who will *not* be crying at my funeral?

- my critics
- people who write me to ask for favors, but whom I never hear from otherwise
- people whose approval I'm constantly trying to gain, but who always withhold it
- rich people who I think might give me something if I get to know them better (but so far it hasn't happened)
- successful people whose success I think might rub off on me if I hang out with them more often
- people who see me frequently but don't remember my name
- people who I think could make me feel important if I could just get them to notice me
- people who are cooler than I am
- users
- famous people I've never actually met
- beautiful women whose pictures are on the Internet, but who don't actually know I'm alive
- people I'm afraid of
- people who are afraid of me

- all the people in the little jury box of my mind whose opinion of me matters so much, but who aren't thinking about me at all because they're wondering what other people are thinking about them

Who *is* likely to cry at my funeral?

- my children and their families
- my wife
- my brother and sister
  (Though my sister is a little older than I am, I still think she'll live longer. She is much shorter, so her heart doesn't have to work nearly as hard.)
- my good friends
- my parents, if I should go before them
- people I have genuinely and personally helped

In other words, the people with whom I have true intimacy.

The question is, *Am I giving the best of my time and my life to the people who will cry at my funeral?*

Martin Seligman recommends five rituals to observe on a daily or weekly basis: *beginnings, reunions, affection, one weekly date,* and *appreciation.*[7] They take only a few minutes a day and can be the difference between intimacy and distance. Although they were originally designed with couples in mind, these practices can be adapted to work with family relationships, friends, roommates, or coworkers.

Beginnings

How do we greet each other? We have to acknowledge the other person's existence in some way—why not do it with joy!

In your first conversation of the morning, find out one thing the other person will be doing during the day.

My wife tells me she has to have a difficult conversation with one of her team members today, and is not looking forward to it. I remind her that she's great at difficult conversations—she has them with me all the time! And at the end of the day, I can check in with her to see how it went. My son tells me he's coaching an ultimate Frisbee game in Palo Alto; when I remember to ask about the results afterward, it makes a tiny but significant statement: *What you do matters to someone.* Seligman points out that if we follow this ritual for two minutes a day, five days a week, we can make a positive difference in our relationships with an investment of only ten minutes a week.

Reunions

At the end of each workday, devote twenty minutes when you first get home to have a "low-stress reunion conversation." "Low-stress" means the goal here is to *relieve* the other person's stress level, not add to it. Nancy and I seek to listen, encourage, empathize, and laugh with each other. We used to do this in the bathroom, with the door locked so the kids couldn't get in. We literally remodeled our bathroom to create a comfortable space to do this, and it was some of the best money we've ever spent. This investment of an hour and forty minutes a week (20 minutes/day × 5 days/week) can pay tremendous dividends.

Affection

The benefits of this one are pretty obvious for establishing and maintaining a connection. Touching, holding, kissing—all combined with tenderness and affection—build feelings of intimacy and safety (5 minutes/day x 7 days/week = 35 minutes).

One weekly date

Just the two of you, in a relaxed atmosphere, updating your relationship. In the early years of our marriage, because we had no money, Nancy and I did this at Carl's Jr.—and had dinner beforehand. The only thing we ordered at the restaurant was iced tea, but we got two hours a week alone together face-to-face.

Appreciation

Every day, find opportunities to express genuine appreciation. Because I'm relatively fashion-challenged, a friend of mine recently picked out a pair of shoes he thought I should get. When I wore them, I actually had someone compliment me on my shoes—the first time in my life that's happened since I was a toddler wearing saddle shoes my mother picked out. The compliment made me feel good, and when I passed it on to my shoe-selecting friend, it made him smile as well. It takes so little to bring delight to someone's heart (5 minutes/day x 7 days/week = 35 minutes).

Truth is, you're going to communicate with your spouse, your friends, and your family anyway. Why not do it in a way that will make sure they cry at your funeral? When you're with the people you love, this means sending them signals that you're connected, and noticing when you're not feeling connected.

Recently, Nancy and I were at dinner with friends, and I said something that I could immediately tell was hurtful to Nancy—you know, that moment when you and the other person are aware that there's been a little wound inflicted even if no one else knows.

A few minutes later, under the table, where no one else could see or know, a little foot came over and started to nudge my foot. It just lingered there playfully for a few seconds. I was pretty sure it was Nancy's foot. (I sure hope it was Nancy's foot.)

That little foot was saying, "I'm okay. We're okay. We can check in with each other later on, but I want you to know I'm not running from you. I will not distance myself from you while we are with our friends to make you feel strained or isolated. We're still together. We're okay."

I'm pretty confident that foot will be crying at my funeral.

THE POWER OF NAMING

Dr. William Betcher notes that creating intimacy is like building a private culture. It's the treasure of a family or a friendship or a marriage. It consists of ritual and language—of "terms of endearment."[8]

Language communicates intimacy.

One family calls their old vacuum cleaner J. Edgar, because it's a Hoover. (If you're twenty years old or under, google it.) I used to read my kids a book about a family whose car was nicknamed Foolish Carriage because the dad said he was foolish to think he could afford it.

The point is, we use nicknames to communicate an intimate attachment to family, friends, or even coworkers.

Betcher has done such an exhaustive study on nicknames that he sorts them into three primary categories: *food, body parts,* and *animals.* Sometimes we combine the categories: Sugar Lips or Honey Bear.

Sometimes nicknames are enigmatic. Anton Chekhov, for example, was constantly coming up with new appellations for his wife, Olga. In one note, he wrote, "I embrace my little cockroach and send her a million kisses."[9] Winston and Clementine Churchill referred to each other as Cat (her) and Pig (him).[10]

Why do we do this?

When you bestow a secret name on someone you love, you are setting that relationship apart from all others. You are staking a claim: "I know you in a way that no one else can quite share." Often, a couple's real names fall into disuse. I have a nickname for Nancy (don't worry; you'll never get it from me) and if I were ever to call her Nancy when we were alone, it would sound like I was addressing her as Dr. Ortberg (which, on the other hand, I'm still trying to get her to call *me*).

The magic of the secret name is not that it's glamorous or even complimentary. It's that it speaks of intimate connection and shared experience. As couples age, the familiarity of that intimacy is often what matters most.

Betcher writes of sitting before a fire on a blustery day, drinking tea with an elderly English couple he was interviewing. They had been married fifty years—through good times, rough times, and many adjustments—and were still together. At one point, the wife turned toward her husband and said, "Why don't you put another log on the scuttle, Old Shoe?"[11] The nickname, like their relationship, was humble and worn with time, and spoke of a world known only to them.

You may have noticed (to get more embarrassing still) that couples in love often speak baby talk. C. S. Lewis writes about this in *The Four Loves*, observing that "it embarrasses many moderns . . . to use a 'little language' or 'baby talk.'"

Lewis also notes that "this is not peculiar to the human

species. Professor Lorenz has told us that when jackdaws are amorous, their calls 'consist chiefly of infantile sounds reserved by adult jackdaws for these occasions.' We and the birds have the same excuse."[12]

Love desires tenderness, and the language associated with babies is the most tender language we have. You may have noticed some people use baby talk with their dogs.

C. S. Lewis says this is stupid.

SOMETHING GREATER THAN OURSELVES

The Boys in the Boat tells the riveting story of how nine working-class boys, during the depths of the Depression, defeated the elite rowers of the Ivy League and then beat Adolf Hitler's rowers to win gold at the 1936 Berlin Olympics. Their goal was not simply to defeat other teams; it was to experience a level of harmony, cooperation, and oneness together as a team that approached transcendence.

There is a thing that sometimes happens in rowing that is hard to achieve and hard to define. . . . It's called "swing." It only happens when all eight oarsmen are rowing in such perfect unison that no single action by any one is out of synch with those of all the others. . . . Sixteen arms must begin to pull, sixteen knees must begin to fold and unfold, eight bodies must begin to slide forward and backward, eight backs must bend and straighten all at once. Each minute action—each subtle turning of wrists—must be mirrored exactly by each oarsman, from one end of the boat to the other. Only then will the boat continue to run, unchecked, fluidly and gracefully between pulls of the oars. Only then will

it feel as if the boat is a part of each of them, moving
as if on its own. Only then does pain entirely give way
to exultation. Rowing then becomes a kind of perfect
language. Poetry, that's what a good swing feels like.[13]

The crew's mentor, George Pocock, explained to them what he
called "the spiritual value of rowing" as "the losing of self entirely
to the cooperative effort of the crew as a whole."[14] He explained
the strange wonder of how—at the moment you are most sacri-
ficing yourself for others—you are also most fully yourself, more
fully alive than you'll ever be again.

"Swing" can happen in a friendship, when two people love,
encourage, enjoy, know, and challenge each other so deeply that
they become better together than either one could ever be on
their own.

It can happen in a marriage, when one partner sacrifices
a career achievement to make space for the other partner's
growth, and in that sacrifice finds more joy than could ever be
derived from climbing one more rung on the corporate ladder.

It can happen in a family, when members care for each
other, speak truth to each other, call out the best in each other,
become masters of observation, and create a community that
seeks to serve others outside of the family.

Swing can happen for a work team or in a neighborhood,
but it's never fully under our control. When it comes, it comes
as a gift. George Pocock said, "When you're rowing well, . . .
it's nearing perfection. And when you near perfection, you're
touching the Divine."[15]

The biblical term for "swing" is *shalom*. Neal Plantinga
calls *shalom* the "webbing together of God, humans, and
all creation in justice, fulfillment, and delight."[16] In *shalom*,
people work in peace, and work to good effect; lambs lie down

safely with lions; swords are beaten into plowshares. In *shalom*, the Internet would be filled with stories of moral beauty and expressions of admiration.

In *shalom*, the human race would be so harmonious that no one would need a password for anything anymore, doors would be left unlocked, and workplaces would be filled with people giving credit to others. Husbands and wives would seek to outdo each other in acts of service. As Dallas Willard said, we would know the joy of "being absorbed in a tremendously creative team effort, with unimaginably splendid leadership, on an inconceivably vast plane of activity, with ever more comprehensive cycles of productivity and enjoyment."[17]

When Ruth gave up her home for the sake of her mother-in-law, Naomi, and Naomi devoted herself to Ruth's well-being; when Jonathan risked his life and his own throne for the sake of his friend David and his nation, Israel; when a little boy gave his meager lunch to Jesus and Jesus turned it into a feast that fed thousands and would have won an episode of *Chopped*—that's *shalom*.

That's *swing*.

OUTIMACY: THE CIRCLE BEYOND

Intimacy does not exist solely for itself. When a man loves a woman (sounds like a song), the result is often a child, upon whom they now can pour out their love. And so it goes. This is the great chain of being that makes up human life.

Intimacy needs to flow beyond itself. It needs "outimacy"— that is, to overflow in love for someone *outside* the circle.

In *A Severe Mercy*, Sheldon Vanauken writes of how he and his wife, Davy, sought to put a wall around their intimacy.

They promised to share everything—friends, interests, work—so that nothing could separate them.

They made the choice to remain childless because they did not want Davy to experience motherhood when Sheldon never could. They erected what they came to call a Shining Barrier around their relationship that would keep their intimacy for themselves.

While studying in England, they came to faith in God. Davy believed first; Sheldon reluctantly followed. He was jealous of the hold that God now had on Davy's life. "I didn't want us to be swallowed up in God," he writes. "I wanted holidays from the school of Christ."[18]

Over time, however, both Davy and Sheldon came to see intimacy in a new way. Now in tune with a higher purpose, they came to believe that intimacy was not merely for the sake of those inside a relationship. As Davy was dying, at the age of forty, in what Sheldon calls "a severe mercy," they realized that any love that seeks to exist for its own sake must die. The Shining Barrier, which looks at first like intimacy's protector, actually becomes its killer in the end.

Jean Vanier, director of the L'Arche community where Henri Nouwen resided for many years, expressed it like this:

> The two great dangers of community [intimacy] are "friends" and "enemies." People very quickly get together with those who are like themselves; we all like to be with someone who pleases us, who shares our ideas, ways of looking at life and our sense of humor. We nourish each other, we flatter each other: "You are marvelous"—"So are you"—"We are marvelous because we are intelligent and clever." Human friendships can very quickly become a club of

mediocrities, enclosed in mutual flattery and approval, preventing people from seeing their inner poverty and wounds. Friendship is then no longer a spur to grow, to go further, to be of greater service.[19]

Intimate friends and families must have a sense of *shared meaning*. They require a purpose nobler than simply their own happiness. In a 2015 article in *Forbes*, writer Liz Ryan argues that for a business, having happy employees "is not a goal worthy of an organization's energy and brainpower."[20] Instead, she says,

> Let's imagine a person completely immersed in his or her work. We'll use the greatest violin maker in the world as our example. I don't know who makes the greatest violins in the world, but we'll imagine that it's an Italian violin maker named Franco and that Franco has a studio where 15 or 20 apprentice and journeyman violin makers work alongside Franco making the most exquisite violins in the world.
> Is Franco happy? He is alternately ecstatic, frustrated, transported, confused, exhausted and lost in the zone. He and his work are inextricable from one another. No one would say about Franco or his employees "They're happy." Instead, people in Franco's town would say "Those guys live and breathe violins, and people around the world rejoice."[21]

Once there was a community of whom it was said, "Those guys live and breathe Jesus, and people around the world rejoice." This is how we are saved from becoming the "you are marvelous" club of mediocrities.

There's a character in the New Testament at the opposite end of the scale from Herod the Great. Her name is Dorcas, and all we know about her is that "she was always doing good and helping the poor."[22]

Dorcas had some resources—the phrase translated "doing good" implies the giving of alms—and she was connected to the people around her. She had money. She had time. She was part of the community. And out of the resources of her life and the intimacy of her community flowed goodness to people who were on the outside.

People who couldn't have afforded clothes were dressed because of her.

People who couldn't afford food were fed because of her.

People who would have been outsiders became insiders because of her.

At some point, Dorcas became sick and died. We're told that her body was washed and placed in an upstairs room—which, if she was a woman of means, may well have been in her own house.

People in the ancient world were very concerned about what would happen to their bodies after they died. Rome was filled with burial societies that people could join (if they paid) to make sure their corpses were cared for. The Romans were confused about what Christianity was; they didn't consider it a religion because it had only one god and offered no sacrifices. A prominent theory held that Christians were part of a burial society, because they took such tender care of the dead.[23]

We're told Dorcas's body was washed, which was part of the Jewish preparation for burial, but there is no mention of anointing, which also would have been part of the custom. It may be that the community allowed the poor widows to prepare Dorcas's body as an act of love and they had no money for burial spices.

And there were people crying at her funeral: "All the widows stood around [Peter], crying and showing him the robes and other clothing that Dorcas had made while she was still with them."[24]

This is what we can learn from Dorcas two thousand years later. We might call it the *paradox of intimacy*: If I aim at *getting* love, I will neither give it nor receive it; if I aim at *giving* love, I will find the gift of receiving it thrown in.

When it comes to love, not only is it more blessed to give than to receive, it turns out that giving is the only path to receiving.

EAT AND GET OUT

Circles of intimacy—marriages, families, friendships, and churches—exist not only for themselves but to enrich the lives of those outside the circle as well.

Here's a phrase you'll never read in the Bible: "Where do you go to church?" In fact, there's no place in the Bible that even says you *should* go to church.

There's an important reason for this.

At the time when the New Testament books were written, nobody thought about calling a *building* a church. The church didn't even have any buildings then. It just had *people*. But then, over the centuries, a strange thing happened. What used to describe a group of people came to be the name of a building.

Sometimes, people will look at a building where a group of people congregate and say, "You have a beautiful church." But to the early Christians, that would have made as much sense as someone looking at a crib and saying, "You have a beautiful baby."

Babies are people. A crib is just a place where you *put* the baby—and not all the time. You put the baby in the crib so that he or she can rest up and recharge to go back into the world. The *world* is where the action is.

If you have a baby, would you want him or her in the crib 24/7? (Actually, if you have a baby, *you* might want to be in the crib 24/7. Speaking from experience.)

The place of intimacy is to be a place of safety and joy, but it is not to be our only place.

We don't gather as the church for our *own* sakes. We come together as the church to rest up, recharge, and get nourished so that we can go *into the world* and *be* the church. The church, not the "you are marvelous" club of mediocrities.

In other words, church isn't something you *go to*, in here; church is something *you are*, out there—outimacy.

The fellowship of the early church centered on the dinner table. Believers shared the Lord's Supper there. It was a place of great intimacy. But the measure of the greatness of their community was not the experience of intimacy; it was the extent to which their intimacy with God and with one another overflowed to the blessing of those not yet at the table.

For two thousand years, followers of Jesus have communed around the table—that is, *communicated intimately*.[25] The ancient Greek word for intimate fellowship is *koinonia*. In the church, we can suffer from what might be called *koinonitus*: fellowship turned in on itself; cliques and enclaves and tight-knit groups that become little cul-de-sacs of relationship. The difference between the life-giving Sea of Galilee and the salty-enough-to-float-on Dead Sea is that the Dead Sea has no outlet for the life flowing into it.

Intimacy without outimacy leads to stagnation and death.

We began this book with the image of a shared meal as a picture of intimacy. When I think about love, I think about a table. But it's not healthy for us to sit at the table forever.

In Chicago—a city with an attitude—there used to be a diner called Ed Debevic's that mirrored the attitude of city. The waitstaff there was deliberately, hilariously sarcastic. They gleefully insulted patrons; they stood on the bar to dance to the Village People's classic "YMCA." The restaurant's slogan was all over the walls: "Eat and get out."

As followers of Jesus, that's what we need to do: Eat and get out.

IT'S NOT YOUR FAULT . . .

The Bible tells us little about Dorcas. Her Greek name was Tabitha; most likely she was a Gentile; most likely the tradition of generosity and servanthood she modeled had to be learned.

I wonder if she ever asked why she should be the one to give up her home and her possessions and her time for the sake of others. It wasn't her fault there was poverty, or nakedness, or homelessness. What did her intimacy have to do with their need?

Barbara Williams-Skinner, a woman who has been a towering presence for Jesus in the fight against racism, says that sometimes these are God's words to his people: "It may not be your fault, but it certainly is your time."[26]

It's not your fault that some people have no place to sleep tonight. It's not your fault that children are going to bed hungry. It's not your fault that orphans have no home or that sick people have no medicine.

It's not your fault, but you *can* do something. You have access. You have privilege. You have gifts. You have a chance to make a difference. Who knows but that you have come to your position for just such a time as this.[27]

It may not be your fault, but it certainly is your time.

I believe that this is Jesus' word to many of us. It's not your fault that the world is full of poverty, inequality, injustice, and suffering. But you can do something to help. You may have money you can donate. You may have time, energy, and expertise you can offer.

It may not be your fault, but it certainly is your time.

It's not your fault that racism came to America. It's not your fault that 250 years of slavery kept millions of God's children in chains; that a century of Jim Crow laws kept them degraded and impoverished. It's not your fault that in 2013, there were about 840,000 black men in prison in the US (compared to 1.4 million black men in college).[28]

But you might be able to help tilt the balance. You might be able to tutor a child. You might be able to help a school. You might have a little education you can share.

It may not be your fault, but it certainly is your time.

It's not your fault that immigrants are being hounded from their homes by modern-day Herods; that parents are putting children on boats so overcrowded that they sink; that people would rather risk dying than wait in their countries to be killed; that young people feel so pressured, or older people so isolated, that they'd rather die than live.

It may not be your fault, but it certainly is your time.

Remember, *intimacy* without *outimacy* leads to stagnation and death. Once you have experienced true intimacy, it is your great commission to share it with others. To help others experience love, joy, acceptance, and belonging.

One more thing about Dorcas—maybe the main reason the book of Acts tells her story: *She didn't stay dead.*

> Peter . . . got down on his knees and prayed. Turning toward the dead woman, he said, "Tabitha, get up." She opened her eyes, and seeing Peter she sat up. He took her by the hand and helped her to her feet. Then he called for the believers, especially the widows, and presented her to them alive.[29]

Here's the thing about death. We're not going to stay dead. Jesus promises those of us who trust Jesus with our lives that death will not be the end. When it comes, he will say, "Get up," and he will take us by the hand and help us to our feet.

And then we will see the tears. Not tears of sorrow. Tears of joy. The joyful tears of God.

I'll see you at the table.

Now eat and get out.

CHAPTER 14

AT LAST

REAL INTIMACY

And then a strange thing happened . . .
MARGERY WILLIAMS, *The Velveteen Rabbit*

THE BEST STORIES are love stories. And the best love stories always come as a surprise.

In the church where I grew up, people often spoke of the Bible as a kind of instruction manual for life.

I've never cared much for instruction manuals.

But what if the Bible is actually a love story rather than a how-to manual?

What if the key to the whole mystery of intimacy—our longing for it and its seeming elusiveness—lies at the heart of the story?

Philip Yancey observes that romantic love is the closest many people ever come to experiencing pure grace: "Someone at last feels that I—*I!*—am the most desirable, attractive, companionable creature on the planet. Someone lies awake at night thinking of *me*."[1]

Sometimes when I hold my wife, she will whisper the phrase, "Closer is better," and we know this to be true. Bodies are made to be close. Bodies are fleshy and soft and messy— and intimacy is that way too.

But that's not how we perceive our relationship with God. For most of us, God is distant and mysterious. He watches and judges. He is serene, unattainable, unapproachable. People have always been afraid of God. They offer sacrifices. They stay at a distance.

The Bible begins with God's love of intimacy. He comes to walk in the Garden in the cool of the day. It is the simplest bid for intimate connection, repeated by every human being who ever lived: "Want to go for a walk?"

But the man and the woman didn't want to. They were hiding.

The first rejected bid.

The history of ancient Israel is the story of a rejected God who will not give up on the people he loves. Instead, he finds a way to break through.

If intimacy is shared experience, then the Incarnation is its greatest expression, its highest articulation, its deepest sacrifice.

In the Incarnation, God shared our experience of loneliness, our tiredness, our fear, our guilt, our joy at having a body, our pain at having it hurt, our comfort in being held, our despair at feeling God-forsaken.

Brené Brown uses a short cartoon video to discuss the difference between *empathy* and *sympathy*. In the video, a little fox in a T-shirt falls into a deep hole.

"I'm stuck," he says. "It's dark. I'm overwhelmed."

From up above, a deer pokes her head down the hole and sympathizes.

"Ooh! It's bad, uh-huh. . . . Want a sandwich?"

Then a bear in a baseball cap appears, but instead of watching from above, he lumbers down a ladder and stands next to the fox in the hole. "Hey, I know what it's like down here," he says. "And you're not alone."[2]

If you watch that video and you can't see Jesus in it, you're not looking closely enough.

People think God is like the deer.

But he's not.

He's the bear. Into the hole. Down the ladder: "I know what it's like down here. And you're not alone."

THE PARABLE OF THE KING

A few decades ago, two mental health clinicians discovered a new disease. They kept finding a similar pattern in their patients: a persistent fear of being exposed as a fraud. They observed that high achievement could not solve it; in fact, high-achieving people were often especially unable to internalize their accomplishments. These people would work hard, tinker, obsess, hide, and figure out positive ways to present themselves to others. But they lived with anxiety, stress, shame, self-doubt, and inner confusion.

This condition was named the Imposter Phenomenon.[3] It's not a mental disorder. It's an epidemic. It's the haunting belief that I'm not as smart or kind or tough or good or successful or happy as I've led other people to believe. That the self I have so carefully crafted for you to see is not *really* me. Ironically, the better I am at crafting this false self—the more applause and approval it wins—the more isolated becomes the true and unloved self I keep carefully hidden.

That's why the first question in the Bible is not posed by people asking where God is; it's the other way around.

"Adam, where are you—the *real* you, the you I made? Who is this frightened, shamed creature hoping not to be seen or known, cutting himself off from love, trying to pretend nothing's wrong?"

I know this phenomenon. On Sunday mornings, I stand before a congregation and speak on behalf of God. Who am I to do this? Sometimes when I'm talking, I think of things I've done wrong during the week. Or I think of doubts that claw at me even when I'm calling other people to believe. I try to find the right amount of self-disclosure—enough to connect with people, but not so much that I alarm them, or look bad, or lose my job. And yet, even when I'm trying to disclose myself, I'm concealing myself.

What I want is the opposite of this. I want:

- to not pretend or hide
- to be the same publicly as privately
- to own my own story
- to understand my own worth
- to rest from trying to live by "impression management"
- to let go of other people's opinions of me
- to be healed of everything that makes me want to hide: greed, lust, judging, deceit, pettiness, envy
- to feel deeply without pettiness or denial
- to be genuine—so that what you see is what you get

I want to be *real*. And yet I can't seem to pull it off. No matter how hard I try, I can't *make* myself real.

The discoverers of this epidemic say that the only healing for Imposter Phenomenon is to do precisely what we don't want to do: make ourselves known. To courageously reveal our fears, our inadequacies, and our shame, so that our *real* selves can be seen and loved.

But this presents a problem—because everyone else is hiding too. In order to truly be healed, someone who is fully real and truly safe would have to become like us, would have to enter our world, so that we could really be loved.

And guess what? That's exactly what happened.

Søren Kierkegaard told the story as a parable:

Suppose there was a king who loved a humble maiden. The king was like no other king. Every statesman trembled before his power. No one dared breathe a word against him, for he had the strength to crush all opponents.

And yet this mighty king was melted by love for a humble maiden who lived in a poor village in his kingdom. How could he declare his love for her? In an odd sort of way, his kingliness tied his hands. If he brought her to the palace and crowned her head with jewels and clothed her body in royal robes, she would surely not resist—no one dared resist him. But would she love him?

She would say she loved him, of course, but would she truly? Or would she live with him in fear, nursing a private grief for the life she had left behind? Would she be happy at his side? How could he know for sure? If he rode to her forest cottage in his royal carriage, with an armed escort waving bright banners, that too would overwhelm her. He did not want a cringing subject. He wanted a lover, an equal. He wanted her to forget that he was a king and she a humble maiden and to let shared love cross the gulf between them. For it is only in love that the unequal can be made equal.

The king, convinced he could not elevate the maiden without crushing her freedom, resolved to descend to her. Clothed as a beggar, he approached her cottage with a worn cloak fluttering loose about him. This was not just a disguise—the king took on a totally new identity. He had renounced his throne to declare his love and to win hers.[4]

The King renounced his throne to declare his love.
Where have we seen this before?

> In the beginning was the Word, and the Word was with God, and the Word was God. . . . The Word became flesh and made his dwelling among us.[5]

In the early centuries of the church, a great thinker named Origen wrote, "Of all the marvelous and splendid things about him, there is one that utterly transcends the limits of human knowledge . . . how this mighty power of the divine majesty . . . can have entered into a woman's womb and been born as a little child and uttered noises like those of crying children."[6]

In Jesus, God became fleshy and messy and needy. God could be touched. God could be hugged. In Jesus, God said, "Closer is better."

Why did God do this? God could have loved us—could have willed our good—from a distance. But he wanted more than to love us. He wanted to be intimate with us.

Intimacy is shared experience.

God became human to share the experience of humanity.

God became fully human to share that experience fully.

Intimacy demands closeness, vulnerability. So God took on flesh. God wanted to have skin in the game.

"Jesus of Nazareth—whom Christians hold to be God incarnate—came into this world in the same bloody, messy, and vulnerable manner as the rest of us."[7]

Mary held God in her arms, kissed God's face, fed God from her body, stroked God's little head. In Jesus, God had to learn how to walk by falling down. The God who said, "Let there be light," and it was so, had to be taught how to speak. In Jesus, God was lonely, God grew tired, God bled, God went through puberty, God hammered nails and hit himself on the thumb. In Jesus, God loved and laughed and hurt and hoped and lived and died.

In Jesus, this distant, untouchable, unapproachable, unattainable God became *real*.

BECOMING REAL

In 1922, Margery Williams, a failed author of grown-up fiction, wrote a children's book called *The Velveteen Rabbit*.

In the story, a boy receives a toy rabbit as a Christmas present, but he doesn't like the rabbit much. In fact, after a few hours, the rabbit is discarded in favor of more high-tech, windup toys, and for a long time, the rabbit sits on a shelf, untouched, unknown, safe.

While on the shelf, the rabbit talks to the Skin Horse, an old shabby toy, who tells the rabbit what it means to become real:

"What is REAL?" asked the Rabbit one day, when they were lying side by side. . . . "Does it mean having things that buzz inside you and a stick-out handle?"

"Real isn't how you are made," said the Skin Horse. "It's a thing that happens to you. When a child loves you for a long, long time, not just to play with, but REALLY loves you, then you become Real."

"Does it hurt?" asked the Rabbit.

"Sometimes," said the Skin Horse, for he was always truthful. "When you are Real you don't mind being hurt."

"Does it happen all at once, like being wound up," he asked, "or bit by bit?"

"It doesn't happen all at once," said the Skin Horse. "You become. It takes a long time. That's why it doesn't happen often to people who break easily, or have sharp edges, or who have to be carefully kept. Generally, by the time you are Real, most of your hair has been loved off, and your eyes drop out and you get loose in the joints and very shabby. But these things don't matter at all, because once you are Real you can't be ugly, except to people who don't understand."[8]

I believe the reason this story is so enduring is because it speaks to a great longing in the human heart—the longing to become our *real* selves. To lay bare all our flaws, weaknesses, and frailties, and—miracle of miracles—to be loved anyway. *Unconditionally.*

The Velveteen Rabbit "longed to become Real, to know what it felt like; and yet the idea of growing shabby and losing his eyes and whiskers was rather sad. He wished that he could become it without these uncomfortable things happening to him."[9]

But becoming real always comes at a cost.

It means risking the fear of being rejected.

It means losing freedom in order to make the promises that allow for relationship.

It means the everlasting humiliation of the never-ending need for confession: "I lied. I betrayed. I belittled. I'm sorry."

It means letting go of the remote control, and of control in general.

It means wrapping our heart around someone else's well-being. It means being wounded when my child is deeply depressed, and I cannot fix it, and I wonder how much I am to blame. It is a woman sitting at the bedside of the husband she has known for sixty years, his once athletic frame now a gaunt parody, holding his hand and telling him it's okay for him to go, when it isn't okay at all.

Getting close means getting hurt.

And yet, no one becomes real without getting close, without being loved. And love, like grace, sneaks up on us mostly when we're unaware.

> Weeks passed, and the little Rabbit grew very old and shabby, but the Boy loved him just as much. He loved him so hard that he loved all his whiskers off, and the pink lining to his ears turned grey, and his brown spots faded. He even began to lose his shape, and he scarcely looked like a rabbit any more, except to the Boy. To him he was always beautiful, and that was all that the little Rabbit cared about.[10]

Ian Pitt-Watson, who taught me how to preach, told another version of this story about his daughter, for it is repeated in the life of every child who loves a toy or a doll or a blanket nearly to death. He said each time we see this behavior repeated, it pierces our heart because it teaches us about the love that matters most.

There is a love that seeks value, he would say. A love that is drawn to its object because that object is shiny or handsome or expensive or useful. A love that seeks value in what is loved.

But there is also a love that *creates* value in what is loved: "This is real love—not that we loved God, but that he loved us and sent his Son as a sacrifice to take away our sins."[11]

And then, one day, the Boy was ill.

His face grew very flushed . . . and his little body was so hot that it burned the Rabbit when he held him close. . . .

Presently the fever turned, and the Boy got better. . . .

Now it only remained to carry out the doctor's orders. . . . The room was to be disinfected, and all the books and toys that the Boy had played with in bed must be burnt. . . .

Just then Nana caught sight of [the Rabbit].

"How about his old Bunny?" she asked.

"*That?*" said the doctor. "Why, it's a mass of scarlet fever germs! Burn it at once." . . .

And so the little Rabbit was put into a sack with the old picture-books and a lot of rubbish, and carried out to the end of the garden behind the fowl-house. . . .

He felt very lonely. . . . He was shivering a little, for he had always been used to sleeping in a proper bed, and by this time his coat had worn so thin and threadbare from hugging that it was no longer any protection to him. . . . He thought of those long

sunlit hours in the garden—how happy they were—
and a great sadness came over him. . . . He thought of
the Skin Horse, so wise and gentle, and all that he had
told him. *Of what use was it to be loved and lose one's
beauty and become Real if it all ended like this?*[12]

Sound familiar? It should. Long before Margery Williams put
pen to paper, Somebody Else became real. He was a Jewish
teacher who lived a surprisingly ordinary life. Blue collar. He
may have been a bit shabby. He loved so much and so deeply
that his heart broke and his tears flowed. And the terminal
condition of the whole human race fell on his shoulders. "He
took up our pain and bore our suffering."[13] He was discarded,
as the Romans discarded troublemakers in that day—on a
cross. And the sound of his heart breaking was the sound of
ultimate suffering.

His disciples were devastated. *Of what use was it to be loved
and lose one's beauty and become Real if it all ended like this?*

And then a strange thing happened. . . .
Quite the loveliest fairy in the whole world
[appeared]. . . . She came close to the little Rabbit and
gathered him up in her arms and kissed him on his
velveteen nose that was all damp from crying.
"Little Rabbit," she said, "don't you know who I
am? . . .
"I am the nursery magic Fairy," she said. "I take
care of all the playthings that the children have loved.
When they are old and worn out and the children
don't need them anymore, then I come and take them
away with me and turn them into Real."
"Wasn't I Real before?" asked the little Rabbit.

"You were Real to the Boy," the Fairy said, "because he loved you. Now you shall be Real to every one."[14]

Williams called it "becoming Real." But perhaps a better word for it is *resurrection.*

A Presence came.

And on the third day, he became Real.

And his friends saw him.

And they knew.

The Velveteen Rabbi.

And if it could happen to him, he promised, it would happen to us as well.

THERE'S THE LOVE

The love that results from true intimacy is what makes us real. Shauna Niequist writes of her four-year-old son, Mac: "When he wants a hug or a kiss, he'll fling out his arms and bellow, 'Bring in the love!' in a deep voice, like a radio deejay. And then when you scoop him up, he pats you over and over on the back with his little hands and says, 'There it is. There's the love. There's the love.'"[15]

There it is.

There's the love.

It's in the marriage and parenting. It's in the family and friends. It's in the murmur of my parents' voices when I'm a drowsy little boy in the back seat of the car and all is right with the world. It's in the joy of my friend Rick, who just became a grandfather and tells me that having a grandchild slows you way down, because you have to adjust to Baby Time. And babies don't do hurry.

There's the love. It comes to me in my memory when my

dad says, "Okay, you kids—you have to go out for ice cream." It's in the quiet *Thees* and *Thous* of my grandmother's prayers. It's in the hymn "What a Friend We Have in Jesus," which was sung years ago at the funeral of a young woman and could not be sung again by her brother Max for decades—but he sings it now in his nineties as he waits to be reunited with her. It's around the table in a little breakfast room on Brendenwood Terrace that time cannot erase from my mind. It's in the neighborhood in Oakland where my daughter lives—where outsiders are sometimes afraid to be, but where people who live there are not in a hurry, have time to stop and talk and smile and care; where they call it home.

God created us to offer love to others because he wants no one to miss out on an intimate connection with him.

He loves the worst person in his world more than you love the best person in yours.

He loves everybody more than you love anybody.

There's the love. The Word became flesh. The bear came down the ladder.

Because all little children do adorable things, I wonder what Jesus did when he was four years old that made Mary and Joseph laugh or cry. I wonder if he said, "Stroke your little head," or "Honey, honey, I know, I know." I wonder if Mary said to him, "It's okay," when he was born. I wonder if he said it to her when he was dying.

I wonder if Jesus ever bellowed, "Bring in the love!" to his disciples when they argued over who was the greatest, or to the crowd of men who gathered to stone a woman caught in an intimate act, or to the religious leaders who didn't want him to heal a leper on the Sabbath. I wonder if he whispered it at the table, at the final meal, just before Judas tiptoed out of the room.

I wonder if he whispers it still.

Just stop.

Be still and know.

Whoever has ears, let them hear: Bring in the love!

INTIMACY LASTS FOR ALWAYS

Sometimes people who pride themselves on being tough-minded dismiss topics like intimacy and faith as ethereal escapism. "We live in the real world," they say.

Often the assumption is that the real world consists only of that which we can see and hear, and the harsh things we experience. The real world is office politics and disappointment, colds and hangovers, scarcity and effort, and "no free lunch" and "every man for himself."

Every human being must decide what counts as the real world. According to a philosopher friend of mine, "Reality is what you can count on. Pain is what you experience when you were mistaken about reality."[16]

When Jesus became human, he did not *become* real. He just brought a tiny little slice of reality to our fake, phony, phantom world. He became real *to us*. He showed us what a real human life looks like. He makes it possible for us to become real.

As we experience intimacy with him—through one shared experience after another—his plan is that we too will begin to become real.

The final book of the Bible offers a promise to God's children that can bring tears to your eyes if you believe it. God says, "I will give to each one a white stone, and on the stone will be engraved a new name that no one understands except the one who receives it."[17]

Your name is your identity, your character, your possibilities. To receive your name is to be known and to be loved; to belong and to be healed.

There's the love.

You don't know your name yet.

But one day you will.

Then you will be his.

Then you will be real.

Here's the best part: "Once you are Real you can't become unreal again. It lasts for *always*."[18]

About the Author

JOHN ORTBERG IS AN AUTHOR, a speaker, and the senior pastor of Menlo Church in the San Francisco Bay Area. A consistent theme of John's teaching is how to follow a Jesus way of life—that is, how faith in Christ can affect our everyday lives with God. His books include *All the Places to Go . . . How Will You Know?*; *Soul Keeping*; *Who Is This Man?*; *The Life You've Always Wanted*; *Faith and Doubt*; and *If You Want to Walk on Water, You've Got to Get Out of the Boat*. John teaches around the world at conferences and churches.

Born and raised in Rockford, Illinois, John graduated from Wheaton College. He holds a master's degree in divinity and a doctorate in clinical psychology from Fuller Seminary, and he did postgraduate work at the University of Aberdeen, Scotland.

John is a member of the board of trustees at Fuller Seminary, where he has also served as an adjunct faculty member. He is on the board of the Dallas Willard Center for Spiritual Formation and has served in the past on the board of Christianity Today International.

Now that their children are grown, John and his wife, Nancy, enjoy surfing in the Pacific to help care for their souls. He can be followed on Twitter: @johnortberg.

Notes

INTRODUCTION: TABLE FOR ONE?

1. Victor Hugo, *Les Misérables*, vol. IV (London: George Routledge and Sons, 1887), 307.
2. Genesis 2:18, NLT
3. Genesis 3:8-9
4. Revelation 3:20, NLT

CHAPTER 1: ARE YOU WITH ME?

1. Helena Horton, "More People Have Died by Taking Selfies This Year than by Shark Attacks," *Telegraph*, September 22, 2015, www.telegraph.co.uk /technology/11881900/More-people-have-died-by-taking-selfies-this-year -than-by-shark-attacks.html.
2. Mark 3:14.
3. Mark 1:16-17, NLT
4. Matthew 9:10
5. Luke 22:15
6. Matthew 5:1-2. See also Matthew 13:36; 15:15; 16:21; Mark 4:34; 8:31; 9:30-31; Luke 24:27.
7. John 13:14
8. Mark 6:31
9. Mark 6:32
10. Mark 9:2
11. Luke 11:1
12. Luke 5:4
13. Acts 2:1, author's paraphrase of the King James Version.
14. Malcolm Gladwell, *Outliers* (New York: Little, Brown, 2008). See particularly chapter 2. Gladwell's work is largely based on a study by Swedish psychologist Anders Ericsson and is somewhat controversial.

15. John 13:34-35
16. Anthony de Mello, *Seek God Everywhere: Reflections on the Spiritual Exercises of St. Ignatius* (New York: Image/Doubleday, 2010), 169.
17. Frank C. Laubach, *The Game with Minutes* (1953 pamphlet); http://hockleys.org/wp-content/uploads/Game_with_Minutes.pdf.
18. Joseph de Beaufort, "The Life of Brother Lawrence," in *The Brother Lawrence Collection*, Kindle edition (Radford, VA: Wilder Publications, 2008), loc. 1521.

CHAPTER 2: LET'S GET THIS STRAIGHT

1. See, for example, www.mtfca.com/discus/messages/257047/304942 .html?1346263614.
2. Nora Ephron, *Heartburn* (New York: Vintage, 1996), 158.
3. Nora Ephron, "What I Wish I'd Known," in *I Feel Bad about My Neck* (New York: Vintage, 2008), 125.
4. Thomas Aquinas, *Summa Theologica*, in *Great Books of the Western World*, vol. 20 (New York: Encyclopedia Britannica, 1952), 483.
5. 1 Corinthians 13:1-3
6. Ephesians 3:17-18
7. 1 Corinthians 13:4, 7-8
8. Song of Songs 4:1-5
9. Philippians 1:9, NLT
10. Cliff Penner, conversation with the author, date unknown.
11. Gary Chapman, *The Five Love Languages* (Chicago: Northfield, 1995), 126.
12. Samuel L. Clemens, letter to Gertrude Natkin, March 2, 1906, in *Mark Twain's Aquarium: The Samuel Clemens Angelfish Correspondence, 1905–1910*, ed. John Cooley, paperback edition (Athens, GA: University of Georgia Press, 2009), 16.
13. Dietrich Bonhoeffer, *Life Together* (New York: Harper & Row, 1954), 38.
14. John 14:22
15. See Matthew 19:28-30.
16. Carol Tavris, *Anger: The Misunderstood Emotion*, rev. ed. (New York: Touchstone, 1989), 129.
17. Deborah Tannen, *You Just Don't Understand: Women and Men in Conversation* (New York: Quill, 2001), 47, 298.
18. Ibid., 24.
19. Mark 9:33-34; Luke 9:46, 22:24
20. Tannen, *You Just Don't Understand*, 25.
21. Ibid., 113–114.
22. Jessie Jones, Nicholas Hope, and Jamie Wooten, *Always a Bridesmaid* (New York: Dramatists Play Service, Inc., 2013), 29.
23. John M. Gottman and Julie Gottman, "Love Maps," www.gottman.com/wp -content/uploads/2016/09/Love-Maps-White-Paper.pdf.

24. John Steinbeck, *The Grapes of Wrath*, Centennial edition (New York: Penguin, 2002), 419.

25. Charles Taylor, *A Secular Age* (Cambridge, MA: Belknap Press, 2007), 25.

26. Lewis B. Smedes, *Union with Christ: A Biblical View of the New Life in Jesus Christ*, rev. ed. (Grand Rapids, MI: Eerdmans, 1983), 58.

27. Jeremiah 2:32

28. Ibid.

29. Cornelius Plantinga Jr., "Pray the Lord My Mind to Keep," *Christianity Today*, August 10, 1998, 2, www.christianitytoday.com/ct/1998/august10/8t9050.html?start=2.

30. See Matthew 25:31-46.

31. Matthew 27:46; Mark 15:34

CHAPTER 3: BORN TO BOND

1. Cornelius Plantinga Jr., *Not the Way It's Supposed to Be: A Breviary of Sin* (Grand Rapids, MI: Eerdmans, 1995), 29.

2. Ibid., 197.

3. James Randerson, "How Many Neurons Make a Human Brain? Billions Fewer than We Thought," *Guardian*, February 28, 2012, www.theguardian.com/science/blog/2012/feb/28/how-many-neurons-human-brain.

4. Daniel J. Siegel, *The Developing Mind: How Relationships and the Brain Interact to Shape Who We Are*, 2nd ed. (New York: Guilford Press, 2012), 13.

5. Ibid., 9–10.

6. Ibid., 48–49. According to Siegel, "cells that fire together wire together" is neurobiologist Carla Shatz's paraphrase of "a simple axiom defined in 1949 by Donald Hebb: Neurons that fire together at one time will tend to fire together in the future." Shatz's version is much catchier.

7. Ibid., 10.

8. Ibid., 155.

9. John M. Gottman and Joan DeClaire, *The Relationship Cure* (New York: Three Rivers Press, 2001), 25–26.

10. Siegel, *The Developing Mind*, 100, 117, 155.

11. Isaiah 41:10, ESV

12. Psalm 139:14

13. Romans 12:9

14. Rankin Wilbourne, *Union with Christ: The Way to Know and Enjoy God* (Colorado Springs: David C. Cook, 2016), 245.

15. Isaiah 49:15

16. Dallas Willard, *Renovation of the Heart: Putting on the Character of Christ* (Colorado Springs: NavPress, 2001), 179.

17. Hosea 11:1, 3, 7

18. Psalm 23:1, 4, ESV

19. Julian of Norwich (1373), *Revelations of Divine Love*, in *Devotional Classics*, ed. Richard Foster and James Bryan Smith (San Francisco: HarperSanFrancisco, 1990), 68–69.
20. Quoted in introduction to Julian of Norwich, *Revelations of Divine Love* (Brewster, MA: Paraclete Press, 2011), ix.

CHAPTER 4: YOUR BID . . .
1. Rachel Feltman, "Stephen Hawking Announces $100 Million Hunt for Alien Life," *Washington Post*, July 20, 2015, www.washingtonpost.com/news /speaking-of-science/wp/2015/07/20/stephen-hawking-announces-100 -million-hunt-for-alien-life/?utm_term=.b9251f88ab60.
2. Charlie Cooper, "Stephen Hawking: There Is 'No Bigger Question' in Science than the Search for Extraterrestrial Life," *Independent*, July 20, 2015, www.independent.co.uk/news/science/stephen-hawking-there-is-no-bigger -question-in-science-than-the-search-for-extraterrestrial-life-10402432.html.
3. John M. Gottman and Joan DeClaire, *The Relationship Cure* (New York: Three Rivers Press, 2001), 4.
4. Ibid.
5. Ibid.
6. Ibid.
7. John 21:19
8. Matthew 25:40
9. Colossians 3:23, esv
10. Psalm 42:7
11. Psalm 42:8
12. Cornelius Plantinga Jr., *Not the Way It's Supposed to Be: A Breviary of Sin* (Grand Rapids, MI: Eerdmans, 1995), 11.
13. Elizabeth Barrett Browning, "Aurora Leigh" (1856), in *Aurora Leigh and Other Poems* (New York: Penguin, 1995), 232.

CHAPTER 5: ME, MYSELF, AND LIES
1. Daniel Goleman, *Emotional Intelligence* (New York: Bantam, 1995), 46.
2. Luke 10:41
3. Luke 12:15, nlt
4. Matthew 7:3
5. St. Augustine, *The Soliloquies of St. Augustine*, book II, I, trans. Rose Elizabeth Cleveland (Boston: Little, Brown, 1910), 51.
6. John Calvin, *Institutes of the Christian Religion*, ch. 1, sec. 3, *Christian Classics Ethereal Library*, www.ccel.org/ccel/calvin/institutes.iii.ii.html.
7. St. Bernard of Clairvaux, "Sermon 37: Knowledge and Ignorance of God and of Self," in *Commentary on the Song of Songs*, trans. Matthew Henry (Altenmünster, Germany: Jürgen Beck), 209.
8. Matthew 25:26

9. Matthew 25:24
10. Psalm 19:12
11. Joseph Butler, "Upon Self-Deceit," in *The Works of the Right Reverend Father in God Joseph Butler, D. C. L.* (London: J. F. Dove, 1828), 103.
12. Frederick Buechner, *Peculiar Treasures: A Biblical Who's Who* (New York: HarperCollins, 1979), 128–30.
13. C. S. Lewis, *The Four Loves* (New York: Harcourt, Brace, 1960), 61.
14. John 14:19-21; 15:4-5
15. Fyodor Dostoyevsky, *Notes from Underground*, University of Adelaide web edition, chapter XI, paragraph 7, trans. Constance Garnett, https://ebooks .adelaide.edu.au/d/dostoyevsky/d72n/chapter12.html.
16. Romans 12:3
17. Daniel Richardson, *Social Psychology for Dummies* (Chichester, West Sussex: John Wiley & Sons, 2014), 125.
18. Mark R. McMinn, *Why Sin Matters: The Surprising Relationship between Our Sin and God's Grace* (Carol Stream, IL: Tyndale House, 2004), 70.
19. This discussion about *self-serving bias* and *fundamental attribution error* is adapted from McMinn, *Why Sin Matters*, 69–75.
20. David Brooks, *The Road to Character* (New York: Random House, 2015), 6.
21. Ibid., 6–7.
22. James 1:22-24
23. Peter F. Drucker, *Managing Oneself* (Boston: Harvard Business School, 2008), 4.
24. Richard Rohr, *Breathing Under Water: Spirituality and the Twelve Steps* (Cincinnati: St. Anthony Messenger Press, 2011), xxi.
25. Brené Brown, *Daring Greatly: How the Courage to Be Vulnerable Transforms the Way We Live, Love, Parent, and Lead* (2012; repr. New York: Avery, 2015), 11. Italics added.
26. John 15:13, NLT
27. Henri J. M. Nouwen, *In the Name of Jesus: Reflections on Christian Leadership* (Chestnut Ridge, NY: Crossroad, 1989), 27–28.
28. C. S. Lewis, *The Voyage of the "Dawn Treader"* (New York: HarperCollins, 1952), 109. Italics in the original.

CHAPTER 6: THE JOY OF JURY DUTY

1. Romans 12:15
2. Daniel Goleman, *Social Intelligence: The New Science of Human Relationships* (New York: Bantam, 2006), 86.
3. Anne Lamott, *Bird by Bird: Some Instructions on Writing and Life* (New York: Anchor, 1994), 122.
4. Proverbs 24:17
5. Emma M. Seppälä, "The Science behind the Joy of Sharing Joy," *Psychology Today*, July 15, 2013, www.psychologytoday.com/blog/feeling-it/201307 /the-science-behind-the-joy-sharing-joy.

6. Nehemiah 8:10

7. Galatians 6:2, ESV

8. Nicholas Wolterstorff, *Lament for a Son* (Grand Rapids, MI: Eerdmans, 1987), 86.

9. Mandy Oaklander, "The Science of Crying," *Time*, March 16, 2016, http://time.com/4254089/science-crying.

10. Robert Herrick, "Tears Are Tongues," in *Hesperides, or Works Both Human and Divine* (London: George Routledge, 1887), 47.

11. Ad Vingerhoets, *Why Only Humans Weep: Unravelling the Mysteries of Tears* (Oxford: Oxford University Press, 2013).

12. Ad Vingerhoets, Niels van de Ven, and Yvonne van der Velden, "The Social Impact of Emotional Tears," *Motivation and Emotion* 40 (2016): 455–63, www.ncbi.nlm.nih.gov/pmc/articles/PMC4882350.

13. Oaklander, "The Science of Crying."

14. John 11:35

15. Psalm 56:8, NLT

16. Dinah Maria Mulock Craik, *A Life for a Life* (Leipzig: Bernhard Tauchnitz, 1859), 270–71. Italics in the original.

17. Paul Ekman, "Basic Emotions," in *Handbook of Cognition and Emotion*, ed. Tim Dagleish and Mick Power (Sussex, UK: John Wiley & Sons, 1999), 45–60. See also, Paul Ekman, *Emotions Revealed* (New York: Holt, 2004).

18. Psalm 38:7-8, MSG

19. Psalm 137:8-9

20. Paul Coleman, *The Complete Idiot's Guide to Intimacy* (New York: Alpha, 2005), 146–48.

21. Adapted from Daniel Goleman, *Emotional Intelligence* (New York: Bantam, 1995), 124–26.

22. James 1:17, NLT

CHAPTER 7: WE SHOULD ALL BE COMMITTED

1. Lewis B. Smedes, *Caring and Commitment* (New York: Harper and Row, 1988), 7.

2. For information about the Circus Center, see http://circuscenter.org.

3. Henri Nouwen, *Our Greatest Gift: A Meditation on Dying and Caring*, first paperback edition (New York: HarperCollins, 1995), 63–64.

4. Andy Stanley, "It's Only Physical" (sermon, North Point Community Church, Alpharetta, GA, September 18, 2009), www.sermoncentral .com/sermons/its-only-physical-andy-stanley-sermon-on-sexuality -139279?page=2.

5. Robert J. Sternberg, "Triangular Theory of Love," www.robertjsternberg .com/love.

6. Smedes, *Caring and Commitment*, 11.

7. G. K. Chesterton, "A Defence of Rash Vows" (1902), in *The Defendant* (Mineola, NY: Dover, 2012), 9.

8. Ibid., 13.
9. Genesis 15:12
10. 1 Kings 19:19-20
11. 1 Kings 19:21
12. Because we're talking about God here, and the truth thing is a big deal to him, I have to say: Cortés didn't actually *burn* the ships; he scuttled them. And it's possible he left one ship intact to carry treasure back to Spain (and possibly take a few leaders back, as well, if it didn't all work out).
13. Adapted from Aaron T. Beck, *Love Is Never Enough: How Couples Can Overcome Misunderstandings, Resolve Conflicts, and Solve Relationship Problems through Cognitive Therapy* (New York: HarperPerennial, 1989), 217ff.
14. Urie Bronfenbrenner, cited in Anne B. Smith, *Understanding Children's Development*, 4th ed. (Wellington, NZ: Bridget Williams Books, 1998), 268.
15. William Law, *A Serious Call to a Devout and Holy Life*, 4th ed. (London: W. Innis and R. Manby, 1739), 15. Italics in the original.
16. Cicero, from *Laelius de Amicitia*, 13.47, quoted in Aelred of Rievaulx, *Spiritual Friendship*, book 2, trans. Lawrence C. Braceland, ed. Marsha L. Dutton (Collegeville, MN: Liturgical Press, 2010), 81.
17. 1 Samuel 20:16-17
18. Samuel Taylor Coleridge, "Youth and Age."
19. Proverbs 18:24
20. Proverbs 17:17
21. Aristotle, cited in Kent Dunnington, *Addiction and Virtue: Beyond the Models of Disease and Choice* (Downers Grove, IL: InterVarsity Press, 2011), 187.
22. Aelred of Rievaulx, *Spiritual Friendship*, 103–5.
23. Hannah Arendt, *The Human Condition*, 2nd ed. (Chicago: University of Chicago Press, 1958), 237.
24. Dallas Willard, in conversation with the author, Catalyst West Roadtrip 2010, Catalyst Podcast, episode 124, http://catalyst.libsyn.com/episode-124-dallas-willard-and-john-ortberg. This part of the conversation begins at 33:30.
25. Adapted from Dallas Willard, *The Great Omission: Reclaiming Jesus's Essential Teachings on Discipleship* (New York: HarperOne, 2006), 151.
26. Chesterton, "A Defence of Rash Vows," 13.

CHAPTER 8: SOMETHING THERE IS THAT DOESN'T LOVE A WALL

1. Cited in Atul Gawande, *Being Mortal: Medicine and What Matters in the End* (New York: Metropolitan Books, 2014), 119.
2. Ibid., 122.
3. Adapted from Atul Gawande, *Being Mortal*, 123.
4. Ibid., 21.
5. Ibid., 18.

6. Ibid., 127; see also http://www.edenalt.org/.

7. John Milton, *Paradise Lost*, book IV, line 143.

8. "Great Wall of China," History.com, 2010, www.history.com/topics/great-wall-of-china.

9. Immanuel Kant, *Fundamental Principles of the Metaphysic of Morals* (1785), trans. Thomas Kingsmill Abbott (Mineola, NY: Dover, 2005), 24.

10. G. J. Mattey, course notes on Kant's *Grounding for the Metaphysics of Morals*, Philosophy 1, University of California–Davis, Spring 2002, http://hume.ucdavis.edu/mattey/phi001/grounding.html.

11. Robert Frost, "Mending Wall," in *North of Boston* (New York: H. Holt, 1915), 11–12.

12. Brené Brown, *Daring Greatly* (2012; repr. New York: Avery, 2015), 150.

13. Olivia B. Waxman, "Church Pastor Starts a 'Tip-Shaming' Website," *Time*, March 11, 2014, http://time.com/18977/church-pastor-starts-a-tip-shaming-website.

14. Steve Corbett and Brian Fikkert, *When Helping Hurts: How to Alleviate Poverty without Hurting the Poor . . . and Yourself* (Chicago: Moody, 2012), 127–28.

15. Mark 6:3

16. John 1:1

17. Yalda T. Uhls et al., "Five Days at Outdoor Education Camp without Screens Improves Preteen Skills with Nonverbal Emotion Cues," *Computers in Human Behavior* 39 (October 2014), www.sciencedirect.com/science/article/pii/S0747563214003227.

18. Cited in Nicholas Kardaras, "Generation Z: Online and at Risk?" *Scientific American*, September 1, 2016, www.scientificamerican.com/article/generation-z-online-and-at-risk.

19. Larry Rosen, "Phantom Pocket Vibration Syndrome," *Psychology Today*, May 7, 2013, www.psychologytoday.com/blog/rewired-the-psychology-technology/201305/phantom-pocket-vibration-syndrome.

20. Brandie Johnson's Facebook page, November 2, 2015, cited in Angel Chang, "This Mom's 28 Tallies Beg Us to Put Down Our Phones," Little Things website, www.littlethings.com/parents-put-down-the-phone.

21. Sherry Turkle, "Connected, but Alone?" TED Subtitles and Transcript, posted April 2012, www.ted.com/talks/sherry_turkle_alone_together/transcript?language=en, starting at 12:41.

22. Psalm 139:1-2

23. Psalm 139:4

24. Psalm 139:8-10

25. John M. Gottman and Nan Silver, *The Seven Principles for Making Marriage Work* (1999; repr. New York: Harmony Books, 2015), 2.

26. Except where otherwise noted, this discussion of the "four horsemen" in

relationships is adapted from Gottman, *The Seven Principles for Making Marriage Work*, 30–33.

27. D. P. Rakel et al., "Practitioner Empathy and the Duration of the Common Cold," *Family Medicine* 41, no. 7 (July/August 2009): 494–501, www.ncbi .nlm.nih.gov/pubmed/19582635.

28. 1 Samuel 18:6-8

29. Frederick Buechner, *Wishful Thinking: A Seeker's ABC* (New York: Harper and Row, 1973).

30. F. Murray Abraham as Antonio Salieri, in *Amadeus* (1984), screenplay by Peter Shaffer, www.youtube.com/watch?v=yencLfqOh5A.

31. F. Murray Abraham in *Amadeus*, www.youtube.com/watch?v=-2ulXbpKaTg. Quote begins at 1:00.

32. Ibid. Quote begins at 1:20.

33. M. Scott Peck, *The Different Drum: Community Making and Peace* (New York: Touchstone, 1988), 88.

34. For a more extensive discussion of chaos in relationships, see M. Scott Peck, *The Different Drum*, 90–94.

35. Anne Lamott, *Bird by Bird: Some Instructions on Writing and Life* (New York: Anchor, 1995), 19.

36. Psalm 46:10

37. Matthew Hutson, "People Prefer Electric Shocks to Being Alone with Their Thoughts," *Atlantic*, July 3, 2014, www.theatlantic.com/health /archive/2014/07/people-prefer-electric-shocks-to-being-alone-with-their -thoughts/373936.

38. 1 Chronicles 23:30

39. Ephesians 2:18

CHAPTER 9: NAKED AND UNAFRAID

1. The charts in this section are adapted from Andy Crouch, *Strong and Weak: Embracing a Life of Love, Risk, and True Flourishing* (Downers Grove, IL: InterVarsity Press, 2016), 13–14.

2. Genesis 1:26

3. Crouch, *Strong and Weak*, 35.

4. Psalm 8:5-6

5. Genesis 2:25

6. Crouch, *Strong and Weak*, 43–44.

7. Ibid., 40. Italics in the original.

8. Wallace Stegner, *Crossing to Safety* (New York: Modern Library, 1987), 4.

9. Matthew 28:18

10. Romans 8:39

11. Walter Brueggemann, "Of the Same Flesh and Bone," *Catholic Biblical Quarterly* 32 (1970): 533.

12. Ibid., 534.

13. Genesis 25:24-25, MSG
14. Genesis 27:13
15. Adapted from Andy Crouch, *Strong and Weak*, 95.
16. Genesis 3:4-5, NLT
17. Genesis 27:18-19
18. Brené Brown, *Daring Greatly* (2012; repr. New York: Avery, 2015), 232.
19. Genesis 33:4
20. Brown, *Daring Greatly*, 5–6.
21. Ibid., 6.
22. Henry Cloud, conversation with the author, May 2016.
23. Madeleine L'Engle, *Walking on Water: Reflections on Faith and Art*, paperback edition (New York: North Point Press, 1995), 190, 193.
24. Quoted in Harold Holzer, "If I Had Another Face, Do You Think I'd Wear This One?" *American Heritage* 34, no. 2 (February/March 1983), www.americanheritage.com/content/%E2%80%9Cif-i-had-another-face-do-you-think-id-wear-one%E2%80%9D.
25. Wendy Farley, *The Wounding and Healing of Desire: Weaving Heaven and Earth* (Louisville: Westminster John Knox Press, 2005), 151.
26. Isaiah 49:15
27. Elizabeth O'Donnell Gandolfo, *The Power and Vulnerability of Love: A Theological Anthropology* (Minneapolis: Fortress Press, 2015), 208.
28. Matthew 25:40
29. Genesis 29:17
30. Ibid.
31. Genesis 29:25
32. Genesis 29:30
33. Genesis 29:31
34. Genesis 29:32
35. Genesis 29:33
36. Genesis 29:34
37. Genesis 30:1
38. R. Kent Hughes, *Genesis: Beginning and Blessing* (Wheaton, IL: Crossway, 2004), 373–80.
39. Genesis 30:15
40. Ibid.
41. Sarah Griffiths, "Babies DO Fake Cry: Infants Pretend to Be Distressed to Get Attention," *Daily Mail*, January 16, 2014, http://www.dailymail.co.uk/sciencetech/article-2540677/Babies-DO-fake-cry-Infants-pretend-distressed-attention.html.
42. Kent Dunnington, *Addiction and Virtue: Beyond the Models of Disease and Choice* (Downers Grove, IL: InterVarsity Press, 2011), 187.
43. Gandolfo, *The Power and Vulnerability of Love*, 229.

CHAPTER 10: THE DEEP DOWN DARK

1. This section adapted from Héctor Tobar, *Deep Down Dark: The Untold Stories of 33 Men Buried in a Chilean Mine, and the Miracle That Set Them Free* (New York: Picador, 2014), 94–104, 121.
2. David Brooks, *The Road to Character* (New York: Random House, 2015), 93.
3. Ibid., 94–96.
4. David Von Drehle, with Jay Newton-Small and Maya Rhodan, "How Do You Forgive a Murder?" *Time* 186, no. 21 (November 23, 2015), http://time.com/time-magazine-charleston-shooting-cover-story.
5. Daniel J. Siegel, *The Developing Mind: How Relationships and the Brain Interact to Shape Who We Are*, 2nd ed. (New York: Guilford Press, 2012), 219.
6. Genesis 40:7
7. Siegel, *The Developing Mind*, 176.
8. Genesis 42:24
9. Genesis 43:30
10. Genesis 45:1-2
11. Genesis 45:14-15
12. Genesis 50:1
13. Genesis 50:16-17
14. Exodus 2:23-25
15. Exodus 6:5
16. Psalm 6:3, 6
17. Ezekiel 21:6
18. Exodus 15:24
19. Deuteronomy 1:27
20. Psalm 106:25
21. Philippians 2:14
22. 1 Corinthians 10:10
23. Deborah Tannen, *You Just Don't Understand: Women and Men in Conversation* (New York: Quill, 2001), 49–73.
24. Brooks, *The Road to Character*, 100.
25. Lewis B. Smedes, *How Can It Be All Right When Everything Is All Wrong?* (San Francisco: HarperSanFrancisco, 1992), 85.
26. Adapted and condensed from Dan B. Allender, "Leading Character," in Bill Hybels, John Ortberg, and Dan B. Allender, *The Call to Lead: Following Jesus and Living Out Your Mission* (Grand Rapids, MI: Zondervan, 2008), 70–77.
27. Nicholas Wolterstorff, *Lament for a Son* (Grand Rapids, MI: Eerdmans, 1987), 90.
28. Romans 8:20, 22, ESV
29. Romans 8:23, 26, ESV
30. Romans 8:26, ESV
31. Isaiah 53:3, ESV
32. Matthew 5:3-11

33. From the Apostles' Creed, Christian Classics Ethereal Library, www.ccel
.org/creeds/apostles.creed.html.

CHAPTER 11: THIS TIME IT'S PERSONAL

1. If you want to see Jia Jiang's Rejection Therapy in action, check out his
"100 Days of Rejection" page at http://rejectiontherapy.com/100-days-of
-rejection-therapy.
2. Jia Jiang, *Rejection Proof: How I Beat Fear and Became Invincible through
100 Days of Rejection* (New York: Harmony Books, 2015), 42–43.
3. Adapted from Douglas Stone and Sheila Heen, *Thanks for the Feedback:
The Science and Art of Receiving Feedback Well* (New York: Viking,
2014), 1.
4. Lewis B. Smedes, *Shame and Grace: Healing the Shame We Don't Deserve*
(San Francisco: HarperSanFrancisco, 1993), 5.
5. Dallas Willard, *The Divine Conspiracy: Rediscovering Our Hidden Life in God*
(San Francisco: HarperSanFrancisco, 1998), 218.
6. Gershen Kaufman, *Shame: The Power of Caring* (Rochester, VT: Schenkman
Books, 1992), 12, 30.
7. John 4:6-7
8. John 4:7
9. John 4:9
10. Ibid.
11. Genesis 24
12. Genesis 29:1-30
13. Exodus 2:15-21
14. Niddah 4:1, in *A History of the Mishnaic Law of Purities*, ed. Jacob Nausner,
part 15, Niddah commentary (Leiden, Netherlands: E. J. Brill, 1976), 63.
15. Luke 10:25-37
16. Luke 9:51-55
17. John 8:48
18. John 4:15-18
19. Ethan Kross et al., "Social Rejection Shares Somatosensory Representations
with Physical Pain," *Proceedings of the National Academy of Sciences USA*
108, no. 15 (April 12, 2011), www.ncbi.nlm.nih.gov/pmc/articles
/PMC3076808.
20. John 4:27
21. John 4:10
22. John 4:28-29
23. John 4:39-40
24. John 4:42
25. Ephrem the Syrian (c. 306–373), cited in J. A. Findlay, *The Fourth Gospel:
An Expository Commentary* (London: Epworth, 1956), 61.
26. Quoted and adapted from Lewis B. Smedes, *Shame and Grace*, 105–7.

27. 1 John 3:1-2
28. Isaiah 53:3

CHAPTER 12: HOUSTON, WE HAVE A PROBLEM
 1. William Betcher, *Intimate Play: Creating Romance in Everyday Life* (New York: Viking, 1987), 2–3. Italics in the original.
 2. John M. Gottman and Nan Silver, *The Seven Principles for Making Marriage Work* (New York: Three Rivers Books, 1999), 23.
 3. Charlie W. Shedd, *Remember I Love You: Martha's Story* (New York: HarperCollins, 1992).
 4. Leviticus 19:17, MSG
 5. G. Stanley Hall, "A Study of Anger," *American Journal of Psychology* 10 (July 1, 1899): 537, https://archive.org/details/jstor-1412662.
 6. Daniel Goleman, *Emotional Intelligence* (New York: Bantam, 1995), 63.
 7. James 1:19
 8. Timothy Keller with Kathy Keller, *The Meaning of Marriage: Facing the Complexities of Commitment with the Wisdom of God* (2011; repr., New York: Penguin, 2013), 160–61.
 9. Ibid., 161.
10. Ibid.
11. Ibid.
12. If you haven't seen the movie *Office Space* (written and directed by Mike Judge, Twentieth Century Fox, 1999), here's a link to catch you up on the backstory: http://mentalfloss.com/article/57338/what-tps-report.
13. Gottman and Silver, *The Seven Principles for Making Marriage Work*, 27.
14. Proverbs 15:1, ESV
15. Philippians 1:3-4
16. Shawn Achor, *The Happiness Advantage: The Seven Principles of Positive Psychology That Fuel Success and Performance at Work* (New York: Crown, 2010), 92.
17. 1 Corinthians 13:5
18. Philippians 4:8
19. Joseph J. Ellis, *Founding Brothers: The Revolutionary Generation* (New York: Vintage, 2002), 163.
20. Ibid., 248.
21. Lewis B. Smedes, *Forgive and Forget: Healing the Hurts We Don't Deserve* (New York: HarperCollins, 1984), 82.
22. 1 John 1:5. See also Psalm 18:12; 104:2; 1 Timothy 6:16.
23. See Philip Yancey, *Disappointment with God: Three Questions No One Asks Aloud* (Grand Rapids, MI: Zondervan, 1988).
24. C. S. Lewis, *Surprised by Joy: The Shape of My Early Life* (New York: Harcourt, 1966), 115.
25. Genesis 6:5-6
26. Matthew 27:46; Mark 15:34

CHAPTER 13: WHO WILL CRY AT YOUR FUNERAL?

1. Adapted from Patrick M. Morley, *The Man in the Mirror: Solving the 24 Problems Men Face* (Grand Rapids, MI: Zondervan, 1997), 99–100.
2. Ibid., 100.
3. Ibid.
4. Darren Hardy, *The Entrepreneur Roller Coaster* (Dallas: Success, 2015), chapter 2, section 4.
5. Ibid.
6. Flavius Josephus, *Antiquities of the Jews*, vol. XVII, chap. 6, para. 5, trans. William Whiston.
7. Adapted from Martin E. P. Seligman, *Authentic Happiness: Using the New Positive Psychology to Realize Your Potential for Lasting Fulfillment* (New York: Simon & Schuster, 2002), 249.
8. William Betcher, *Intimate Play: Creating Romance in Everyday Life* (New York: Viking, 1987), 219ff.
9. Ibid., 236.
10. Thomas Mallon, "Dear Cat, Dear Pig," Books section of *New York Times on the Web*, May 9, 1999, http://www.nytimes.com/books/99/05/09/reviews/990509.09mallont.html.
11. Betcher, *Intimate Play.*
12. C. S. Lewis, *The Four Loves* (New York: Harcourt, Brace, 1960), 35.
13. Daniel James Brown, *The Boys in the Boat: Nine Americans and Their Epic Quest for Gold at the 1936 Berlin Olympics* (New York: Penguin, 2013), 161.
14. Ibid., 353.
15. Ibid., front matter.
16. Cornelius Plantinga Jr., *Not the Way It's Supposed to Be: A Breviary of Sin* (Grand Rapids, MI: Eerdmans, 1995), 10.
17. Dallas Willard, *The Divine Conspiracy: Rediscovering Our Hidden Life in God* (San Francisco: HarperSanFrancisco, 1998), 399.
18. Sheldon Vanauken, *A Severe Mercy: A Story of Faith, Tragedy, and Triumph* (New York: Bantam, 1977), 134.
19. Jean Vanier, *Community and Growth*, rev. ed. (New York: Paulist Press, 1989), 31.
20. Liz Ryan, "Why Employee Happiness Is the Wrong Goal," *Forbes*, March 22, 2015, www.forbes.com/sites/lizryan/2015/03/22/why-employee-happiness-is-the-wrong-goal/#3aa39f2028c5.
21. Ibid.
22. Acts 9:36
23. Some information for this section is adapted from Ben Witherington III, *The Acts of the Apostles: A Socio-Rhetorical Commentary* (Grand Rapids, MI: Eerdmans, 1998), 331–33.
24. Acts 9:39
25. Thank you to Merriam-Webster's *11th Collegiate Dictionary* for backing me up on this definition of *commune.*

26. Barbara Williams-Skinner, conversation with the author, 2016.

27. See Esther 4:14.

28. Ivory Toldson, interview with Michel Martin on *Tell Me More*, NPR, April 23, 2013, www.npr.org/2013/04/23/178601467/are-there-really-more-black -men-in-prison-than-college. This is contrary to the widely held belief that a male baby born to an African American mother today is more likely to end up in prison than in college.

29. Acts 9:40-41

CHAPTER 14: AT LAST

1. Philip Yancey, *What's So Amazing about Grace?* (Grand Rapids, MI: Zondervan, 1996), 39.

2. "Brené Brown on Empathy," YouTube, published December 10, 2013, www.youtube.com/watch?v=1Evwgu369Jw.

3. Pauline Rose Clance and Suzanne Imes, "The Imposter Phenomenon in High Achieving Women: Dynamics and Therapeutic Intervention," *Psychotherapy Theory, Research and Practice* 15, no. 3 (Fall 1978), www.paulineroseclance.com/pdf/ip_high_achieving_women.pdf.

4. This version of Søren Kierkegaard's essay "The King and the Maiden" was adapted by Nick Watts for his blog *Reading Theology*, April 18, 2011, www.readingtheology.com/?s=king+and+the+maiden. A translation of the full text can be found in Søren Kierkegaard, *Parables of Kierkegaard*, ed. Thomas C. Oden (Princeton, NJ: Princeton University Press, 1978), 40–45.

5. John 1:1, 14

6. Origen, *On First Principles*, trans. G. W. Butterworth (Notre Dame, IN: Ave Maria Press, 2013), 136–37.

7. Elizabeth O'Donnell Gandolfo, *The Power and Vulnerability of Love: A Theological Anthropology* (Minneapolis: Fortress Press, 2015), 231.

8. Margery Williams, *The Velveteen Rabbit: Or How Toys Become Real* (Garden City, NY: Doubleday, 1922), http://digital.library.upenn.edu/women/williams /rabbit/rabbit.html.

9. Ibid.

10. Ibid.

11. 1 John 4:10, NLT

12. Williams, *The Velveteen Rabbit*. Italics added.

13. Isaiah 53:4

14. Williams, *The Velveteen Rabbit*.

15. Shauna Niequist, *Present over Perfect: Leaving Behind Frantic for a Simpler, More Soulful Way of Living* (Grand Rapids, MI: Zondervan, 2016), 231.

16. Dallas Willard, conversation with the author.

17. Revelation 2:17, NLT

18. Williams, *The Velveteen Rabbit*. Italics added.

JOHN ORTBERG INVITES SMALL GROUPS TO GREATER CONNECTIONS WITH GOD AND OTHERS

Following the ideas of John Ortberg's book *I'd Like You More if You Were More like Me*, this six-week study includes biblical insights, group questions, personal journaling prompts, and at-home activity ideas. Small-group members will learn how to connect on a deeper level with the people God has placed in their lives, both inside and outside the group, as they grow closer to the One who made them for relationships.

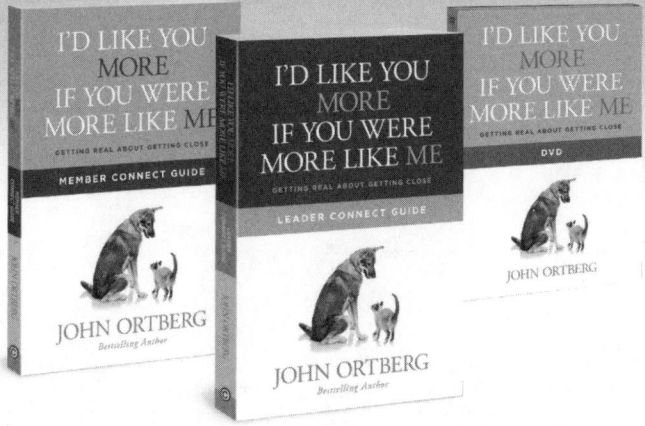

Small Group Connect Guide — Part discussion guide and part workbook, this creative resource offers small-group members opportunities to grow closer to one another and to God.

Leader Connect Guide — A practical guide for small-group leaders who want to gently encourage their groups toward greater closeness with God and one another.

DVD — In this six-session DVD, John Ortberg's conversational style sets the stage for great discussion starters to get to know one another more deeply.

GetRealGetClose.com

Available in print and digital editions everywhere books are sold

David C Cook
transforming lives together

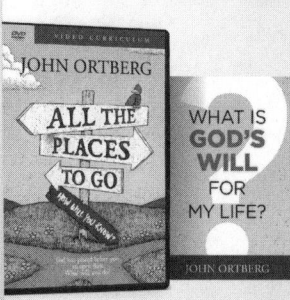